Greening Trade and Investment
Environmental Protection Without Protectionism

Eric Neumayer

Earthscan Publications Ltd, London and Sterling, VA

For my parents, in gratitude

First published in the UK and USA in 2001
by Earthscan Publications Ltd

Copyright © Eric Neumayer, 2001

All rights reserved

ISBN: 1 85383 788 1 paperback
        1 85383 787 3 hardback

Typesetting by PCS Mapping & DTP
Printed and bound in the UK by Creative Print and Design
Cover design by Richard Reid

For a full list of publications please contact:
Earthscan Publications Ltd
120 Pentonville Road, London, N1 9JN, UK
Tel: +44 (0)20 7278 0433
Fax: +44 (0)20 7278 1142
Email: earthinfo@earthscan.co.uk
http://www.earthscan.co.uk

22883 Quicksilver Drive, Sterling, VA 20166–2012, USA

Earthscan is an editorially independent subsidiary of Kogan Page Ltd and publishes in
association with WWF-UK and the International Institute for Environment and
Development

A catalogue record for this book is available from the British Library

Library of Congress Cataloging-in-Publication Data
Neumayer, Eric, 1970-
    Greening trade and investment : environmental protection without
protectionism / Eric Neumayer.
        p. cm.
    Includes bibliographical references and index.
    ISBN 1-85383-787-3 – ISBN 1-85383-788-1 (pbk.)
    1. Free trade–Environmental aspects. 2. Investments, Foreign–Environmental
aspects. 3. Environmental policy–Economic aspects. 4. Environmental
policy–Developing countries. 5. Environmental protection–Developing countries.
6. World Trade Organization–Developing countries. I. Title.
HF1713.N42 2001
333.7–dc21

                                                                                        2001001379

Contents

List of Tables and Boxes

Tables

Box

Preface

Foreign investment and international trade are regarded with great suspicion by some environmentalists. They fear that a free flow of capital and goods and services might significantly harm the environment. Consequently, they demand that the multilateral investment and trade regimes should allow nation states to intervene for the protection of the environment.

Representatives from developing countries in turn regard these demands with great suspicion. They fear that the developed countries will use strong interventionist rights to their own advantage and to the detriment of developing countries. Consequently, they oppose most, if not all, demands for a 'greening' of the multilateral investment and trade regimes.

As someone who cares about the environment, believes in the merits of a liberal investment and trade regime, and is sympathetic to the concerns of developing countries' representatives, it was no easy task to write this book on investment, trade and the environment. I have tried to show ways in which the multilateral investment and trade regimes could be made more environmentally friendly without unnecessarily restricting the free flow of capital and goods and services, and without detriment to the economic development aspirations of developing countries. Winning developing countries' support is the greatest challenge ahead for a successful greening of the multilateral investment and trade regimes – a challenge that this book tries to meet.

I hope that I have written a book that is accessible to many people without prior specialist knowledge in the issues. However, this book would not have been possible without the help of many. It has benefited much from constructive comments from others. My special thanks go to Duncan Brack from the Royal Institute of International Affairs in London, Dan Esty from the Yale Center for Environmental Law and Policy, Jonathan Krueger from the John F Kennedy School of Government at Harvard University, David Pearce from University College London, Nick Mabey from WWF, Tim Forsyth, Gilles Duranton and Simon Batterbury from the London School of Economics and Political Science, as well as several anonymous referees. Thanks for their support also go to Jagdish Bhagwati, Vudayagi Balasubramanyam, Steve Charnovitz and Aaron Cosbey, and finally to the Earthscan team. All errors are mine, as are all the views expressed in this book.

Shorter and revised versions of various parts of this book have been previously published in journals. My thanks go to the editors of these journals for their willingness to accept publication of these articles.[1]

Dr Eric Neumayer
London School of Economics and Political Science
London, March 2001

List of Acronyms and Abbreviations

AEA	American Electronics Association
AFL-CIO	American Federation of Labor-Congress of Industrial Organizations
AFTA	ASEAN Free Trade Area
APEC	Asia-Pacific Economic Cooperation
ASEAN	Association of Southeast Asian Nations
BDI	Bundesverband der Deutschen Industrie
BIT	Bilateral Investment Treaty
BSE	bovine spongiform encephalopathy
BTA	border tax adjustment
BTU	British Thermal Unit
CAFE	corporate average fuel economy
CARICOM	Caribbean Community
CBD	Convention on Biological Diversity
CEC	Commission for Environmental Cooperation
CEPA	Canadian Environmental Protection Act
CFC	chlorofluorocarbon
CITES	Convention on International Trade in Endangered Species of Wild Fauna and Flora
CO	carbon monoxide
CO_2	carbon dioxide
COMESA	Common Market for Eastern and Southern Africa
CTE	Committee on Trade and Environment
DDT	dichlorodiphenyltrichloroethane
DSB	dispute settlement body
DSU	dispute settlement understanding
EC	European Communities
EC	European Community
EFTA	European Free Trade Association
EKC	Environmental Kuznets Curve
EPA	Environmental Protection Agency
EU	European Union
FDI	foreign direct investment
FTAA	Free Trade Area of the Americas
GATS	General Agreement on Trade in Services
GATT	General Agreement on Tariffs and Trade
GCC	Global Climate Change Coalition
GDP	gross domestic product
GMO	genetically modified organism

GNP	gross national product
HCFC	hydrochlorofluorocarbon
IBRD	International Bank for Reconstruction and Development
ICC	International Chamber of Commerce
ICSID	International Center for the Settlement of Investment Disputes
IDCP	International Dolphin Conservation Programme
IISD	International Institute for Sustainable Development
IMF	International Monetary Fund
ITO	International Trade Organization
IUCN	World Conservation Union (formerly International Union for Conservation of Nature and Natural Resources)
LCA	life-cycle analysis
MAI	Multilateral Agreement on Investment
MEA	Multilateral Environmental Agreement
Mercosur	Mercado Común del Sur
MMPA	Marine Mammal Protection Act
MMT	methylcyclopentadienyl manganese tricarbonyl
MTBE	methyl tertiary butyl ether
NAAEC	North American Agreement on Environmental Cooperation
NAFTA	North American Free Trade Agreement
NGO	non-governmental organization
NO_2	nitrogen dioxide
NO_x	nitrogen oxides
ODA	official development assistance
ODS	ozone-depleting substance
OECD	Organization for Economic Co-operation and Development
PCB	polychlorinated biphenyl
PIC	Prior Informed Consent
POP	persistent organic pollutant
PPM	process and production method
SADC	Southern African Development Community
SME	small and medium enterprise
SO_2	sulphur dioxide
SO_x	sulphur oxides
SPS	sanitary and phytosanitary
TBT	Technical Barriers to Trade
TED	turtle excluder device
TNC	transnational corporation
TREM	Trade-Related Environmental Measure
TRIM	Trade-Related Investment Measure
TRIP	Trade-Related Intellectual Property Right
UN	United Nations
UNCED	United Nations Conference on Environment and Development
UNCLOS	United Nations Convention on the Law of the Sea
UNCTAD	United Nations Conference on Trade and Development
UNEP	United Nations Environment Programme
UPOV	Union for the Protection of New Varieties of Plants
US	United States
WEO	World Environment Organization
WTO	World Trade Organization
WWF	*formerly known as* World Wide Fund For Nature

Introduction

At the start of a new millennium, humankind finds itself confronted with many challenges, one of which is to find a solution to the environmental problems that are manifold both within nation states and internationally. Developing countries in particular are faced with severe environmental problems that directly affect human health and welfare: restricted access to clean drinking water and sanitation; heavy air and water pollution; erosion and destruction of local renewable resources, to mention just a few. The problem of global ozone depletion has more or less been resolved through successive international agreements but the community of nation states is only beginning to formulate an adequate response to international and global environmental problems such as climate change, biodiversity loss and toxic pollutants.

Greening Trade and Investment examines how this environmental challenge is affected by a phenomenon commonly referred to as 'globalization'. The term describes the fact that countries are increasingly linked with each other via foreign investment and international flows of trade. Many environmentalists and academics alike fear that globalization will affect the environment negatively and will render a successful meeting of the environmental challenge more difficult, if not impossible (Daly 1993; Nader 1993; Røpke 1994; Mander and Goldsmith 1996). They also regard the multilateral investment and trade regimes – that is, the institutions and rules that have been set up to govern the international flow of investment and trade – as well as their representatives as insensitive or even hostile towards environmental interests.[1] This book provides an analysis of these fears and will be guided by the following questions. First, what are the issue areas, where significant environmental problems caused by foreign investment or trade allegedly exist? Second, what is the evidence with respect to these allegations? Third, what policies can be recommended to solve these problems?

In examining these questions, much emphasis is put on the multilateral investment and trade regimes and, consequently, on whether or not these regimes need to be reformed. However, a solution to environmental problems is not the only challenge to be met by humankind. Billions of people in developing countries live in appalling conditions and, due to population growth, many more are about to join them. They all have a basic human right to a decent standard of living. In my view at least, the fate of people in developing countries has to be taken into account when considering how the multilateral investment and trade regimes can be made more environmentally friendly. We need to ensure that the 'greening' of the multilateral investment and trade regimes can be reconciled with rising living standards via increased foreign investment and trade for developing countries, which in general are rather hostile towards any form of 'greening'. The challenge is to make investment and trade regimes more environmentally friendly, without opening the floodgates for potential protectionist abuse by the developed world.

Greening Trade and Investment differs from other writings on the subject with respect to two major aspects. First, it takes a comprehensive approach and examines both investment and trade together. The vast majority of authors concentrate on one (mostly trade), thereby neglecting the interlinkages between investment and trade. Second, the book's objective is to derive policy proposals for a greening of the multilateral investment and trade regimes that can be acceptable to developing countries. The real challenge is to overcome their hostility towards such greening, which can only be met if the suggested policies do not endanger the economic development aspirations of developing countries.

Greening Trade and Investment is based on the implicit assumption that foreign investment and international trade will lead to a narrowing of income disparities among nations and to an alleviation of poverty in poor countries if the multilateral trade and investment regimes are not biased against developing countries and adequate policies are put in place. There is much evidence in favour of this assumption, as discussed and summarized comprehensively in Ben-David, Nordström and Winters (2000). Nevertheless, it is contested by opponents to and critics of foreign investment and trade liberalization (Dunkley 1997; Oxfam 1999). It would be beyond the scope of this book to provide a detailed justification for this assumption or a discussion of the wider issues. In the following, it will therefore simply be assumed that the assumption holds true.

The structure of the book's analysis is as follows. Chapter 1 portrays foreign investment and trade in an integrating world economy in historical perspective. It shows that while the world has seen already a similar form of globalization at the transition of the 19th century to the 20th century (which was aborted abruptly with the outbreak of the First World War), the current wave of globalization is exceeding this first wave. The extent and quality of the integration currently taking place are a consequence of the major institutions and the rules that came to govern the multilateral investment and trade regimes after the Second World War and which had no equivalent counterpart in the first wave of globalization. Chapter 1 briefly introduces these institutions and Chapter 2 describes in detail the rules embodied in the multilateral investment and trade regimes. Together Chapters 1 and 2 provide the foundations for the major discussion of the ideas put forward in the book.

This discussion is contained in Parts One and Two which deal with investment and trade separately.

Foreign investment affects the environment in many ways. In resource-based industries, especially oil extraction and mineral mining, it can lead to significant local environmental degradation as demonstrated in, for example, Nigeria, Indonesia and Papua New Guinea. Foreign investment in the manufacturing sector, on the other hand, can lead to the employment of later vintage and possibly less resource- and pollution-intensive technology. However, many environmental effects are more indirect and therefore more difficult to trace. The possibility of capital to relocate to other countries via foreign investment can tempt some, especially developing countries that are keen (or sometimes even desperate) to receive a higher inflow of foreign investment, to lower their environmental standards or to fail to enforce them (see Chapter 3). The same possibility of capital to relocate to other countries can exert pressure on domestic environmental policy-makers, especially in developed countries as the major sources of foreign investment, not to raise environmental standards for fear of capital loss if these higher standards are seen as a burden to internationally mobile capital (see Chapter 4). In addition, some of the potential indirect environmental effects of foreign investment are closely linked to the way that foreign investment is governed. Many bilateral investment treaties and the investment protection provisions in the North American Free Trade Agreement (NAFTA) allow foreign private investors to challenge host countries for measures, environmental or other. These investor-to-state dispute settlement provisions therefore can potentially be employed by foreign private investors to knock down existing environmental regulations or to deter countries from enacting future environmental regulations which they regard as an undue encroachment into their rights as a foreign investor (see Chapter 5). The multilateral agreement on investment (MAI) that OECD countries attempted to negotiate in the mid-1990s is examined as a case study of the various investment issues in Chapter 6. Its draft included many provisions that critics regarded as facilitating the relocation of capital to low standard countries, the deterrence of environmental standard raising and the knocking down of existing environmental regulations.

International trade also affects the environment in many ways. Trade liberalization is likely to have many different effects on the environment, some of which are positive, such as a more efficient allocation of resources, while others are negative, such as the detrimental consequences of increased transportation. The net effects on the environment are far from clear (for more detail see Chapter 7). As with foreign investment, many of the environmental effects of international trade are more indirect and difficult to trace, however. In addition, they are inextricably linked with the way that multilateral trade is governed. If the multilateral trade regime is biased against environmental interests and employs a strong dispute settlement system that makes it costly for countries to avoid their trade obligations, then countries can be restricted in their domestic or unilateral environmental policy-making to the detriment of the environment – an issue which is discussed in Chapter 8. Similarly, if multilateral environmental agreements need to employ trade measures or substantive provisions to achieve their environmental objective, but these trade measures or provisions contradict the rules of the multilateral trade regime, then countries will not only be restricted in their domestic, but also in their multilateral environmental policy-making (see Chapter 9).

Parts Two and Three of the book not only try to assess the validity of the alleged problematic aspects but also provide chapter-by-chapter recommendations for policies on how to solve the problems that have been identified. Chapter 10 provides conclusions and a summary of these policy recommendations.

Investment and trade are dealt with in separate parts for analytical clarity, although to some extent this obscures the fact that the two are inextricably linked. For once, foreign investment and trade can be substitutes or complements. In other words, increased foreign investment, especially in the form of foreign direct investment (FDI), can either decrease or increase international trade flows and vice versa.[2] The setting up of a new plant in a foreign country via foreign investment might crowd out exports into that country from the country in which the investing company resides. This is sometimes described as horizontal foreign investment as it represents investment into similar production units for the production of essentially the same product in various countries (WTO 1997b, p3). It can be encouraged by high trade barriers in the host country as foreign investment is a means to circumvent these barriers. On the other hand, foreign investment is often undertaken with the intention to export the goods produced in the foreign plant back into the country where the investment comes from, or into third countries, so that it might enhance trade. Furthermore, transnational corporations (TNCs) which set up affiliations in various countries tend to increase international trade flows as they normally import and export intermediate goods for the production of consumer goods and services to a greater extent than companies that reside in only one country. This is sometimes described as vertical foreign investment as it represents investment in units for the production of different stages of a product in various countries (ibid). This type of foreign investment will be encouraged if host countries have low trade barriers. A third type of so-called distribution foreign investment takes place if investment aims to set up local distribution, sale and service points to facilitate exports from the home country. The net effect of these opposing trends is probably a trade-enhancing one. A World Trade Organization (WTO) survey of different studies comes to the conclusion that while they differ with regard to the net effect on home country exports, most studies suggest a trade-enhancing effect of foreign investment (ibid).

Investment and trade have close linkages also from an environmental perspective, however. For example, countries can only attract foreign capital with low or non-enforced environmental standards if goods can be re-exported to the country where the foreign investment came from, or to other third countries, as otherwise the market in the host country would usually be too small to make the foreign investment profitable. Companies can only threaten policy-makers with capital flight if they can serve the domestic market also from another location. In restricting international trade in specific goods with non-members, multilateral environmental agreements also take away the incentive for companies to relocate into these free-riding countries as these goods cannot be exported into countries that are members to the agreement.

This book only deals with the multilateral investment and trade regimes. It does not deal in detail with regional agreements such as the European Union (EU), the Mercado Común del Sur (Mercosur) or the North American Free Trade Agreement (NAFTA).[3] A comparative discussion of the multilateral with regional investment and trade regimes would be vastly beyond the limits of this book and is the subject of ongoing research by the author. This book does, however, address a few provisions within the Maastricht Treaty on European Union in Chapter 3 and some of the NAFTA rules in various chapters, as they are of great importance to some of the issues discussed here.[4] Also, the Appendix presents a short overview of environmental provisions contained in some regional and bilateral trade and investment agreements.

As this book refers repeatedly to developed and developing countries, it is necessary to define these terms. Developed countries are the currently 15 EU member countries, plus Norway, Iceland and Switzerland, Australia, New Zealand, Canada, Japan and the US. Developing countries encompass the remaining countries of the world, with the exception of the former Communist countries in Eastern Europe. These so-called economies in transition stand somewhere between developed and developing countries, with those likely to join the EU in the near future (especially Poland, the Czech Republic and Hungary) being closest to developed country status.

I hope that I have written a book that is easily accessible to all interested readers, whether they are students, scholars, policy-makers or representatives from non-governmental organizations (NGOs), without sacrifice in terms of analytical depth. I also hope that the book contributes to a better understanding of how investment, trade and environmental issues are inter-linked and what kind of policy reform is necessary to achieve a development-friendly 'greening' of the multilateral investment and trade regimes – ie environmental protection without protectionism. If we can help policy-makers to achieve this, then we have done our best. If this book has contributed even slightly towards this task, then it has fulfilled its objective.

Part One

Foundations

Part One provides the foundations for the main analysis that follows in Parts Two and Three. It is written for those who are unfamiliar with the major issues. Chapter 1 puts the discussion into historical context in illuminating the development of trade integration and investment flows from about 1870 to 2000. It also introduces the main institutions and agreements encountered in the book. Finally, it examines why developing countries are so hostile towards greening the multilateral investment and trade regimes in the context of the World Trade Organization (WTO) Ministerial Meeting in Seattle in late 1999 and the failed attempt to launch a new 'Millennium Round' of trade negotiations.

Chapter 2 looks at the current regulatory regime in presenting the major rules of the multilateral trade and investment regimes with respect to the environment. The main analysis in Parts Two and Three will frequently refer back to these rules. However, the reader who is familiar with the multilateral trade and investment regimes may omit Chapters 1 and 2, or consult various sections and subsections only.

Globalization: Investment, Trade and the Environment in an Integrating World Economy

Trade integration and investment flows in historical perspective

A defining character of the 1990s has been the continuation and strengthening of what has become known as economic globalization: international trade has grown faster than world economic output in every decade after 1950, and since around the mid-1980s foreign direct investment (FDI) flows are growing faster still on average than international trade flows (UNCTAD 1993, Annex Table 1; UNCTAD 1994, p127; UNCTAD 1998a, Annex Table B.1). Indeed, whereas the difference in growth rates of world trade and world output had decreased in each decade since the 1960s, the last decade of the 20th century has seen a sharp increase in this growth differential (UNCTAD 1991, 1995, 1998c). As a consequence, the economies of nation states all over the globe are becoming integrated at a high pace.

At the same time, however, the extent to which international economies are already interlinked is often exaggerated. For example, the exports share of gross domestic product (GDP) was about 7.6 per cent for the US in 1996, 9.3 per cent for Japan and 21.3 per cent for Germany (UNCTAD 1999b; OECD 1999b). While the speed of integration is fast and accelerating, it is still at a relatively low level and it is unclear for how long it can prolong its own momentum into the future.

It is sometimes even suggested that what we describe as economic globalization nowadays has already been a defining character of the period 1870–1913, when world gross product grew at an average annual rate of 2.5 per cent, while world trade increased at 3.9 per cent and international flows of capital grew significantly – now, as then, made possible by tremendous falls in transportation and communication costs (see Maddison 1991; UNCTAD 1994, pp120–122). Sachs and Warner (1995) suggest that:

... global capitalism has emerged twice, *at the end of the nineteenth century as well as the end of the twentieth century. The earlier global capitalist system peaked around 1910 but subsequently disintegrated in the first half of the twentieth century, between the outbreak of World War I and the end of World War II. The reemergence of a global, capitalist market economy since 1950, and especially since the mid-1980s, in an important sense reestablishes the global market economy that had existed one hundred years earlier* (p5, emphasis in original).

The system was highly integrative, as in the present. A network of bilateral trade treaties kept protectionism in check in most countries (the United States and Russia, where tariff rates were relatively high, being the exceptions). Nations as diverse as Argentina and Russia struggled to adjust their economic policies, and especially their financial policies, to attract foreign investment, particularly for railway building (p8).

Bairoch and Kozul-Wright (1996) actually doubt the validity of the historical analysis provided by Sachs and Warner (1995) in support of their claims, arguing forcefully that continental European countries already became highly protectionist after 1879 and that most non-European advanced countries never adopted a liberal trade regime at all. However, here we will merely further examine the question whether the world about one century ago had the same or at least a very similar extent of trade integration as the current world. At first sight, the available historical data seem to support such an inference – see Table 1.1 adapted from Feenstra (1998, p33). Countries like Australia, Sweden and the UK had a higher ratio of merchandise trade to GDP in 1890 than in 1990. For others, like Japan and the US, the 1990 ratio is not that much higher than the 1890 ratio.

However, to conclude from these historical data that in terms of trade integration current economic globalization is merely a revival of a similar phenomenon from about a century ago would be too hasty because it might be misleading to focus on the trade to GDP ratio, as GDP includes many sectors that do not enter the merchandise trade statistics. As Irwin (1996, p42) points out:

When GNP[1] is disaggregated by industry, it typically includes the following sectors: agriculture (including forestry and fisheries); mining; construction; manufacturing; transportation and public utilities; wholesale and retail trade; finance, insurance, and real estate; other services; and government. Of these categories only agriculture, mining, and manufacturing really produce merchandise goods that enter into standard trade statistics. Over the past few decades, the sectoral composition

Table 1.1 *Ratios of merchandise trade to GDP in per cent*

Country	1890	1990
Australia	15.7	13.4
Canada	12.8	22.0
Denmark	24.0	24.3
France	14.2	17.1
Germany	15.9	24.0
Italy	9.7	15.9
Japan	5.1	8.4
Norway	21.8	28.8
Sweden	23.6	23.5
United Kingdom	27.3	20.6
United States	5.6	8.0

Source: Adapted from Feenstra (1998, p33)

of nominal GNP has shifted away from the production of merchandise goods toward the production of services.

He therefore concludes that '[P]erhaps a better indication of the importance of international trade is to consider merchandise exports as a share of the production of these tradable goods' (ibid). Table 1.2, taken from Feenstra (1998, p35) shows the ratios of merchandise trade to merchandise value added. As can be seen in comparing Table 1.2 to Table 1.1, for most countries the increase in the ratios of merchandise trade to merchandise value added between 1890 and 1990 is much more significant than the increase in the ratios of merchandise trade to GDP over the same time period.

As with trade integration, some have doubted whether current international flows of investment are significantly higher than what they were in the period before 1913. According to Bairoch and Kozul-Wright (1996, p11), in terms of international capital flows, by 1913 about 5 per cent of the gross national product (GNP) of the capital exporting countries was invested abroad, mostly into railways, utilities and public works, and international capital markets were integrated to a considerable extent. Baldwin and Martin (1999, pp10ff) claim that foreign investment was more long-term oriented than in the current phase of globalization, however, due to the much higher costs of communication which hindered the rapid movement of highly liquid investments.

The period before 1913 knew already the phenomenon of TNCs – for example, the famous East India Company – and foreign investment was growing rapidly, with FDI amounting to one-third of overseas investment. Bairoch and Kozul-Wright (1996, p10) point out that their 'own estimate suggests that the stock of FDI reached over 9 per cent of world output in 1913, a figure which had not been surpassed in the early 1990s'. However, the 1980s and 1990s have seen a tremendous increase in foreign investment.

The worldwide inward FDI stock has increased from 4.6 per cent of world GDP in 1980, to 6.5 per cent in 1985, 8 per cent in 1990 and 10.6 per cent in 1996 (UNCTAD 1999a, Statistical Annex, Table B.6). International private flows of financial resources have increased from US$33 billion in 1986 to US$252 billion in 1997 (OECD 1988, Statistical Annex, Table 12; OECD 1999a, Statistical Annex, Table 1).

While the rather volatile and often speculative portfolio equity flows have risen at a tremendous speed in the early 1990s, still more than 50 per cent of private flows consist of FDI and about 15 per cent of commercial bank loans (UNCTAD 1998a, p14).[2] Contrary to the first phase of globalization when FDI mainly flew from advanced countries to more backward countries and mainly into their primary and transportation sectors (Baldwin and Martin 1999, pp18ff), the developed countries are now both the dominating source and the major recipient of FDI, and investment mainly flows into the manufacturing and services sector. However, the dominance of developed countries in terms of FDI recipients has decreased over time, with developing countries in the 1990s receiving almost 40 per cent of FDI as opposed to only about 20 per cent in the 1980s (UNCTAD 1993, Annex Table 1, and UNCTAD 1999a, Annex Table B.1). Indeed, FDI inflows per unit of GDP are much higher in developing as opposed to developed countries. While the latter received FDI in 1996 of around 10 per cent per unit of output, Africa receives 13.7 per cent, Latin America and the Caribbean 23.7 per cent, South, East and South-East Asia 27.5 per cent, and Central and Eastern Europe 15 per cent (UNCTAD 1998a, p10). There was only one developed country (New Zealand) among the top 30 recipients of FDI inflows as measured per unit of GDP (ibid, p11).

Private international flows of financial resources have become increasingly important to developing countries as official development assistance from the developed world has dried up because of tight budgets and a decreased willingness to assist. The official development assistance (ODA) share of the total net resource flows to developing countries has decreased from 64.1 per cent in 1988 to merely 23.6 per cent in 1997 (OECD 1999a, Statistical Annex, Table 1). It is often asserted, however, that contrary to the ODA international investment flows benefit mainly about a dozen developing countries in Asia and Latin America, whereas the vast majority of poor countries, especially in Africa, are left out. This assertion is correct in the sense that countries like Brazil, Mexico, Argentina, Chile and Venezuela in Latin America, and China, Singapore, Indonesia, Malaysia, Thailand and India in Asia, together received almost 72 per cent of all the FDI flowing to the developing world in 1998 and more than 40 times more than the combined FDI to all of the least developed countries together (UNCTAD 1999a, Annex Table B.1). However, the picture is much less uneven if FDI is looked at as a percentage of gross fixed capital formation rather than as absolute figures. This percentage was 8.3 for Africa in 1997, only slightly lower than the developing countries' average of 10.3, and

Table 1.2 *Ratios of merchandise trade to merchandise value-added in per cent*

Country	1890	1990
Australia	27.2	38.7
Canada	29.7	69.8
Denmark	47.4	85.9
France	18.5	53.5
Germany	22.7	57.8
Italy	14.4	43.9
Japan	10.2	18.9
Norway	46.2	74.8
Sweden	42.5	73.1
United Kingdom	61.5	62.8
United States	14.3	35.8

Source: Adapted from Feenstra (1998, p35)

higher than either India's (4.2) or Thailand's (6.8) (UNCTAD 1999a, Annex Table B.5).

It is true that a large share of FDI inflows to developing countries consists of cross-border mergers and acquisitions rather than the setting up of a new plant by a transnational corporation (TNC). According to the United Nations Conference on Trade and Development (UNCTAD) (1998a, p19), the share of mergers and acquisitions has been on average about 50 per cent of FDI inflows between 1985 and 1997. This need not be bad for developing countries, however, as the inflow of capital into existing companies together with their restructuring typically leads to efficiency and profitability improvements.

The expansion of private investment flows has been accompanied by policy changes towards a more investment-friendly environment that makes countries more receptive for these flows. The relationship between the economic and political dimension is not fully clear, but changes in both dimensions seem to have gone hand in hand and to have mutually enforced themselves. According to UNCTAD (1998a, p57), since 1991 on average about 50 countries each year enacted on average about 100 regulatory policy changes every year, the vast majority of which were favourable towards FDI. However, because competition for scarce financial resources is tough and countries fear to lose out in the bid for foreign investment, the last 15 years or so have also seen an increase in incentives that are supposed to lure investment, especially FDI, into a specific location rather than elsewhere. An UNCTAD (1996, p17) study comes to the conclusion that 'the range of incentives available to TNCs, and the number of countries that offer incentives, have increased considerably since the mid-1980s, as barriers to FDI and trade have declined'.

The proliferation and inflation of these incentives are often regarded as socially wasteful as in general they do not increase the overall amount of FDI available, but merely distort the efficient allocation of flows among recipient countries.[3] Investments still flow to the location with the highest return on investment; however, this return is not fully justified by economic productivity but artificially created via governmental incentives, financial or other. Countries are caught in a so-called Prisoner's Dilemma where all would be better off if nobody granted the incentives, but everybody fears to lose out if only the others grant them, so that all end up providing incentives, thus making everybody worse off. The World Trade Organization (WTO) (1998g, p17) makes clear why such a Prisoner's Dilemma is undesirable:

> *The lasting effect is only to redistribute income from host countries to the shareholders of the home countries. This has negative repercussions on global income distribution since some of the gains that would have accrued to poorer developing countries (that are net recipients of FDI) are squandered on incentives to richer developed countries (that are net outward investors).*

It does not matter much that studies of the determinants of FDI flows generally indicate that incentives have only a very minor role to play in international investment decisions (UNCTAD 1996, p41; WTO 1998g). This is for two reasons: first, these incentives can make a difference at the margin, and second, and more importantly, what matters is that, against the received wisdom of empirical studies, policy-makers apparently do believe in the power of incentives to attract investment.

To conclude, while it is often overlooked that the world economy before 1913 was already integrated significantly both in terms of trade and investment flows, the current extent and pace of trade and investment integration seem to signify that the world has entered an unprecedented phase of what is commonly described as economic globalization. Investment and trade do matter and will do so more and more. Next we will briefly present how the creation of a multilateral trade regime has helped to bring about economic globalization and how in turn it has been influenced by globalization, as well as how the links between investment, trade and the environment were addressed.

The institutions governing economic globalization

GATT, ITO and WTO

When a couple desperately want to have a baby girl, but have a boy instead, the parents usually accept the child after their initial disappointment. In some sense, in 1947 the General Agreement on Tariffs and Trade (GATT) resembled such a baby boy: it was not exactly what its founding countries wanted to have, but they settled for it for lack of an alternative.

What was originally envisaged by over 50 countries was a sister organization for the International Bank for Reconstruction and Development (IBRD, nowadays better known as the World Bank) and the International Monetary Fund (IMF), which are called the 'Bretton Woods' institutions because they were founded in 1944 at a conference in the town of Bretton Woods in the US state of New Hampshire. This envisaged sister organization already had a name, International Trade Organization (ITO), and was supposed to be a specialized agency of the United Nations. It was also supposed to be a comprehensive organization with extensive competences for the regulation of world trade in products and services, and international investment, as well as for commodity agreements, restrictive business practices and employment rules. Its charter was finally agreed upon at a UN Conference on Trade and Employment in March 1948 in Havana, which is why it is commonly referred to as the 'Havana Charter'. However, ratification of the charter proved to be impossible in many countries. Most importantly, the US government, which had been one of its strongest proponents, announced in 1950 that its ratification in the US Congress would be impossible, which gave the final death blow to the ITO. Right-wing critics saw too many elements of economic planning, for example in its call for action to maintain full employment in its Article 3, and a sacrifice of US principles and interests in the charter (Brown 1950). One critic went as far as calling it a threat to human freedom and an 'economic Munich', alluding to the de facto resignation of the English democracy to the expansionary aggression of the Nazi regime against the Czechs in 1938 (Cortney 1949).

Enter the GATT. Two years before the Havana conference, 23 of the 50 countries that participated in the ITO negotiations had started negotiations on the reduction and binding of customs tariffs. These, together with some of the trade rules of the draft ITO charter, formed the GATT, which was signed by the 23 countries in 1947 and came into force in January 1948 – that is, before the Havana conference finally approved the ITO charter. As the GATT was never meant to be a substitute for the ITO, its institutional structure was much weaker than the ITO's structure was supposed to be. It was a rather ad hoc agreement, a contract between countries, not an organization as the planned ITO, which meant that it did not need ratification in members' parliaments and its founding members were actually called 'contracting parties', rather than members, in official language.

For an ad hoc agreement with a rather weak institutional structure, the GATT was astonishingly persistent. Over time, more and more countries became contracting parties and several GATT trade rounds further decreased tariffs, and extended the scope and reach of trade rules. While earlier rounds had focused exclusively on tariff reductions, the so-called Kennedy Round of trade negotiations, which took place between 1964 and 1967, extended GATT rules to cover anti-dumping measures. The so-called Tokyo Round, negotiated between 1973 and 1979, brought about a number of so-called 'codes', which dealt inter alia with subsidies and countervailing measures and various forms of non-tariff barriers. (Non-tariff barriers are barriers to trade which do not take the form of tariffs – for example, standards that require certain characteristics for products before they can enter a market.) The Uruguay Round, negotiated between 1986 and 1994, and therefore also the longest lasting trade round so far, brought about the most far-reaching changes. Rules on non-tariff measures were strengthened and new rules were established for new areas such as services, intellectual property, textiles and agriculture that had not been subjected to multilateral rules before. The Uruguay Round also strengthened the existing GATT dispute settlement mechanism. Most importantly, however, it led to the creation of the WTO, with its headquarters in Geneva. Its highest decision-making body is the Ministerial Meeting, which takes place about every two years in various places. Below is the General Council, which meets several times per year in Geneva and normally is attended by ambassadors and the heads of a country's delegation to the WTO.

The WTO finally gave a formal organizational structure to the multilateral trade regime. It also enhanced its legal security as the WTO agreements – that is, the series of agreements resulting from the Uruguay Round – were ratified in members' parliaments. In some sense it is a resurrection of the aborted ITO, even though almost 50 years later the agreed rules were, of course, different and the WTO does not deal with, for example, employment issues, as the ITO was supposed to. The GATT, as a legal text, still exists in a revised form as one of the WTO agreements (and arguably still its most important one). Therefore, while the GATT as an institution with weak organizational structure was superseded by the WTO, the GATT as an agreement that establishes rules for the trade in products still exists. At the time of writing, the WTO had 140 member countries, which account for approximately 90 per cent of world trade, and 28 applicant countries. The two most important among these current non-members are China and the Russian Federation, but China is likely to become a WTO member soon. The WTO therefore encompasses the vast majority of trading countries, which further strengthens its perceived legitimacy. Contrary to the original GATT from 1948, it is no longer an exclusive developed countries' club. Indicative of this shift is that after an exhaustive period of frustrating deadlock, the developed countries finally accepted that in September 2002 Supachai Panitchpakdi of Thailand will become its first Director General from a developing country in the history of the GATT and the WTO.

Committee on Trade and the Environment (CTE)

Already in 1971 – that is, even before the United Nations Conference on the Human Environment took place in Stockholm in 1972 – the GATT contracting parties agreed to establish a so-called Group on Environmental Measures and International Trade. However, as the group was supposed to convene only upon request and no GATT party submitted such a request, it lay dormant for 20 years. Finally, in February 1991 contracting parties to the European Free Trade Association (EFTA) asked the then GATT Director General Arthur Dunkel to convene the group in order to inquire into the trade–environment nexus and make a contribution to the 1992 United Nations Conference on Environment and Development (UNCED) in Rio de Janeiro.[4] Consequently, the group met several times between November 1991 and January 1994 to discuss the consistency of trade provisions in multilateral environmental agreements (MEAs) with GATT rules, the trade effects of national environmental regulations and the trade effects of product packaging and eco-labelling rules (see WTO 1999a, annex 1).

At their Ministerial Meeting in Marrakesh in April 1994 trade ministers decided to widen and intensify the debates on the trade and environment linkage, and to request the next meeting of the General Council of the WTO to establish a Committee on Trade and Environment (CTE) for that purpose. The Marrakesh Decision set up a list of ten items to be examined by the CTE. This list encompassed all the major areas of the international trading system including goods, services and intellectual property, the relationship between the GATT rules including its dispute settlement mechanisms and MEAs and their dispute settlement mechanisms, as well as market access for developing countries and the arrangement for relations with NGOs and the transparency of WTO documentation.

The CTE met for the first time on 31 January 1995 and has met since then, at the time of writing, almost 35 times and is scheduled to meet regularly in the future. The results of these meetings have been rather disappointing as no conclusive and definite results have emerged so far. Thus, the CTE reports usually tend to list the disagreements among the GATT parties concerning the items on their agenda, which, for lack of consensus, agree that nothing should be changed and the issues should be subject to further inquiry. Instead of being a front-runner in triggering reform of the multilateral trade regime to make it more environmentally friendly, as hoped for by some environmental groups, the CTE has proved to be more of a paper tiger.

There is one area, however, where substantial progress has been achieved: transparency of WTO documentation. The debates within the CTE are reported in publicly available so-called 'Trade and Environment Bulletins'. More generally, the WTO General Council has changed the rules on derestriction of WTO documents. Whereas the GATT documents were restricted if they were not specified otherwise, WTO documents are now in principle unrestricted if they are not specified otherwise. However, critics maintain that documents are still often unavailable until after decisions have been made, that WTO members can determine arbitrarily and uncontestedly to keep documents restricted and that currently existing restriction periods are both unnecessary and arbitrary (Van Dyke and Weiner 1997). Canada has made a far-reaching proposal to derestrict all secretariat working papers, formal contributions from members, dispute panel and appellate body submissions, as well as opening dispute settlement hearings to the public and allowing NGOs to submit so-called amicus curiae briefs, which are position papers, to panels and appellate bodies (Canada 1999a). This proposal has received sympathy among some developed countries, especially the US, but has met fierce opposition by most countries, especially developing ones, which view the calls for more transparency at the WTO with suspicion (ICTSD 1999e).

North American Free Trade Agreement (NAFTA)

On 1 January 1994 the North American Free Trade Agreement between Canada, Mexico and the US came into effect. It has been hailed by some as the most environmental regional free-trade agreement ever, and condemned by others for its alleged environmental insensitivity and weak environmental enforcement mechanisms. As one environmentalist has put it: 'The NAFTA has been designed to create a low wage, weak environmental regulatory enforcement haven for manufacturing' (quoted in CEC 1996, p17). The rift went right through the environmental movement, especially in the US, with some, like WWF, in favour of it, while others, like Greenpeace, were strictly opposed (WWF 1993; Greenpeace 1993a, 1993b).

NAFTA and its environmental side agreement, the North American Agreement on Environmental Cooperation (NAAEC), do indeed contain some provisions which are novel for a free trade agreement.[5] These environmental provisions were at the time of conclusion widely regarded as the price proponents of free trade had to pay to overcome some of the opposition to NAFTA and to get the agreement ratified in the US Congress. As this book does not deal explicitly with plurilateral regional trade agreements and focuses instead on the multilateral trade and investment regime, we will not examine these provisions here in detail (for good analyses see Johnson and Beaulieu (1996) and Saunders (1997)). However, some of these provisions are so interesting to a study of investment, trade and the environment that they will be dealt with in other sections of the book (which is the reason for briefly introducing NAFTA here).

At the time of writing, seven years after NAFTA came into force, views on NAFTA's and its side agreement's environmental performance are still divided. Maybe not surprisingly, the Commission for Environmental Cooperation, the main body established by the environmental side agreement, draws a mainly positive balance:

> *Most of the NAFTA institutions with specific environmental responsibilities or relevance have moved into operation, with a takeoff in activity in 1996. There is considerable cooperation, openness and trust emerging on a trilateral basis ... There have been concrete environmental achievements in some cases, notably the transportation of dangerous goods and pesticides.*

> Yet performance varies. In some areas, such as automotive emissions, slow progress has been made in meeting mandatory targets and timetables (CEC 1999, p20).

Others, especially some NGOs, speak of NAFTA as a failed experiment and blame it for broken promises (Public Citizen 2000). Many NGOs are particularly concerned about the investor-to-state dispute settlement provision in NAFTA's Chapter 11 and the impact that pending cases will have on the government's ability to set stringent environmental standards (see Chapter 5).

Bilateral Investment Treaties (BITs)

The economic and political changes towards a more investment-friendly global economy have been legally backed by a tremendous increase in Bilateral Investment Treaties (BITs), the objective of which is to grant foreign investors security and legally enforceable rights for their investments. Since West Germany negotiated the first two treaties in 1959, the number of BITs has increased to over 1300 by the end of 1996, with almost 1000 treaties coming into effect after 1990 (UNCTAD 1998b, p9). 162 countries now participate in one or more treaty (ibid, p10). The majority of treaties are concluded between a developing or country in transition from planned to market economy and a developed country. Contrary to NAFTA's Chapter 11 which deals with investment issues, BITs usually do not contain any environmental provisions.

Multilateral Agreement on Investment (MAI)

In the mid-1990s representatives from the Organization for Economic Co-operation and Development (OECD) countries tried to base the plethora of BITs on a more multilateral basis in negotiating a Multilateral Agreement on Investment (MAI) among themselves with the intent to persuade non-OECD countries to accede to the MAI later on.[6] The MAI sought to establish binding rules on the treatment of foreign investment by host countries. Its draft clauses were not altogether new as most of them can be found already in many BITs. But some of these clauses were rather novel and it was the declared intention of negotiators to conclude a treaty of the highest level. However, a short sentence informed the public about the failure of over three years of intensive negotiations in a press release on 3 December 1998: 'Negotiations on the MAI are no longer taking place' (OECD 1998d).

While it is true that negotiations also failed because of substantial disagreements among the negotiating parties, as can be seen by the many alternative formulations and points to be agreed on in the draft treaty text (OECD 1998a), the rising tide of opposition against the MAI from both members of parliaments and especially from NGOs was presumably decisive in bringing down the negotiations (Henderson 1999).[7] The failure of the

MAI might mark a watershed for future international negotiations on issues such as investment or trade, as presumably for the first time negotiators were challenged by a global network of NGO activists who were hostile towards the outcome of negotiations. Due to the revolutionary changes in communications technology, these activists could communicate with each other all over the globe via electronic mail at an enormous speed and could publish their acid critique of the draft MAI on the internet, thus giving access to their statements and position papers to any computer-literate at the push of a button. Representatives from WTO members got a first taste of this form of opposition when the initial ceremony at the Seattle Ministerial Meeting in November 1999 was ambushed by street blockades.

Many of the NGOs and many trade unionists were not only fundamentally opposed to any form of MAI, but they opposed more generally the very idea of trade liberalization and the concept of economic globalization.[8] Indeed, the draft MAI seems to have served the function of a rallying device for NGOs, trade unionists and all other groups and individuals opposed to a liberal world economic order. This observation is confirmed by NGO activist Clarke (1998) who assures his readers that the fight against the MAI is 'part of the much larger struggle against the forces and institutions of economic globalization itself'.

The OECD negotiators were rather unlucky that, at the time, their negotiations coincided with fundamental economic and financial crises in East Asia, Russia and Latin America that were perceived by many people, and certainly by most NGOs, as the catastrophic but inevitable consequences of economic globalization. These crises made members of parliament and the wider public alike more receptive of the NGOs' radical criticism of the MAI and of everything connected to economic globalization. It is pure irony, however, that the NGOs could only collaborate so intensively worldwide and disseminate their critique so quickly because they profited from the revolutionary changes in communications technology that represent another form of globalization.

The failure of MAI negotiations at the OECD level does not mean that a multilateral agreement on investment is off the table. Indeed, the same press release by the OECD that makes public the failure of negotiations goes on to state that 'officials reaffirmed the desirability of international rules for investment' (OECD 1998d). Efforts now focus on a substantial revision and extension of the existing WTO Agreement on Trade Related Investment Measures, with both Japan and the European Union being committed to negotiations on investment as part of their broader push for a new so-called Millennium round of negotiations at the WTO.[9] The prospects for the success of this demand are unclear as many, but not all, developing countries appear to be opposed to a new round of WTO negotiations in general and a multilateral investment agreement in particular, and the US is at best lukewarm to this proposal.

Why are developing countries hostile towards greening the multilateral investment and trade regimes?

There exists a fundamental clash of priorities between developed and developing countries about whether the multilateral investment and trade regime is in need of 'greening' – that is of incorporating new environmental elements. On the one hand, practically all developed countries – partly by conviction, partly due to pressure from NGOs – are to some extent in favour of such greening. These proposals encompass a strengthening of the stance of the Committee for Trade and the Environment within the WTO system, reductions in environmentally harmful subsidies, the liberalization in the trade of environmental goods and services, environmental assessments of new trade agreements, the reconciliation of trade measures in Multilateral Environmental Agreements (MEAs) with WTO rules, the role of eco-labelling and, in the case of the European Communities, also a strengthening of the precautionary principle (see, for example, Canada 1999b; United States 1999; European Communities 1999).

On the other hand, practically all developing countries are either strictly opposed or at least most reluctant to accept even negotiation of such reform proposals. This became crystal clear at a WTO high-level symposium on trade and the environment on 15–16 March 1999 (ICTSD 1999a). Developing countries regard the proposals to 'green' these regimes with dire suspicion and that meeting was by far not the first occasion that they had voiced their opposition. They do not trust the alleged idealistic intentions of the proponents. Instead they regard the proposals as motivated by economically protectionist reasons.[10] In their view, they are either intended by design as protectionism under green disguise or will have such unintended, but de facto, consequences. Whether in the form of eco-labels, unilateral trade sanctions for allegedly environmental reasons or trade measures in MEAs, the fear is that these will be used to restrict developing countries' access to developed countries' markets. Representative of this stance is presumably a quotation from a communication of Kenya (1999a, para 52ff):

> *It is important to emphasize that Kenya is a keen proponent of environmental conservation. However, Kenya objects to any move to use environmental measures as a barrier to trade … It is Kenya's view that environmental norms and standards are a function of the stage of development of the economy. Therefore, to impose on low income developing countries environmental standards prevailing in advanced countries would, internally, artificially raise their costs of production and, externally, extinguish their comparative advantage in the export sector.*

One cannot understand this sometimes embittered hostility towards practically any form of greening of the multilateral investment and trade regimes without understanding at the same time that developing countries' suspicions with regard to the proper intentions of developed countries are rooted in a much deeper frustration with the distribution of benefits in these multilateral regimes. In the view of developing countries, the developed countries benefit much more from these than they themselves do. In particular, they believe that the developed countries have benefited quite substantially from the Uruguay Round of trade negotiations in including topics in the agreements that they favour: intellectual property rights, investment, services, telecommunications, restriction of production and export subsidies, strengthening of anti-dumping measures, increased access to developing countries' markets, to mention just a few. The developing countries, on the other hand, have hardly benefited, if at all, from trade liberalization enacted by the Uruguay Round.

But is this perspective correct? How do developing countries currently fare in the WTO? On paper they are privileged. The WTO agreements of the Uruguay Round guaranteed them 'special and differential' treatment (WTO 1999b). Developed countries are encouraged to grant developing countries trade preferences and a number of WTO agreements contain special provisions that are supposed to safeguard developing countries' interests. For example, in the Agreement on Technical Barriers to Trade (TBT Agreement) the preparation and application of technical regulations and standards are supposed to take into account the special needs of developing countries (Articles 11 and 12). The same applies to measures taken in pursuance of the Agreement on Sanitary and Phytosanitary Measures (SPS Agreement) (Articles 9 and 10). Furthermore, most of the WTO agreements allow developing countries a transitional period of grace until the provisions have to be implemented. For example, in the Agreement on Subsidies and Countervailing Measures, developing countries were given eight years to phase out the relevant subsidies, and a number of the least developed countries and other poor developing countries with an annual per capita income of less then US$1000 were totally exempted from the prohibition of export subsidies (Article 27). Lastly, a couple of WTO agreements envisaged the provision of trade-related technical assistance to developing countries either by developed countries on a bilateral basis or through multilateral institutions.

Developing countries welcomed their 'special and differential treatment' at the time of the conclusion of the WTO agreements, but have by now grown disillusioned about their actual effects. They rightly complain that the special provisions that were supposed to safeguard their interests have been largely ineffectual in reality, that the transitional periods were too short for them to adjust to the requirements of the WTO agreements and that the promised technical assistance was too little and too unsystematic to strengthen their capacity to comply with trade obligations. In a high-level symposium on trade and development held by the WTO in Geneva on 17–18 March 1999, the developing countries were united in their suggestion that, by and large, 'special and differential treatment' has proved to be a 'dead letter' (ICTSD 1999b).

This does not mean, however, that developing countries have not benefited at all from the Uruguay Round. Substantial gains have already arisen and are bound to rise further over time due to the gradual phasing in of agriculture and textiles into the WTO, for which developing countries have a clear comparative advantage. But the very fact that liberalization in agriculture and textiles remains rather limited and has been delayed to a later period than most other liberalizations, shows that developed countries successfully managed to shield themselves to some extent from increased competition in the markets that were most relevant to developing countries.

Developing countries have also benefited from a further clarification and formalization of dispute settlement rules, including some special provisions for developing countries, such as the participation of a panelist from the developing world upon a developing country's request and the provision of qualified legal assistance to developing countries. This has led to increased participation from a broader range of developing countries trying to defend their trade rights, whereas the former GATT dispute settlement was mostly only invoked by large developing countries such as Argentina, Brazil, Chile, Hong Kong and India (Kuruvila 1997).

Nevertheless, it seems fair to say that the developed countries have benefited much more relative to developing countries from the Uruguay Round, a conclusion that was tentatively accepted even by then WTO Director General Renato Ruggiero at the mentioned high-level symposium on trade and development (ICTSD 1999b). Given this imbalance, it is understandable why developing countries are desperate to seek access to developed countries' markets, and regard any reform proposals that could lead to a restriction of this access with great suspicion and outright hostility – even if it comes in the name of saving 'our common environment'.

WTO Ministerial Meeting in Seattle and the 'Millennium Round'

The perceived imbalance in the distribution of benefits from the Uruguay Round of trade negotiations and the suspicion of developing countries towards the proper intentions of developed countries' proposals to green the multilateral investment and trade regimes became an important factor when delegates from WTO members convened for the Ministerial Meeting in Seattle in late November and early December 1999. Many were anxious for the results that this meeting would generate. The EU and Japan went to Seattle with the most comprehensive proposal: to initiate a new so-called 'Millennium Round' of trade negotiations covering a broad range of issues from the traditional ones, such as tariff reductions for goods and services, to an inclusion of new (or as yet only marginally covered) topics, such as competition policy, government procurement and investment. Other developed countries, most notably the US and Canada, also wanted a new round of trade negotiations to be enacted, but were reluctant to include many new topics. The same is true for some developing countries with traditionally good links to developed countries, such as Brazil, Mexico and other Latin American as well as a few Asian countries. One of the reasons for this reluctance to embark on a very comprehensive new round of trade negotiations was the expressed opposition of most other developing countries – most notably that of Egypt, Zimbabwe, India, Bangladesh, Pakistan and Malaysia. In essence, their objective was to merely renegotiate the Uruguay Round agreements and to correct some of what they perceived as its imbalances.[11]

For the first time in the history of the GATT/WTO, non-governmental organizations (NGOs) played a prominent and clearly visible role at a ministerial meeting. They had mobilized their activists months before with impressive organizational skills. That there would be massive protests in the streets of Seattle, attempted disturbances of meetings and even violent riots was clear to everybody who observed the networked mobilization via the internet – everybody but the Seattle police force, that is.

Obviously, there are non-negligible differences between environmental NGOs and more development-orientated NGOs, as well as differences between 'Northern' NGOs, whose activists mainly come from developed countries, and 'Southern' NGOs. Nevertheless, on some substantive issues, most NGOs had a common stance. For example, they clearly supported the majority of developing countries in their opposition to a new round of trade negotiations and in their call for a renegotiation of the existing agreements. On the other hand, at least the 'Northern' NGOs clearly supported the developed countries in their call for incorporating environmental elements into the multilateral trade regime, whereas some 'Southern' NGOs, which were by far less represented in Seattle than their 'Northern' counterparts, opposed such proposals (see, for example, CUTS 1999). Indeed, on many accounts the reform proposals from 'Northern' NGOs were much more far reaching and extended to the multilateral investment regime as well, which was practically ignored by developed countries' governments (see, for example, Greenpeace 1999 and WWF 1999a).

The support for the environmental agenda of developed countries and the fact that some environmental activists made it into developed countries' delegations to the Seattle meeting prompted developing countries to regard the NGOs as a whole with suspicion. On top of this came the fact that some, but not all, NGOs rejected the WTO and the very idea of gains from trade liberalization itself. Developing countries want to gain more from the multilateral trade regime, want the WTO to become 'their' institution as well and they are glad for any NGO support they might receive for this objective. But they had nothing to do with and felt alienated by the fundamental opposition towards virtually any form of trade liberalization expressed by some of the more radical activists and NGOs at Seattle (see, for example, Peoples' Global Action 1999; World Development Movement 1999).

However, the single factor that prompted developing countries to regard some of the especially environmental NGOs positively as enemies was their cooperation with and support of trade unions, together with their mutual calls for an inclusion of strong labour rights into the WTO system (ICTSD 2000k; Alliance for Sustainable Jobs and the Environment 1999). In the view of developing countries, this link confirmed their suspicion that behind the seemingly idealist environmentalist agenda stood massive economically protectionist interests. It confirmed their view that the greening of the multi-lateral investment and trade regime is just a Trojan horse, and yet another mechanism to protect jobs in developed countries from competition from the South.

After Seattle: Quo vadis the WTO?

The WTO ministerial meeting in Seattle ended in turmoil and no new round of trade negotiations was enacted – not even a final declaration was passed. The last section above concentrated on NGOs and the role played by their critique of and opposition to a new trade round. It would be grossly misleading, however, to suggest that this had been the major reason for the Seattle failure. Instead, the more fundamental reasons are manifold, of which three of the most important are as follows:

1   There were substantive disagreements among the major trading groups. The European Union (EU), for example, together with Japan tried to keep agriculture in general and genetically modified organisms (GMOs) in particular as far as possible out of the liberalization efforts, and insisted on a broad negotiating agenda that included such issues as the environment, investment, government procurement and competition policy, eventually leading to the simultaneous conclusion of a comprehensive new round of trade negotiations ('single undertaking'). The US, on the other hand, together with the so-called Cairns Group of major agricultural exporting nations, insisted on further liberalization in agriculture in general and GMOs in particular, and was sceptical towards the inclusion of some of the new issues such as competition policy as it feared strong-headed opposition from developing countries. It also wanted to see early negotiation results in these and other sectors, such as services and products, under the banner of 'early harvest' and 'accelerated tariff liberalization'. Developing countries wanted to see a correction of the perceived imbalances of past trade rounds as outlined above and to restrict the use of anti-dumping measures which they perceived as being abused by developed countries to shield themselves

against cheaper imports from developing countries. They also wanted to fight off the inclusion of new issues (especially the environment and labour rights), and to gain extended deadlines for the implementation of trade-related intellectual property rights (TRIPs) and other agreements.

2   Many, especially from the developing world, were angered by the way that negotiations in Seattle were undertaken. Often, a selection of 10–20 major trading powers held separate negotiations in so-called 'Green Room' meetings that excluded the majority of developing countries, which in turn accused the WTO and the US hosts of holding negotiations in a non-transparent and undemocratic manner. The difficulty with open negotiations is, of course, that to reach consensus is easier among 10 or 20 countries than among the totality of WTO members. Neither the WTO nor the US hosts had found a convincing means to achieve constructive negotiations at low transactions cost without leaving the vast majority of countries with the impression of exclusion from the negotiations.

3   The US hosts achieved further alienation of developing countries when US President Clinton, faced with angry trade unionists, spoke out for a WTO Working Group on Trade and Labour that was supposed to develop labour rights that eventually were to be backed up by trade sanctions. This move, which was triggered by domestic US policy considerations, prompted many developing countries' representatives to fear that a new trade round would bring about further imbalances at their expense rather than increased opportunities.

Does this mean that a new Millennium Round of trade round is off the table forever? Of course not. It is just a question of time that sooner or later a new round will be enacted. Past trade negotiations, such as the Uruguay Round, had suffered from similar initial setbacks that delayed negotiations for years. A new round will also be facilitated by the fact that many of the Uruguay Round agreements have a so-called 'built-in agenda' that automatically requires new rounds of negotiations and reviews of the agreements.

In closing ranks with trade unions some of the environmental NGOs and activists might have done a great disservice to the environment. There will only be substantial progress for the global environment if it will be possible to convince the developing world that an incorporation of environmental elements into the multilateral investment and trade regime can be done in a way that does not harm their trade and economic development aspirations. The challenge is to make the multilateral investment and trade regimes more environmentally friendly, without opening the floodgates for potential protectionist abuse by the developed world. It lies at the heart of the objective of this book to persuade readers that this challenge can be met successfully. I hope that the following chapters will achieve this objective. The next chapter starts with an outline of the current regulatory multilateral trade and investment regimes in which environmental policy takes place.

2

The Current Multilateral Trade and Investment Regimes

Trade and the environment

The agreement establishing the WTO and the GATT

The preamble

The preambular language to the GATT 1947 leaves readers in no doubt why environmentalists, especially those who are pessimistic about the environmental effects of economic growth, are suspicious towards the General Agreement on Tariffs and Trade. In the preamble the GATT parties state their desire to strive for, among other things, 'a *large and steadily growing volume* of real income and effective demand, developing the *full* use of the resources of the world and *expanding* the production and exchange of goods' (emphasis added). The rhetoric of this quotation is one of 'frontier economics' (Colby 1991), for which limitless economic growth is both possible and desirable, and environmental constraints are non-existent.

Of course, such a rhetoric might not be surprising, given the time at which the GATT was negotiated. When almost 50 years later countries concluded negotiations on the Agreement Establishing the World Trade Organization, in its preamble the 'full use of the resources of the world' had given way to 'the *optimal* use of the world's resources in accordance with the objective of sustainable development' (emphasis added). Furthermore, the World Trade Organization (WTO) parties assured that they were 'seeking both to protect and preserve the environment and to enhance the means for doing so in a manner consistent with their respective needs and concerns at different levels of economic development'. However, what is often overlooked by many who focus on the WTO's espousal of sustainable development and environmental protection is that the WTO parties still state their desire to strive for 'a large and steadily growing volume of real income and effective demand, and expanding the production of and trade in goods and services' in the preamble of this agreement.

A preamble does not have the same legal status as the substantive rights and obligations of WTO members codified in the GATT articles and other WTO agreements themselves. However, the preamble is far from irrelevant and is frequently invoked in interpreting these articles. For example, in the so-called shrimp/sea turtle dispute (see p136), the appellate body explicitly referred to the preamble's espousal of the objective of sustainable development to determine that, 'in the light of contemporary concerns', sea turtles constitute 'exhaustible natural resources' in accordance with Article XX(g) of the GATT (WTO 1998b, paragraph 129). Furthermore, the panel insisted that the preamble 'must add colour, texture and shading to our interpretation of the agreements annexed to the WTO Agreement' (ibid, paragraph 153).

Article I (Most favoured nation treatment)

Articles I and III of the GATT codify two of its most important principles. Article I grants, with exceptions, most favoured nation treatment to all members of the WTO, which means that:

> *any advantage, favour, privilege or immunity granted by any contracting party to any product originating in or destined for any other country shall be accorded immediately and unconditionally to the like product originating in or destined for the territories of all other contracting parties.*

In other words, *like* products must in principle be treated exactly the same, no matter which trading partner supplied the products, as long as they are WTO members. It forbids discrimination between trading partners.

Most favoured nation treatment can be in conflict with multilateral environmental agreements (MEAs). Often MEAs employ some form of trade measure against non-parties. If these non-parties are WTO members, they could challenge these provisions before a WTO dispute settlement panel, claiming that its products are unfairly discriminated against. No such dispute has arisen – yet – but the potential for conflict is clearly there (see Chapter 9 for more detail).

Article III (National treatment)

Article III goes one step beyond Article I in not only forbidding discrimination between various like foreign products, but also forbidding discrimination of foreign products relative to domestic ones. It grants, with exceptions, national treatment to foreign products:

> *The products of the territory of any contracting party imported into the territory of any other contracting party shall not be subject, directly or indirectly, to internal taxes or other internal*

*charges of any kind in excess of those applied, directly or
indirectly, to like domestic products* (Article III, para 2).

*The products of the territory of any contracting party imported
into the territory of any other contracting party shall be
accorded treatment no less favourable than that accorded to
like products of national origin in respect of all laws, regulations and requirements affecting their internal sale, offering for
sale, purchase, transportation, distribution or use* (Article III,
para 4).

Of course, national treatment only applies to foreign products after they
have entered the market. A tariff on imported products does not constitute a
violation of national treatment.

Article III is also of direct environmental relevance to MEAs. Often they
employ some distinction of products according to their process and production methods (PPMs) – that is, according to the way in which these products
were produced. The Montreal Protocol, for example, distinguishes between
products manufactured with and without ozone-depleting substances (see
p162). The WTO rules by and large do not allow a distinction of products
according to their PPMs as far as differences in environmental standards are
concerned. Instead, it demands national treatment – that is, non-discrimination for 'like products', where 'like products' has been interpreted by various
GATT and WTO panels narrowly, explicitly denying that otherwise identical
products are 'unlike' if they are produced by different PPMs (see p138).

Article XI (General elimination of quantitative restrictions)

Article XI is also of importance. Its objective is the general elimination of
quantitative restrictions:

*No prohibitions or restrictions other than duties, taxes or other
charges, whether made effective through quotas, import or
export licences or other measures, shall be instituted or
maintained by any contracting party on the importation of any
product of the territory of any other contracting party or on the
exportation or sale for export of any product destined for the
territory of any other contracting party* (Article XI, 1).

Environmentally motivated import restrictions that violate the national treatment provisions, as well as export restrictions, can be challenged as
prohibited quantitative restrictions if they take the form of bans, embargoes
and other prohibitions of trade (Caldwell 1994, p184).

Article XX (General exceptions)

The three mentioned articles are also of indirect environmental relevance as they themselves, as well as any other GATT article, may be violated under certain conditions which are set out in Article XX of the GATT. This article includes the following 'general exceptions' to the otherwise binding obligations of WTO members:

> Subject to the requirement that such measures are not applied in a manner which would constitute a means of arbitrary or unjustifiable discrimination between countries where the same conditions prevail, or a disguised restriction on international trade, nothing in this Agreement shall be construed to prevent the adoption or enforcement by any contracting party of measures:
>
> ...
>
> (b) necessary to protect human, animal or plant life or health;
>
> ...
>
> (g) relating to the conservation of exhaustible natural resources if such measures are made effective in conjunction with restrictions on domestic production or consumption;

Article XX provides a 'limited and conditional exception from obligations under other provisions of the General Agreement, and, as opposed to the positive provisions of the General Agreement, does not establish obligations in itself' (WTO 1998d, p2). Importantly, the burden of proof lies with the party invoking one of the exceptions of Article XX – that is, it is on the party that introduced a disputed measure to prove that in case other GATT articles are violated, the measure may nevertheless be justified under one of the exceptions of Article XX (ibid, p3). Dispute panels have to decide first whether the disputed measure is covered by one of the exceptions and, if so, then to assess whether it also satisfies the requirements of the preamble to Article XX (ibid, p4).

As concerns Article XX(b), for a measure to be covered by this exception, the policy in respect of which the measure was invoked must actually 'protect human, animal or plant life'. The GATT and WTO panels have tended to interpret the term 'necessary' narrowly, usually requiring that no other less trade-restrictive measures exist, which could also achieve the protection of human, animal or plant life or health (see p124).

As concerns Article XX(g), for a measure to be covered by this exception, it must fulfil three requirements (ibid, p16):

1   The policy in respect of which the measure was invoked must actually be related to the conservation of exhaustible natural resources.
2   The same must apply to the measure itself.
3   The disputed measure must have been undertaken 'in conjunction' with restrictions on domestic production or consumption.

As concerns the first two conditions, the already mentioned appellate body in the shrimp/sea turtle dispute has significantly extended the reach of the meaning of 'exhaustible natural resources'. It noticed that while the term might have encompassed merely exhaustible mineral or other non-living natural resources by the time of drafting in 1947, the words of Article XX(g) 'must be read by the treaty interpreter in the light of contemporary concerns of the nations about the protection and conservation of the environment' (WTO 1998b, paragraph 129). It ruled that 'exhaustible natural resources' should therefore encompass both living and non-living resources (ibid, paragraph 131).

As concerns the preamble, its objective is to prevent the abuse of the exceptions contained in Article XX. The appellate body in the shrimp/sea turtle-dispute noted that:

> [t]he task of interpreting and applying the chapeau[1] is ... essentially the delicate one of locating and marking out a line of equilibrium between the right of a Member to invoke an exception under Article XX and the rights of the other Members under varying substantive provisions (eg Article XI) of the GATT 1994, so that neither of the competing rights will cancel out the other and thereby distort and nullify or impair the balance of rights and obligations constructed by the Members themselves in that Agreement (WTO 1998b, para 158).

As concerns the substance of the preamble, under what conditions measures represent 'an arbitrary or unjustifiable discrimination between countries where the same conditions prevail, or a disguised restriction on international trade' depends very much on the specific case. We will therefore have a closer look at it when we examine specific relevant dispute panel and appellate body reports in Chapter 8.

The General Agreement on Trade in Services

The General Agreement on Trade in Services (GATS) is basically for services what the GATT is for products. In its Article II:1 it has a most-favoured nation treatment clause for 'like services and service suppliers' analogous to GATT Article I:1. In its Article XVII:1 it provides national treatment for 'like services and service suppliers' analogous to GATT Article III:2. Finally, its Article XIV provides general exceptions to the substantive GATS obligations analogous to GATT Article XX. There are two differences, however. First, while the wording of the preamble to both articles is otherwise identical, Article XX of GATT subjects measures to the requirement that they 'are not applied in a manner which would constitute a means of arbitrary or unjustifiable discrimination between countries where the *same* conditions prevail', whereas Article XIV of GATS refers to '...where *like* conditions prevail' (emphasis added). Second, whereas GATS Article XIV(b) is identical to GATT Article XX(b), there is no exception analogous to GATT Article XX(g) – that is, measures 'necessary to protect human, animal or plant life or health' are exempted, but not measures 'relating to the conservation of exhaustible natural resources'.

At the time of writing, no WTO member has ever challenged an environmentally related trade measure as inconsistent with GATS. Hence no environmentally relevant case law exists with special reference to GATS. However, as the substantive clauses as well as the exceptions are analogous to the GATT, the same rules for interpretation, as laid down in the last section, are likely to apply.

The Agreement on Technical Barriers to Trade (TBT Agreement)

The major objective of the Agreement on Technical Barriers to Trade (TBT Agreement) is the setting of rules for the establishment and application of technical regulations and standards. The major definitional divide between the two is that whereas compliance with technical regulations is mandatory, compliance with standards is voluntary (Annex 1). Both regulations and standards may also include '... labelling requirements as they apply to a product, process or production methods' (Annex 1, paragraphs 1 and 2). Box 2.1 deals with eco-labelling and WTO rules.

In its preamble, the TBT Agreement explicitly recognizes that 'no country should be prevented from taking measures ... for the protection of human, animal or plant life or health, or the environment...'. Article 2:2 proclaims the 'protection of human health or safety, animal or plant life or health, or the environment' as legitimate objectives for technical regulations as long as they are not 'prepared, adopted or applied with a view to or with the effect of creating unnecessary obstacles to international trade', and as long as they are not 'more trade-restrictive than necessary to fulfil a legitimate objective'. Also, all measures are required to be consistent with non-discrimination and national treatment (Article 2:1) similar to GATT Article III. While the TBT Agreement encourages the adoption of international technical regulations (Article 2:4), the harmonization of regulations (Article 2:6) and even the adoption of foreign regulations (Article 2:7), it specifically allows deviation from international standards 'when such international standards or relevant parts would be an ineffective or inappropriate means for the fulfilment of the legitimate objectives pursued – for instance, because of fundamental climatic or geographical factors or fundamental technological problems'

BOX 2.1 ECO-LABELLING SCHEMES AND WTO RULES

WTO rules with respect to eco-labelling schemes are not particularly straightforward. In the most common case, eco-labels will be related to product characteristics, for which the TBT Agreement applies. However, if they are not related to product characteristics, but purely PPM related, the TBT Agreement does not apply and the general GATT rules come into play. If, however, eco-labels are 'directly related to food safety', no matter whether or not they are related to product characteristics, then the Agreement on the Application of Sanitary and Phytosanitary Measures (SPS Agreement) applies – see the next section. To make things even more complicated, the WTO system further distinguishes between eco-labelling schemes that are voluntary and schemes that are mandatory.

The TBT Agreement in principle allows mandatory eco-labelling schemes if they are related to product characteristics, do not include PPM relevant aspects and fulfil all the requirements of its Article 2 (see the accompanying text). The TBT Agreement's Code of Good Practice for the Preparation, Adoption and Application of Standards in Annex 3 also allows inclusion of PPM relevant aspects as long as the eco-labelling is voluntary and subject to the same requirements. The exact extent to which this code allows eco-labels to include PPM relevant aspects, as well as connected aspects of implementation, effects on international trade and poor countries, and so on are issues that are the object of ongoing discussions both within the CTE and the TBT Committee. At the time of writing, no conclusion has been reached yet. The negotiation history of the TBT Agreement seems to suggest that many countries were of the view that standards based on PPMs, even if voluntary, should only be allowed if they were somehow related to the characteristics of a product, but not if they were unrelated (WTO 1995a).

Strictly speaking, therefore, the TBT Agreement only applies to eco-labelling schemes that are related to or affect product characteristics. Purely PPM related eco-labels – that is, eco-labels that target PPMs without being related to or affecting product characteristics – lie outside the scope of the TBT Agreement. The same is presumably true for eco-labelling schemes which are neither purely product, nor purely non-product related. Examples of this type of eco-labels are those that are based on life-cycle analysis (LCA) of products which try to assess the environmental impacts of goods from 'cradle to grave' – that is, from their production up until their consumption and disposal. Whether voluntary or mandatory, their legality under the WTO system is not entirely clear. If such an eco-labelling scheme was *mandatory*, it would most likely clash with GATT Article III as it distinguishes between 'like products' on grounds that are not related to a product's characteristics and could probably not be justified by invoking one of the environmental exceptions in GATT Article XX (Appleton 1997). At the time of writing, no country seemed to have had such a purely PPM related mandatory eco-labelling scheme in place. A *voluntary* eco-labelling scheme, on the other hand, could be deemed GATT-consistent. In the famous first GATT dispute settlement on US import restrictions of tuna, the panel upheld the Dolphin Protection Consumer Information Act which gave tuna processors access to a voluntary 'dolphin safe' label, if they could demonstrate that the tuna was actually caught without harm to dolphins. However, as this ruling never became formally adopted (see p134), the legality or otherwise of purely PPM related voluntary eco-labelling schemes remains somewhat unclear. It should be noted here, however, that if the eco-labelling scheme is administered by a purely private body without any form of government involvement, then the question of the violation of WTO rules does not pose itself at all (Cheang 1997, p157).

(Article 2:4). Article 2:9–2:12 set out rules for notification of trading partners if countries set up technical regulations and standards.

The first dispute to be decided by a WTO panel with explicit reference to the TBT Agreement was 'European Communities – Measures affecting asbestos and products containing asbestos' (see p132 for details). The next potential dispute over provisions of the TBT Agreement looming on the horizon relates to an EU directive in preparation on waste from electrical and electronic equipment (European Commission 2000a). The proposal intends to ban electronic products if they contain a number of hazardous materials, and requires companies that sell electrical and electronic equipment to set up take-back systems for their worn out products or to contribute financially to a collective take-back system where such a system exists. The American Electronics Association (AEA) has condemned the planned directive, claiming that it violates several of the obligations under the GATT and the TBT Agreement, including quantitative restrictions in violation of GATT Article XI and technical regulations that are more trade-restrictive than necessary in violation of TBT Agreement Article 2, without being justified under one of the general exceptions in GATT Article XX (AEA 1999). The US Representative to the European Union and some Asian governments share these concerns, which seems to suggest that either they or, more likely, the US might challenge the directive before the WTO should it be passed (US Representative 1999; ICTSD 2000g; BNA 2000f).

The Agreement on the Application of Sanitary and Phytosanitary Measures (SPS Agreement)

The TBT Agreement is relevant for technical regulations and standards, except when these are sanitary or phytosanitary measures, for which the Agreement on the Application of Sanitary and Phytosanitary Measures (SPS Agreement) is relevant. Its Annex A defines SPS measures as any measure applied:

> *(a) to protect animal or plant life or health within the territory of the Member from risks arising from the entry, establishment or spread of pests, diseases, disease-carrying organisms or disease-causing organisms;*
>
> *(b) to protect human or animal life or health within the territory of the Member from risks arising from additives, contaminants, toxins or disease-causing organisms in foods, beverages or feedstuffs;*
>
> *(c) to protect life or health within the territory of the Member from risks arising from diseases carried by animals, plants or products thereof, or from the entry, establishment or spread of pests; or*

(d) to prevent or limit other damage within the territory of the Member from the entry, establishment or spread of pests.

Article 2:1 of the SPS Agreement says that 'Members have the right to take sanitary and phytosanitary measures necessary to protect human, animal or plant life or health'. Similar to the TBT Agreement, Article 3:1 of the SPS Agreement encourages the harmonization of standards and the adoption of international standards, but Article 3:3 explicitly acknowledges that countries may introduce stricter measures than those provided by international standards. Article 5:5 makes clear that

With the objective of achieving consistency in the application of the concept of appropriate level of sanitary or phytosanitary protection against risks to human life or health, or to animal and plant life or health, each Member shall avoid arbitrary or unjustifiable distinctions in the levels it considers to be appropriate in different situations, if such distinctions result in discrimination or a disguised restriction on international trade...

According to an appellate body ruling (WTO 1998c, para 212), this article needs to be read in context, an important part of which is Article 2:3, which basically states the same requirements:

Members shall ensure that their sanitary and phytosanitary measures do not arbitrarily or unjustifiably discriminate between Members where identical or similar conditions prevail. Sanitary and phytosanitary measures shall not be applied in a manner which would constitute a disguised restriction on international trade.

According to Article 2:2, members shall ensure that 'any sanitary or phytosanitary measure is applied only to the extent necessary to protect human, animal or plant life or health, is based on scientific principles and is not maintained without sufficient scientific evidence, except as provided for in paragraph 7 of Article 5'. Scientific evidence and the requirements to demonstrate sufficient evidence thus play a central role in the SPS Agreement. Its Article 5:1, which according to an appellate body ruling should constantly be read together with Article 2:2 (WTO 1998c, para 180), demands that SPS measures are based on a risk assessment: 'Members shall ensure that their sanitary or phytosanitary measures are based on an assessment, as appropriate to the circumstances, of the risks to human, animal or plant life or health, taking into account risk assessment techniques developed by the relevant international organizations'. Paragraph 4 of Annex A defines risk assessment as:

> *the evaluation of the likelihood of entry, establishment or spread of a pest or disease within the territory of an importing Member according to the sanitary or phytosanitary measures which might be applied, and of the associated potential biological and economic consequences; or the evaluation of the potential for adverse effects on human or animal health arising from the presence of additives, contaminants, toxins or disease-causing organisms in food, beverages or feedstuffs.*

The requirement of a risk assessment can only be temporarily suspended. Article 5:7 gives some space to the precautionary principle without explicitly calling it thus.[2] The article says that

> *in cases where relevant scientific evidence is insufficient, a Member may provisionally adopt sanitary or phytosanitary measures on the basis of available pertinent information, including that from the relevant international organizations as well as from sanitary or phytosanitary measures applied by other Members. In such circumstances, Members shall seek to obtain the additional information necessary for a more objective assessment of risk and review the sanitary or phytosanitary measure accordingly within a reasonable period of time* (emphasis added).

All SPS-relevant dispute cases so far have revolved around whether the challenged measures are based on sufficient scientific evidence which ultimately needs to be demonstrated via a risk assessment. For example, in its report concerning 'Japan – Measures Affecting Agricultural Products' (WTO 1998e) an appellate body panel decided against Japan's effective prohibition, under quarantine measures, to import agricultural products. It came to the conclusion that the scientific evidence provided by Japan was so weak that it provides a clear violation of Article 2:2 of the SPS Agreement and that its trade measures are not based on a risk assessment as demanded by the Agreement's Article 5.1. Also in 1998 an appellate body ruled on 'Australia – Measures Affecting Importation of Salmon' that Australia has prohibited the import of fresh, chilled or frozen ocean-caught Pacific salmon without providing a proper risk assessment within the meaning of Article 5:1 of the SPS Agreement (WTO 1998f; for more detail see p130). Similarly, in possibly the most famous case concerning SPS measures so far, an appellate body found that the European Communities import ban on beef from cattle raised with growth hormones was not based on a proper risk assessment (WTO 1998c; for more detail see p127). But the biggest clash is likely to arise with respect to GMOs. Some WTO members, including the European Community and Japan, would like to impose SPS measures to restrict or ban the use of (certain types of) GMOs, as they regard their use as dangerous to human, animal or plant life or health. In Chapter 8 I will argue that the best way to deal with these and other conflicts is to reform the SPS Agreement and to integrate fully the precautionary principle into the Agreement.

The Agreement on Subsidies and Countervailing Measures

The WTO's Agreement on Subsidies and Countervailing Measures imposes disciplines on the use of subsidies and controls the use of countervailing measures to offset damage caused by subsidized imports. It distinguishes between subsidies that are widely available within the economy and subsidies that are specific to certain enterprises, industries or regions (Article 2). It imposes rules only on the latter category. Specific subsidies are prohibited if they are contingent on export performance or local content (Article 3). Otherwise, with few exceptions, they are actionable – that is, subject to challenge if they cause adverse effects to the interests of another WTO member country and are amenable for the imposition of countervailing measures. To cause adverse effects, a subsidy must cause injury and serious prejudice to the industry of another member country which would nullify or impair its benefits under the GATT treaty (Article 5). As serious prejudice is difficult to prove, there exists a presumption of serious prejudice if subsidies are greater than 5 per cent ad valorem, cover operating losses or accrue in the form of direct forgiveness of debt (Article 6).

One of the types of subsidy exempted from these rules, and therefore non-actionable, is assistance to adapt existing industries to new environmental requirements, so-called 'green light' provisions (Article 8.2(c)), provided that the assistance:

(i)   is a one-time non-recurring measure; and
(ii) is limited to 20 per cent of the cost of adaptation; and
(iii) does not cover the cost of replacing and operating the assisted investment, which must be fully borne by firms; and
(iv) is directly linked to and proportionate to a firm's planned reduction of nuisances and pollution, and does not cover any manufacturing cost savings which may be achieved; and
(v)   is available to all firms which can adopt the new equipment and/or production process.

However, as notification and approval are not obligatory, few countries have done so. At the time of writing, no environmentally related subsidies have been challenged.

The Agreement on Agriculture

The Agreement on Agriculture aims to reduce subsidies to agricultural production. Its preamble notes that 'commitments under the reform programme should be made in an equitable way among all members, having regard to non-trade concerns, including food security and the need to protect the environment'. In Article 20(c) WTO members pledge that in the built-in reform process of the Agreement, the objectives mentioned in the preamble, including the protection of the environment, shall be taken into account. Annex 2 lists a whole range of subsidies that are exempted from the reduction commitments of the Agreement. This list is non-exclusive in the sense that other subsidies can be exempted as well. The criterion for being eligible for exemption is that 'domestic support measures for which exemptions from the reduction commitments is claimed shall meet the fundamental requirement that they have no, or at most minimal, trade-distorting effects or effects on production' (paragraph 1).

Paragraph 2 lists a number of exempted general services – that is, expenditures that provide services to agriculture or the rural community as a whole rather than direct payments to individual producers or processors. Exempted are, inter alia, 'research in connection with environmental programmes' (paragraph 2(a)) and 'infrastructure works associated with environmental programmes' (paragraph 2(g)). Furthermore, paragraph 12 exempts payments, which need not be general, under environmental programmes if these payments are 'part of a clearly-defined government environmental or conservation programme' (paragraph 12(a)). At the time of writing, no environmentally-related agricultural subsidies have been challenged.

The Agreement on Trade-Related Aspects of Intellectual Property Rights (TRIPs Agreement)

The Agreement on Trade-Related Aspects of Intellectual Property Rights (TRIPs Agreement) sets up rules for, inter alia, the granting of copyrights and related rights, trademarks, patents and layout designs of integrated circuits. It seeks a balance between the rights and obligations of those who hold intellectual property rights:

> *The protection and enforcement of intellectual property rights should contribute to the promotion of technological innovation and to the transfer and dissemination of technology, to the mutual advantage of producers and users of technological knowledge and in a manner conducive to social and economic welfare, and to a balance of rights and obligations* (Article 7).

Article 27 of the TRIPs Agreement has important environmental implications with respect to the conservation of biological diversity, which will be examined in more detail in Chapter 9, p180. Article 27:1 defines the criteria of eligibility for patents: '... patents shall be available for any inventions, whether products or processes, in all fields of technology, provided that they are new, involve an inventive step and are capable of industrial application'. However, Article 27:2 states that *members may exclude from patentability inventions, the prevention within their territory of the commercial exploitation of which is necessary to protect ordre public or morality, including to protect human, animal or plant life or health or to avoid serious prejudice to the environment, provided that such exclusion is not made merely because the exploitation is prohibited by their law.*

Furthermore, Article 27:3 allows members to exclude from patentability:

(a) diagnostic, therapeutic and surgical methods for the treatment of humans or animals;

(b) plants and animals other than micro-organisms, and essentially biological processes for the production of plants or animals other than non-biological and microbiological processes. However, Members shall provide for the protection of plant varieties either by patents or by an effective sui generis[3] system or by any combination thereof. The provisions of this subparagraph shall be reviewed four years after the date of entry into force of the WTO Agreement.

Article 30 allows 'exceptions to the exclusive rights conferred by a patent, provided that such exceptions do not unreasonably conflict with a normal exploitation of the patent and do not unreasonably prejudice the legitimate interest of the patent owner, taking account of the legitimate interests of third parties'. Furthermore, countries can allow for 'use of the subject matter of a patent without the authorization of the right holder, including use by the government or third parties authorized by the government' (Article 31) if 'prior to such use, the proposed user has made efforts to obtain authorization from the right holder on reasonable, commercial terms and conditions and that such efforts have not been successful within a reasonable period of time' (Article 31(b)). In any case, 'the right holder shall be paid adequate remuneration in the circumstances of each case, taking into account the economic value of the authorization' (Article 31(h)). The time period of the patent shall be a minimum of 20 years (Article 33).

Foreign investment and the environment

The regulatory regime with respect to foreign investment is less comprehensive than the one with respect to international trade. Here we assess the relevant provisions in the North American Free Trade Agreement (NAFTA), in the Bilateral Investment Treaties (BITs), in the draft, but ultimately failed, Multilateral Agreement on Investment (MAI) and in the WTO Agreement on Trade Related Investment Measures (TRIMs). The assessment proceeds in the order of decreasing comprehensiveness.

Investment provisions in the NAFTA

Article 1101 defines the scope and coverage of rules governing investment provisions contained in NAFTA's Chapter 11. It states that 'This Chapter applies to measures adopted or maintained by a Party relating to...' an investment, where Article 201 of NAFTA defines 'measures' rather broadly as including 'any law, regulation, procedure, requirement or practice'. Similarly broad is the definition of 'investment' contained in Article 1139, encompassing an enterprise, an equity security of, debt security of or loan to an enterprise, a claim on income or profits or assets or property, both tangible or intangible, of an enterprise in the expectation of economic benefit, interests arising from the commitment of capital or other resources, contracts involving the presence of an investor's property as well as contracts where remuneration depends substantially on the production, revenues or profits of an enterprise.

Article 1102 grants national treatment, Article 1103 most favoured nation treatment and Article 1104 the better of the two treatments to investments of investors from another NAFTA party. Article 1105 establishes a minimum standard of treatment in demanding that '[E]ach Party shall accord to investments of investors of another Party treatment in accordance with international law, including fair and equitable treatment and full protection and security'. Importantly, these investor rights do not only apply to already established investments, but also to the pre-establishment phase – that is, they apply to the phase of the investment entering a NAFTA party's market as well and thereby establish a right of entry. However, for the case of Mexico, Article 1101:2 in conjunction with Annex III of NAFTA exempts a number of activities from the permission of the establishment of investment.

Article 1106 regulates the imposition of performance requirements. According to Article 1106:1 no NAFTA party may 'impose or enforce'

- export requirements (Article 1106:1(a));
- domestic content requirements (Article 1106:1(b));
- requirements restricting the purchase or use of goods (Article 1106:1(c));
- requirements restricting access to imported products and foreign exchange (Article 1106:1(d));
- restrictions on the export of products (Article 1106:1(e));
- technology, production process or other proprietary knowledge requirements (Article 1106:1(f));
- exclusive supply requirements (Article 1106:1(g)).

Article 1106:3 goes one step further in forbidding the conditioning of the receipt or continued receipt of an advantage on certain performance requirements. In other words, these requirements are banned *even if investors were compensated for the restrictions imposed on them* and regarded it in their own interest to comply with the restrictions in exchange for advantages. These requirements include domestic content requirements (Article 1106:3(a)), as well as requirements restricting the purchase or use of goods (Article 1106:1(b)), access to imported products (Article 1106:1(c)) and foreign exchange or the export of products (Article 1106:1(d)).

Article 1106:6 contains an important environmental exceptions clause to the performance requirements, the wording of which is very similar to GATT's Article XX exceptions:

> *Provided that such measures are not applied in an arbitrary or unjustifiable manner, or do not constitute a disguised restriction on international trade or investment, nothing in paragraph 1(b) or (c) or 3(a) or (b) [of Article 1106, EN] shall be construed to prevent any Party from adopting or maintaining measures, including environmental measures:*
>
> *(a) necessary to secure compliance with laws and regulations that are not inconsistent with the provisions of this Agreement;*
>
> *(b) necessary to protect human, animal or plant life or health; or*
>
> *(c) necessary for the conservation of living or non-living exhaustible natural resources.*

Furthermore, Article 1114:1 contains a more general clause on environmental measures establishing the rights of parties to maintain or enforce environmental measures:

> *Nothing in this Chapter shall be construed to prevent a Party from adopting, maintaining or enforcing any measure otherwise consistent with this Chapter that it considers appropriate to ensure that investment activity in its territory is undertaken in a manner sensitive to environmental concerns.*

Article 1114:2 contains a non-binding clause whose objective is to dissuade NAFTA parties from lowering environmental standards in order to attract foreign investment:

> *The Parties recognize that it is inappropriate to encourage investment by relaxing domestic health, safety or environmental measures. Accordingly, a Party should not waive or otherwise derogate from, or offer to waive or otherwise derogate from, such measures as an encouragement for the*

establishment, acquisition, expansion or retention in its terri-
tory of an investment of an investor. If a Party considers that
another Party has offered such an encouragement, it may
request consultations with the other Party and the two Parties
shall consult with a view to avoiding any such encouragement.

Article 1110 regulates the expropriation of investment and compensation
for expropriation. Article 1110:1 reads:

No Party may directly or indirectly nationalize or expropriate
an investment of an investor of another Party in its territory or
take a measure tantamount to nationalization or expropriation
of such an investment ('expropriation'), except:

(a) for a public purpose;

(b) on a non-discriminatory basis;

(c) in accordance with due process of law and Article 1105(1);
and

(d) on payment of compensation in accordance with paragraphs
2 through 6.

The rather vague formulation of a 'measure tantamount to nationalization
or expropriation' has caused several investor-to-state disputes over measures
that the complainants regarded as tantamount to expropriation, which has
hit the NAFTA parties by surprise. Some fear that clauses like these, as well
as the very existence of an investor-to-state dispute settlement, open the
floodgates for private companies to knock down existing environmental
regulations and deter countries from enacting future regulations (for more
detail see Chapter 5).

   The rules of the investor-to-state dispute settlement process are laid down
in detail in section B of NAFTA's Chapter 11. The process is non-public and
decisions of the arbitration panel, or tribunal as it is called in that chapter,
which consists of one member nominated by each party to the dispute, plus
a consensual member as the chair (Article 1123), are binding. The arbitration tribunal may award monetary damages as well as the restitution of
property, but may not impose payments for punitive damages (Article 1135).

The regulatory regime in BITs and the draft MAI

Obviously, BITs vary from country to country. Also, BITs have become more
and more comprehensive and substantial regarding the rights and obligations they provide since the first two treaties that West Germany negotiated
in 1959. Modern state-of-the-art BITs usually have the following major
characteristics in common (see UNCTAD 1998b and Vandevelde 1998 for
more detail):

- The definition of investment is broad and not restricted to FDI.
- Foreign investment is granted fair and equitable treatment as well as protection and security.
- Arbitrary or discriminatory measures against foreign investors are prohibited.
- Foreign investors are granted national treatment with qualifications and the important exception of tax treatment.
- Foreign investors are guaranteed most favoured nation treatment with the important exception of tax treatment.
- Expropriation is only allowed with due compensation, for a public purpose, subject to non-discrimination and in accordance with due process. In some BITs the relevant clause also covers measures 'tantamount to expropriation' as NAFTA's Article 1110:1 does.
- A prohibition of foreign currency exchange controls, except for periods of balance of payments crises.
- Contrary to NAFTA and the WTO's Agreement on Trade Related Investment Measures (see below) most BITs do not explicitly restrict performance requirements.
- A right of entry or right of establishment of foreign investment is rarely guaranteed and states are not required to allow investments to flow out of the country.
- A state-to-state as well as an investor-to-state dispute settlement provision enables an arbitration tribunal to make binding decisions in case of conflict.

At the time of writing, around 65 cases of investors alleging a violation of BIT rules in one of the more than 1300 signed BITs so far had been registered with the International Center for Settlement of Investment Disputes (ICSID), which is the most common mechanism for dispute settlement (ICSID 1999a). To my knowledge, none of them was related to environmental measures.

As concerns the draft MAI, the negotiators from the Organisation for Economic Co-operation and Development (OECD) countries had always argued that they aspired to create an agreement of the highest standard (OECD 1998b). Indeed, the draft for the MAI contained several main characteristics that distinguished it sharply from most BITs (see OECD 1998a). The two most important ones are as follows:

- The principles of treatment, such as fair, national and most favoured nation, were supposed to apply not only to existing investment, but granted already in the so-called pre-establishment phase. Thus potential investors were supposed to gain significant rights of entry.
- A comprehensive range of performance requirements were supposed to be prohibited and others allowed only if they were accompanied by financial compensation. This means that foreign investors could not be

required to meet conditions such as employing local staff or using local production inputs.

The MAI is the topic of more detailed examination in Chapter 6.

The Agreement on Trade-Related Investment Measures (TRIMs Agreement)

The Agreement on Trade-Related Investment Measures (TRIMs Agreement) imposes some rudimentary disciplines on the regulation of foreign investment with respect to products.[4] It is by far not as comprehensive as many BITs or NAFTA's Chapter 11.

Over a period of time differentiated according to a country's level of development, WTO members are supposed to abolish TRIMs aimed at foreign investment which, according to an illustrative list in the Annex to the agreement

- set minimum levels of local content in products;
- restrict the extent of purchase or use of imported products;
- restrict access to foreign exchange;
- restrict the export of products.

Article 2:1 provides national treatment and the abolition of quantitative restrictions in simply stating that 'no Member shall apply any TRIM that is inconsistent with the provisions of Article III or Article XI of GATT 1994'. Contrary to GATT, NAFTA's investment provisions and most BITs, the TRIM Agreement does not grant most favoured nation treatment. Article 3 of the TRIMs Agreement states that all exceptions from GATT shall apply to this agreement as well. Of environmental interest is especially GATT's Article XX. At the time of writing, no environmentally relevant TRIMS-related disputes have been brought before the WTO.

Part Two

Investment

This second part of the book looks at investment. Environmentalists are concerned about three issues here: pollution havens, regulatory chill and roll back. Chapter 3 examines the validity of the first and major claim made by environmentalists: that developing countries provide pollution havens in either setting inefficiently low environmental standards or failing to enforce standards in order to attract investment from developed countries. Chapter 4 analyses a related, but nevertheless distinct, second claim, which is also quite common: that developed countries fail to raise environmental standards because they fear that doing so would lead to a capital flight out of their countries. Chapter 5 addresses the third claim: that companies use investor-to-state dispute settlement to knock down or roll back environmental regulations. This third claim is somewhat specific to the investment provisions contained in the North American Free Trade Agreement (NAFTA), but also played a significant role in the environmentalists' opposition to the conclusion of a Multilateral Agreement on Investment (MAI). Chapter 6 provides a kind of case study of this failed attempt to conclude such an MAI as many of the issues raised in the other three chapters can be found together there.

3

Pollution Havens: Do Developing Countries Set Inefficient Environmental Standards to Attract Foreign Investment?

Proponents of the pollution haven hypothesis visualize internationally mobile capital as a ship on the high sea that is looking for a haven to disembark at unrivalled low costs. The owners of various havens compete with each other in, among other things, offering ever higher pollution allowances via ever lower environmental standards to reduce the regulatory burden on the desperately wanted investment inflow. A 'race to the bottom' emerges with respect to environmental standards and, eventually, the capital settles in the country with the lowest standards – the greatest pollution haven – a true investor's paradise and an environmentalists' nightmare.[1]

In spite of the popularity of the hypothesis, the term pollution haven is rarely defined. Public opinion seems to favour the belief that any country with less strict environmental standards than its own is guilty of providing a pollution haven, but such a definition is misleading as all the countries of the world cannot be expected to have the same environmental standards independently of whether or not they want to attract foreign capital (see below). A more sophisticated definition, but one that is inspired by the same kind of reasoning, is provided by Eskeland and Harrison (1997, p4):

> The pollution haven hypothesis is, perhaps, best seen as a corollary to the theory of comparative advantage: as pollution control costs begin to matter for some industries in some countries, other countries should gain comparative advantage in those industries, if pollution control costs are lower there (for whatever reason).

Again, in focusing on cost differentials as such and ignoring the reasons for these differentials, this definition does not capture what seems to be the essence of the pollution haven hypothesis: that countries set inefficiently low environmental standards or set efficient standards, but fail to enforce them in order to attract foreign capital. In the following I will therefore employ the following definition: a country provides a pollution haven if it sets its environmental standards below the socially efficient level or fails to enforce its standards in order to attract foreign investment from countries with higher environmental standards or countries that enforce their standards more rigorously. In formal economic terms, environmental standards are at their socially efficient level if for each different pollutant the standard is set such that the marginal social benefit of an increase in pollution is just equal to the marginal social cost of such an increase.[2] Avoiding economic jargon, this broadly translates into the requirement that the pollution levels are in accordance with the preferences of people living in a political community (here: country). Hence if environmental standards are inefficiently low, then there is excessive pollution relative to people's preferences.

There has been much academic debate on the pollution haven phenomenon (see, for example, Lucas, Wheeler and Hettige 1992; Birdsall and Wheeler 1993; Thompson and Strohm 1996; Porter 1999). This chapter differs from other writings on two major accounts. First, it aspires to provide a more comprehensive analysis of which factors might give rise to pollution havens and what systematic empirical evidence tells us on their existence. As we will see, pollution havens are an elusive phenomenon in the sense that their existence is difficult to demonstrate both theoretically and empirically. Second, and more importantly, it aspires to move forward the debate in providing an analysis of policy options for dealing with this elusive phenomenon. What options do policy-makers have for dealing with pollution havens and how would one evaluate those options?

The next section argues that even if environmental standards were at their efficiency levels everywhere, there would still be international differences in those environmental standards. This is because of differences in the amount of existing emissions, differences in the pollution absorptive capacity of the environment in different countries as well as differences in the intensity of environmental preferences of the people living in a country. Apart from differences in the amount of existing pollution, none of these factors would suggest systematically lower environmental standards in developing as opposed to developed countries, however. Then a number of factors are examined that could lead to pollution havens as defined above. Of these, by far the most important one is that developing countries might suffer from political–institutional deficiencies that could create a bias against environmental preferences such that their environmental standards are set inefficiently low or are non-enforced.

These theory-oriented considerations are important in the sense that they help to clarify analytically when international differences in environmental standards are justified by international differences in the efficient level of standards and when they are not. However, the question is whether such a distinction is useful for empirical analysis which after all represents the only way of knowing whether and to what extent pollution havens exist in actual reality. Ideally, one would try to assess environmental standards internationally, compare the actually existing standards to what would constitute the efficient standards and evaluate whether developing countries' standards are further away from their efficiency standards than is the case in developed countries. If so, then they would provide a pollution haven relative to developed countries. Unfortunately, such an empirical analysis is next to impossible, mainly because it is extremely difficult to say what the efficient environmental standards for each country would be. Studies analysing the pollution haven phenomenon empirically have therefore invariably taken recourse to testing one of three proxy propositions or hypotheses that would need to hold if pollution havens did exist:

1 Differences in environmental standards affect the allocation of investment flows.
2 Developing countries' production and exports have become increasingly pollution-intensive.
3 Pollution-intensive industries flee the high-standards countries.

Reviewing the available empirical literature leads to the conclusion that there is very limited evidence in favour of either of these three propositions and several reasons are presented for why there might be such limited evidence for pollution havens.

It follows from both theoretical considerations and a review of the empirical evidence that pollution havens represent an elusive phenomenon. While their existence is difficult to demonstrate, it would be overhasty to dismiss them completely, however. Maybe insufficient data availability prevents our empirical methods from tracing them. Also, policy-makers and environmental activists alike seem to be concerned about pollution havens independent of the weak empirical evidence for their actual existence. In times of 'globalization' and increasing flows of capital to developing countries, this concern is even likely to become stronger. If one is concerned about policy then it is simply not enough to refer to the weak statistical evidence for pollution havens found in empirical studies. Rather, one needs to take these concerns seriously and offer policy options to address them.

This chapter therefore goes one important step beyond the existing literature. Since the existence of pollution havens is likely to remain a hotly debated issue, it seems more than pertinent to evaluate policy options for tackling potential or actually existing pollution havens. The last section of this chapter therefore examines a wide range of policy options according to a number of clearly specified criteria. It argues that assistance for political–institutional capacity-building and local empowerment of people represent the best policy option.

Theoretical considerations and evidence on factors causing pollution havens

Efficient international differences in environmental standards

As mentioned in the last section, countries might have different environmental standards even if those standards are set at their efficient level. Environmental standards can differ because of at least three reasons:

1   *Differences in emissions of pollutants.* All other things being equal, a country with higher emissions should have stricter environmental standards than a country with lower emissions. Unfortunately, data on international differences in emissions of pollutants are not directly available on an aggregate basis. However, the differences in energy consumption per capita can be used as a first proxy to differences in emissions of pollutants.[3] According to the World Bank (1999, Table 3.7) low- and middle-income countries had a commercial energy use per capita of 1766kg of oil equivalent in 1996, whereas high income countries used 5259kg of oil equivalent per capita. *Ceteris paribus*, we would therefore, on average, expect developing countries to have laxer environmental standards due to lower emissions.

2   *Differences in pollution absorptive capacity.* In principle, different environments can have different capacities to absorb or assimilate and therefore to cope with pollution. This much is undisputed. Going one step further, it is sometimes tentatively suggested that the environment in developing countries might be characterized by higher pollution absorptive capacity (for example, Snape 1992, p88). However, from a natural science perspective there is no justification for such a presumption as the pollution absorptive capacity depends on the meteorological and topographical conditions of the local environment and also on the relevant pollutant.

3   *Differences in the intensity of environmental preferences.* It is often presumed that the intensity of environmental preferences is lower in developing countries. Kriström and Riera (1996, p45) suggest that 'most economists would argue intuitively that environmental quality is a luxury good'. Such a presumption is in conflict with the available evidence, however. In Gallup et al (1993), a cross-national survey encompassing 24 developed as well as developing countries, there is no statistically significant correlation between expressed personal concern about the environment and real gross domestic product (GDP) per capita in purchasing power parity in 1992 (taken from UNDP 1995, Table 1). There is a correlation, statistically significant at the .01 level, between support for stronger environmental laws for business and industry, as well as for citizens. However, it contradicts the common view as individuals in poor countries actually express stronger support for these laws

than individuals in rich countries (Pearson Correlation −0.550 for laws for business/industry, −0.744 for laws for citizens).[4]

These findings are not confined to the Gallup et al (1993) survey.[5] In the 'World Values Survey' (Inglehart, Basanez and Moreno 1998), another cross-national survey conducted in 43 developed and developing countries, there is no statistically significant correlation between income levels and individuals' support for environmental protection – as measured in various formulations asking for people's willingness to accept price or tax or cost increases for the reduction of environmental pollution. More systematically, Kriström and Riera (1996) have surveyed the available evidence from contingent valuation studies – all coming from European countries, however. Somewhat to their own surprise, they find that individuals in lower income brackets express a higher willingness-to-pay as a share of their income than individuals in higher income brackets. It seems fair to say, therefore, that there is no strong evidence showing that the environmental preferences of individuals in poor countries are less intense than those of individuals in rich countries.

Inefficient international differences in environmental standards

International differences in environmental standards need not be in accordance with differences in the efficiency of environmental standards, however. There are a number of reasons that could cause such standards to inefficiently differ internationally, as follows:

Transboundary environmental pollution

If environmental pollution crosses national boundaries, then incentives exist to provide a pollution haven as some of the burden connected to low or badly enforced environmental standards is borne by other countries. Note that for pollution havens to arise in the strict sense a necessary condition is the asymmetry of spill-over effects. Only if one country's environmental pollution affects another country more than vice versa has one country an incentive to set inefficiently low environmental standards *to attract foreign investment from the country with the higher standards*. If, on the other hand, there is no asymmetry of spill-over effects, then both countries will set their environmental standards inefficiently low, but since they set their standards equally inefficiently low, none of them attracts foreign investment from the other country relative to the reference point in which both countries set their standards at the efficient levels. What is true for transboundary spill-overs holds true more generally for other factors giving rise to pollution havens as well: countries must be asymmetrically affected by these factors, otherwise both countries allow inefficiently high pollution levels, but none of them provides a pollution haven relative to the other country.

Note also, however, that the pollution need not spill over into the country with high standards itself for a country to have incentives to provide a pollution haven. Instead, the pollution can spill over into a third country. With reference to the real world, we would not expect pollution from developing countries to spill over into developed countries to any great extent due to geographical separation.[6] But it is sufficient if pollution spills over from one developing country into another to give it an incentive to set inefficiently low environmental standards and attract foreign investment from developed countries with high standards.

What evidence do we have on pollution spill-over effects? To my knowledge, there is no evidence that pollution spill-over effects are more prevalent in the developing world per se. However, we do have evidence on whether affected countries have found an agreement and have tried to internalize the pollution externality. On this account, developing countries fare worse than developed countries. According to Sand (1992), de facto participation of developing countries in international legally binding environmental agreements is in general (but not in each and every case) much less than that of developed countries. Similarly, in cross-country statistical analysis, Roberts (1996) found that wealthy countries are much more likely to sign and ratify international environmental treaties than poor countries. *Ceteris paribus*, we would therefore expect developing countries' pollution spill-overs to be less internalized via international environmental agreement than those of developed countries.

Bias against environmental preferences

Pollution havens can also arise if a country's standard-setting institution – that is, its government or its national environmental authority – is biased against environmental preferences. Why might this be the case? First, the agents causing and therefore benefiting from environmental pollution might be less in number than the victims of pollution. There is a whole strand of public choice theory going back to Olson (1965) arguing that small groups find it easier to organize themselves and therefore to lobby the political process than big number groups. Business groups from pollution-intensive industries, for example, are usually much better lobbyists with much more money and influence available than environmental pressure or consumer groups. However, there is a drawback to this argument. If the number of pollution beneficiaries is much smaller than the number of pollution victims, then at democratic elections the victims have a comparative advantage over the former group. Presumably, therefore, this first argument is not sufficient to explain political bias against environmental preferences. Of course, many, especially developing, countries do not hold democratic elections in the full sense, hence the beneficiaries of pollution need not fear that they will lose out at the ballot box. Freedom House (1999) publishes an annual index of political freedom measured on a one-to-seven scale covering the existence and fairness of elections, the existence of opposition and the possibility to take over power via elections. For a selection of the 52 most important developed and developing countries, the 1996–1997 index is highly correlated with real 1997 GDP per capita in purchasing power parity (Pearson Correlation .865; Spearman's r .847; both are significant at the .01 level; GDP figures taken from UNDP 1999, Table 1). Developed countries therefore tend to have higher political freedoms than developing countries.

Second, and connected to the last point, if the political system is characterized by corruption and is easily amenable to manipulation by powerful and wealthy special interest groups, then the beneficiaries of pollution are likely to be more influential than the comparatively less wealthy environmental pressure or consumer groups. 'Regulatory capture' becomes easier if lobbyists from pollution-intensive industries can bribe officials from environmental agencies. Porter (1999) argues forcefully that developing countries are much more likely to suffer from this kind of failure of political system than developed ones. Transparency International (1999) publishes an index of perceived corruption, defined as the perceived corruption in the public sector in terms of the abuse of public office for private gain, measured on a zero-to-ten scale. For the same 52 developed and developing countries as above, the 1996 index is highly negatively correlated with real 1997 GDP per capita in purchasing power parity (Pearson Correlation −0.638, Spearman's r −0.743, both significant at the .01 level; GDP figures taken from UNDP 1999, Table 1). Developing countries therefore tend to be perceived as being more corrupt than developed countries.

Third, whereas the benefits of pollution are present, tangible and highly visible in terms of the goods and services that are produced and the jobs that are created or secured, the costs of pollution are often invisible, intangible, uncertain and occur in the future. Myopic policy-makers whose interests might primarily revolve around the prospects of re-election in the near future might therefore tend to focus on the benefits of pollution at the expense of its costs. They might be encouraged to do so if, because of economic hardship, the electorate regards problems other than environmental pollution to be the more pressing ones. Maybe surprisingly, there is no systematic evidence demonstrating that individuals in developing countries regard other problems more pressing relative to environmental problems. In the already mentioned Gallup et al (1993) study, the percentage of respondents volunteering to state environmental problems as the most important problem facing the nation is not statistically significantly correlated with GDP per capita. Similarly, in the World Values Survey (Inglehart, Basanez and Moreno 1998) approval rates for the statement 'If we want to combat unemployment in this country, we shall just have to accept environmental problems' is not significantly negatively correlated with GDP per capita.

Fourth, bias against environmental preferences can stem from the political–institutional failure of a country. Even if policy-makers are not biased against environmental preferences per se and try to satisfy the true preferences of their citizenship, a country, especially a developing country, might not have the advanced political, legal, administrative and regulatory capacity to provide environmental protection at the efficiency level. Political–institutional failure might lead either to inefficiently low environmental standards or to the non-enforcement of standards. Birdsall and Wheeler (1993, p138) suggest that 'the relative costs of monitoring and enforcing pollution standards are higher in developing countries, given scarcity of trained personnel, difficulty of acquiring sophisticated equipment, and the high marginal costs of undertaking any new governmental activity when the policy focus is on reducing fiscal burdens'. In using a multidimensional survey analysis of national environmental reports to the United Nations Conference on Environment and Development (UNCED) in Rio de Janeiro in 1992, Dasgupta et al (1995) find that a country's overall institutional environmental performance as measured by environmental awareness, scope of policies adopted, scope of legislation enacted, control mechanisms in place and the degree of success in implementation is positively correlated with its income per capita and the development of its legal and regulatory system.

Fifth, policy-makers can be biased against environmental preferences if this allows domestic firms to reap profits from international imperfectly competitive markets. Barrett (1994b) shows that if firms in these markets compete with each other in quantities (so-called Cournot competition), then lowering environmental standards allows domestic firms to expand their output and increase their profit share at the expense of foreign firms. This is often called 'ecological dumping' and in so far as countries do not tax away all the additional firm profit, foreign investors will find it attractive to invest in countries with low environmental standards. However, whether 'ecological dumping' can explain the provision of pollution havens is rather dubious for two reasons. First, Barrett (1994b) shows as well that if companies compete with each other in prices rather than in quantities (so-called Bertrand competition), then governments have an incentive actually to raise environmental standards as this will allow domestic firms to raise their prices and increase their profit share at the expense of foreign firms. In other words, instead of 'ecological dumping' there can be 'ecological over-pricing' as well, depending on the form of competition. Second, even if firms compete in quantities, all countries have an incentive to lower their environmental standards. Hence, all countries will have inefficiently low environmental standards, but there is no reason to expect that developing countries will provide pollution havens relative to developed countries.

Dependency on capital tax revenue

Oates and Schwab (1988) and Chao and Yu (1997) show that countries have an incentive to set environmental standards inefficiently low if their government's tax revenue depends in part on capital taxation. Lowering environmental standards is a means of attracting foreign capital and keeping domestic capital which raises tax revenue. The International Monetary Fund

(IMF) (1998, pp4–5) provides evidence on the types of governmental revenue as percentages of total revenue in general and on corporate taxation as a proxy to capital taxation in particular. While the percentage of total revenue that stems from corporate taxation obviously varies considerably from country to country, it is striking that a number of developing countries derive above 15 per cent of their total revenue from corporate taxation, whereas in developed countries the dependency ratio is usually below 15 per cent, with the exception of Australia which has a rate of almost 17 per cent. *Ceteris paribus*, we would therefore expect that some developing countries might have lower environmental standards.

Jurisdictional market power in the market for capital

Van Long and Siebert (1991) and Rauscher (1994) have shown that if countries are 'large' so that they can exercise market power in the capital market (a possibility we have implicitly excluded so far), then a capital exporting country has an incentive to lower its environmental standards in order to restrict its capital export and raise its rate of return on its foreign investment. A capital importing country with market power has the opposite incentives. This argument can hardly give rise to developing countries providing pollution havens, however. First, there is hardly a developing country that is large enough to raise or lower the rate of return on capital. If at all, then developing countries could merely exercise market power in a concerted joint effort, which is non-existent at the moment. Second, and more importantly, developing countries are net capital importers, so that instead of having an incentive to provide pollution havens they would have an incentive to set inefficiently strict environmental standards!

Summary of findings

Table 3.1 sums up the findings on how we would expect developing countries' environmental standards to be relative to developed countries' standards under efficiency conditions. Only the lower emissions in developing countries would clearly prompt us to expect them to have laxer environmental standards. The evidence on the pollution absorptive capacity of the environment and the intensity of environmental preferences is indeterminate.

Table 3.2 sums up the findings on the factors that could give rise to pollution havens. The higher prevalence of pollution spill-overs, the more pronounced bias against environmental preferences and the greater dependency of government revenue on capital taxation are all factors that could give rise to developing countries having inefficiently lax or badly enforced environmental standards relative to developed countries. Jurisdictional market power in the capital market is a potentially counteracting factor, but its practical relevance is highly questionable.

As can be seen from Tables 3.1 and 3.2, the existence of laxer or badly enforced environmental standards in the developing countries might, but

Table 3.1 *Developing countries' environmental standards relative to developed countries' standards under* efficiency *conditions*

Factor	Evidence
Emissions	Laxer
Pollution-absorptive capacity	Indeterminate
Intensity of environmental preferences	Indeterminate

need not, represent the provision of a pollution haven. Next we move to a review of the more systematic empirical evidence related to pollution havens.

Systematic empirical evidence

How to detect pollution havens? Ideally, following from the definition of pollution havens one would want to compare existing environmental standards to their efficiency levels. In practice, providing a reliable estimate of these efficiency levels would be next to impossible for most countries due to lack of reliable data and valuation studies. Invariably therefore empirical studies have simply examined whether countries with low environmental standards manage to attract capital from high standards countries. If pollution havens exist, then we would expect to find such evidence. Note, however, that such evidence is only a necessary, not a sufficient condition for proving the existence of pollution havens as the environmental standards in countries attracting investment while lower than in other countries need not be inefficiently low.

Practically all relevant empirical studies have examined one of three questions: First, whether differences in environmental standards affect the allocation of investment flows; second, whether production and exports in developing countries (the supposed pollution havens) are becoming more pollution-intensive; and third, whether pollution-intensive industries leave countries with high environmental standards at any significant level.

Do differences in environmental standards affect the allocation of investment flows?

Pollution havens only matter if differences in environmental standards affect the allocation of investment flows. While there are few studies on the international level, some more studies examine the effects of environmental regulation on investment flows within a nation, mainly in the US. Mani, Pargal and Huq (1996) find that differences in the stringency of environmental enforcement in different states of India do not have a significant impact on the location of new manufacturing plants in 1994. Similarly for the US, Bartik (1998) does not find any statistically significant effect of variations in the stringency of state environmental standards on the location

Table 3.2 *Developing countries' environmental standards relative to developed countries' standards under* non-efficiency *conditions*

Factor	Evidence
Pollution spill-overs	Laxer
Bias against environmental preferences	Laxer
Dependency on revenue from capital taxation	Laxer
Jurisdictional market power	Stricter

decisions of new manufacturing plants owned by the Fortune 500 companies throughout the 1970s. Levinson (1996) examines locational choice that encompasses all the manufacturing industries. He finds that the investment decisions of only very few industries were significantly affected by differences in environmental standards and that the effect is rather small. McConnell and Schwab (1990) look at the impact of environmental regulation on location decisions for new plants of just one industry, the motor vehicle industry during 1973–1982. Their results are ambiguous. Depending on the definition of environmental stringency, they find either no statistically significant evidence or weak evidence that some firms may be deterred at the margin from investing in regions with high environmental compliance costs.

Keller and Levinson (1999) look specifically at foreign direct investment (FDI) inflows to the United States and examine whether states with low environmental standards attract a higher share of this investment inflow than other states. Keller and Levinson find that they do, but estimate the effect to be small. Their results stand in marked contract to List and Co (2000) who also look at the effects of environmental regulations on FDI inflows to the US. Using measures of environmental stringency that differ from Keller and Levinson (1999), they find quite large effects of stringent environmental standards lowering a state's share of receiving FDI.

In moving to the international level, the first thing to note is that the empirical evidence from the national level, even if it was unambiguous, need not carry over as nation-states are much more diverse in many respects than the states of the US. Before we look at two studies that employed systematic statistical analysis, it is interesting to note that environmental compliance costs do not figure in the 49 Competitiveness Indicators, published by the World Bank (1998b). Neither do they play a role in the competitiveness ranking of 59 countries provided by the World Economic Forum (1999). In as far as competitiveness is a metaphor for the attractiveness to invest in a country, then, in the World Bank's and World Economic Forum's view at least, environmental factors do not seem to play a role. In the IMD's (1999) 'World Competitiveness' rankings, the extent to which existing laws to protect the environment hinder businesses is one of the criteria, but it is merely one out of 288 and four other criteria reward countries for good environmental performance.

More systematically, Xing and Kolstad (1998) find that countries with low environmental standards tend to attract a higher share of US FDI outflows than countries with high standards. However, they admit that this result might not be robust as their number of observations is quite low. Eskeland and Harrison (1997) examine how the pattern of foreign investment in four developing countries (Mexico, Morocco, Côte d'Ivoire and Venezuela) is affected by environmental regulation. They find two things: first, differences in pollution abatement costs are insignificant in determining FDI flows to these countries. Second, high-polluting sectors do not attract more FDI than cleaner sectors – sometimes even the opposite effect is statistically significant.

Are developing countries' production and exports becoming increasingly pollution-intensive?

If developing countries provide pollution havens, then we would expect that, *ceteris paribus*, their production, and possibly their exports as well, become more pollution-intensive over time as dirty industries migrate to these havens. Lucas, Wheeler and Hettige (1992) and Birdsall and Wheeler (1993) provide evidence that developing countries had high growth rates of pollution intensity of industrial production in the 1970s and 1980s, whereas the pollution intensity has decreased in developed countries. Similarly, Abimanyu (1996) finds that pollution intensive sectors have expanded faster than average in some developing countries in East and South East Asia. However, it is not clear whether this relative change is due to the relocation of pollution-intensive industries towards developing countries or represents the environmental consequences of the industrialization process (Thompson and Strohm 1996). It is also not clear whether, even if this relative change was due to migration of pollution-intensive industries towards developing countries, relocated industries increased the exports of goods from pollution-intensive production to countries with high environmental standards. First, Lucas, Wheeler and Hettige (1992) and Birdsall and Wheeler (1993) find that closed developing countries had a much higher growth in the pollution intensity of industrial production than export-oriented countries – a finding that is disputed by Rock (1996), however, who claims that this result is due to statistical misspecification. Second, Mani and Wheeler (1997, p20) provide evidence suggesting that the consumption of pollution-intensive goods in the developed world has decreased hand-in-hand with their decreasing pollution-intensity of production so that the 'consumption/production ratios of dirty-sector products in the developing world have remained close to unity'.

Tobey (1990) analyses directly the effects of differences in environmental standards on patterns of world trade, finding that developed countries' stringent standards have not significantly affected international trade patterns in the most polluting industries. He uses data from the late 1960s and early 1970s – that is, before the major wave of raising environmental standards in developed countries. But his result is confirmed by a similar analysis by Beers and Bergh (1997) for 1992. However, whereas they find no significantly negative impact of the stringency of environmental standards on exports of pollution-intensive industries as a whole, they do find such an impact with respect to the subset of 'non-resource based' pollution-intensive industries.

The World Bank (1998a, p113) also provides more recent evidence on the pollution-intensity of exports from developed and developing countries. It computes the export–import ratio for six heavily polluting sectors – iron and steel, non-ferrous metals, industrial chemicals, petroleum refineries, non-metallic mineral products and pulp and paper products – for 53 countries *in monetary terms*. The export–import ratio of low-income countries increased by 71 per cent to about 0.3 between 1986 and 1995, that of both lower and higher middle-income countries decreased, and the ratio of high-income countries increased by 29 per cent to 1.32.[7] The result for low-income countries leaves open the possibility that these countries provided pollution havens in the 1980s and early 1990s (and possibly before). Notably, however, the lower the income group of countries, the lower the export–import ratio. Production of dirty industries takes place predominantly in the richer countries. What is true for income groups holds true on a disaggregated level as well: the World Bank (1998a, p113) finds that, with very few exceptions, developed countries export more goods from highly polluting sectors than they import from developing countries, both in 1986 and in 1995. A possible explanation for this rather striking result might be that dirty sectors are about twice as capital intensive as clean sectors, which in turn are about 40 per cent more labour intensive (Mani and Wheeler 1997, p6), and developed countries are more capital abundant and less labour abundant than developing countries.

The evidence submitted by the World Bank is contested by Muradian and Martinez-Alier (2001), however. They argue that one needs to look at the export–import ratio in physical rather than monetary terms and submit some initial evidence that European Union countries are likely to be net importers of pollution intensive products if measured in physical terms.

Weakly supportive evidence for the latter result can also be found in Kahn (2000) for the US. He looks at the pollution intensity of exports and imports in 1972, 1982 and 1992, where pollution intensity is measured according to information provided by the US Toxic Release Inventory Data. He finds that the growth in pollution-intensive imports is mainly due to growth in trade with rich nations, not with developing countries. However, he also finds that 'when poorer nations engage in trade liberalization dirty trade with the United States grows faster than clean trade with the United States' (ibid, pp3ff).

Do pollution-intensive industries flee the high standards countries?

Pollution havens, if existent, will attract foreign investment from countries with higher standards. Do we observe pollution-intensive industries leaving countries with high environmental standards? Evidence on this aspect exists mainly for the US only. Leonard (1988), in one of the earliest comprehensive qualitative studies, did not find evidence of pollution-intensive US industries moving to Ireland, Spain, Mexico and Romania. More systematic and very strong evidence against the hypothesis that pollution-intensive industries migrate towards countries with lower standards is provided by Albrecht (1998): he looks at the US inflows and outflows of investment from clean, medium polluting and dirty industries between 1991 and 1995. He finds that dirty industries are the only ones for which more investment comes to than leaves the US, whereas there is a massive net outflow of investment in clean industries. As this result is not due to dirty industries growing faster than other US industries, Albrecht (ibid, p191) concludes that 'dirty industries are not at all leaving the USA en masse'.

The period of Albrecht's analysis is quite small. More importantly, it is for the US only. Unfortunately, for the other G7 countries FDI data are not available on a detailed industrial basis.[8] The exception is Germany, for which the following looks at FDI flows of eight pollution-intensive manufacturing sectors over the period 1989 to 1997 (data taken from the Bundesbank (1994, 1997, 1999)).[9] While the cumulative direct investment of foreigners into Germany in these sectors amounts to approximately DM 224 billion, the cumulative flow of direct investment out of Germany amounts to DM 376 billion. It would be wrong, however, to regard this as evidence for a massive flight of pollution-intensive industries out of Germany with its high environmental standards. This is because these industries simply follow the general trend of the overall German manufacturing sector, which is characterized by massive net outflows of direct investment. Indeed, the share of pollution-intensive FDI among all German manufacturing sector FDIs has remained relatively close to its average share of about 41 per cent between 1989 and 1997. That there is a net outflow of investment in pollution-intensive sectors is therefore in itself no evidence for this flight being induced by high environmental standards. However, the same average share of pollution-intensive among all manufacturing sectors is about 39 per cent for FDI into Germany. The difference of two percentage points could be tentatively interpreted as evidence for a net outflow of investment in these sectors, even after the net outflow of investment of the overall manufacturing sector has been taken into account. It is weak evidence at best, however, as this rather small difference of two percentage points might be caused by many other factors besides high environmental compliance costs in Germany.

In search of an explanation: Why is there so little evidence for pollution havens?

It follows from this overview of empirical studies that the evidence for pollution havens is relatively weak at best and inconclusive or even negative at worst. As a next step, one might ask why low standard countries do not manage to attract more capital from high standard countries.

1   The first and perhaps most obvious explanation is that some of the dirtiest industries cannot migrate as they are dependent on being close to their product market. This explanation applies, for example, to electricity generation, but does not apply to the majority of industries in the manufacturing sector.

2   Second, the costs of environmental compliance might be too low to play a significant role in investment decisions. According to the Organization for Economic Co-operation and Development (OECD) (1996, Table 1), while pollution abatement expenditures as a percentage of GDP have slightly increased between 1985 and 1992, they are estimated at well below 2 per cent in most countries in 1992. Potential cost savings of that order might very well be too small to induce foreign investors to move to pollution havens for two reasons.[10] First, migration itself is costly because of dismantling, transportation and new establishment costs. Second, factors other than differences in environmental compliance costs are likely to be much more important in determining international investment location decisions (Wheeler and Mody 1992). Potential pollution havens might have disadvantages with respect to these other factors – for example, they might have a badly trained workforce, a poor infrastructure and political as well as economic instability. Doing business carries many more risks in developing as opposed to developed countries. Even if industries move to developing countries, factors such as proximity to natural resources and financial as well as tax incentives might play a more important role than potential savings on environmental compliance costs. However, there are three caveats to keep in mind:

(i)   How high pollution abatement expenditures are depends on what the point of reference is and varies substantially from sector to sector. If we look at pollution abatement capital expenditures as a percentage of total new capital expenditures in 1993 in the US, these can be as low as 1.52 per cent for rubber and miscellaneous plastics products, but as high as 42.39 per cent for petroleum and coal products and 13.31 per cent for chemicals and allied products (US Bureau of Census 1996, Table 1).

(ii) Should environmental compliance costs in countries with high standards rise further in the future, then things could change dramatically from what they were before. Markusen, Morey and Olewiler

(1995) show that in industries with increasing returns to scale, costs can rise up to a certain threshold without causing any major relocation. However, because increasing returns industries tend to make discrete rather than marginal location decisions, if costs rise beyond this threshold industries might shut down and transfer their operations to countries with lower standards.

(iii) Most studies look at environmental compliance costs in the form of pollution abatement expenditures. However, much modern environmental regulation comes in the form of raising the price of energy use. Whether differences in international energy costs can induce a statistically significant relocation of industries has not been really examined yet to my knowledge.

3   Third, even where environmental compliance costs are significant, international investors might not be deterred, as long as the environmental standards provide clear and reliable rules that apply equally to everybody. What investors dislike most is uncertainty about the future and the unreliability of policy-makers.

4   Fourth, and connected to the last point, rational forward-looking investors might anticipate that environmental standards in countries that currently have low standards might very well increase over time. It might therefore be cheaper to establish already in the present production facilities that comply with these potential future higher standards.

5   Fifth, if pollution abatement is characterized by scale economies, then increasing environmental standards need not induce migration. Eskeland and Harrison (1997, p28) argue that 'if abatement costs fall with the scale of output, then the home country firm may find it more advantageous to expand locally when facing tougher environmental regulations'.

6   Sixth, if TNCs have similar plants in both countries with high standards and countries with low standards, then it might be cheaper to install the same pollution-abatement technology as exists in the countries with high standards everywhere. This is because the costs of dismantling the already established technology might outweigh the benefits from saving on abatement costs. This will be especially true if the abatement technology is an integral part of the production process. If instead the abatement technology is of the add-on end of pipe type, it will be quite cheap to get rid of it in order to save on abatement costs.

7   Seventh, foreign investors might fear for their international reputation if they are perceived as environmental villains exploiting low standards in poor countries. In migrating to these poor countries, it might therefore be worthwhile to exceed voluntarily local environmental standards. It is sometimes argued by economists that foreign investors not only tend to apply better environmental management than required by the host country, but also tend to demand compliance with higher environmental standards from their domestic suppliers. This positive effect on the environmental standards of the recipient country has been coined the

'pollution halo' effect and it stands in stark contrast to the pollution haven hypothesis: Instead of exploiting low environmental standards, foreign investment leads to a rise in environmental standards. Anecdotal evidence supports this hypothesis (Leonard 1988; Gentry 1999; Zarsky 1999). More systematic testing provides more ambiguous evidence. Whereas Eskeland and Harrison (1997) find that foreign-owned plants in Côte d'Ivoire, Mexico and Venezuela are more energy efficient than domestically owned plants, and therefore as a first approximation also less pollution intensive, Dasgupta, Hettige and Wheeler (1997) and Hettige et al (1996) find no evidence that foreign ownership has a significant influence on environmental performance in Mexico and South and Southeast Asia respectively.

8   Eighth, investors might fear the negative effects on their capital market value if information about poor environmental performance becomes available. Hamilton (1995) demonstrates negative stock market reactions for US companies that had to report toxics release inventory data to the US Environmental Protection Agency (EPA). Dasgupta, Laplante and Mamingi (1997) show that negative capital market reactions are not confined to the developed world when they examined how firm-specific environmental information affected capital markets in Mexico, Chile, Argentina and the Philippines. Dowell, Hart and Yeung (2000) demonstrate that US based TNCs that abide by high environmental standards in their foreign operations carried higher market values than TNCs that adopt lower than domestic environmental standards abroad. More generally, Gentry (1999, p16) refers to a recent review of 70 studies exploring the link between environmental and financial performance, which found that 'companies with the environmental practices were rewarded with higher stock market returns than their peers, by up to two percentage points. Moreover, positive environmental performance *never* translated into negative returns'.

Policy recommendation: A plea for assistance to institutional capacity-building

In considering theoretical issues concerning pollution havens, we have seen that several factors can give rise to their existence in developing countries. Of these, bias against environmental preferences is probably the most important one. In examining the empirical evidence we have also seen, however, that there is only weak statistical evidence for their existence. Pollution havens therefore represent a rather elusive phenomenon. While environmentalists insist on the existence and relevance of the phenomenon, their claim is not convincingly backed by available empirical evidence, at least not so far.

Should analysis stop here? No. I would submit that it is important to take the analysis one step further and evaluate policy options for tackling (potential) pollution haven problems. Why? First of all, in spite of the relatively weak systematic evidence, pollution havens might very well exist. For example, limits to data availability might prevent us from detecting them. Besides, we have seen that some empirical studies do lend some support in favour of their existence. Second, and more importantly, no matter what systematic empirical evidence tells us, as a matter of fact both policy-makers and environmentalists are unimpressed and remain concerned about the phenomenon. If anything, the ongoing trend towards increased foreign investment in developing countries will strengthen those concerns. There exists and is bound to remain a wide gap between those who strongly believe in the pollution haven phenomenon and others, among them many economists who believe that pollution havens are either irrelevant or simply non-existent.

Given the limitations of our current empirical knowledge and the strength of concern, it seems to me that an evaluation of policy options for dealing with (potential) pollution haven problems is indispensable. This section therefore goes one step further than most other writings on the topic and engages in an analysis of available policy options. I briefly list a fairly comprehensive range of policy options available and provide some examples for existing policies. I then introduce five criteria with which those policy options become evaluated. Three out of these criteria – namely that options should be development friendly, closed to abuse and not unnecessarily restrictive – are heavily influenced by the fact that the evidence with respect to pollution havens is rather shaky. This is because they are likely to ensure that policy options are chosen that are favourable to developing countries which should not be punished for something that might either not exist or be of little relevance. The inclusion of these criteria should also help in reconciling those who strongly disagree with the relevance of the pollution haven phenomenon with such an analysis. As we will see below, the policy option that fares best on our five criteria – namely assistance for capacity-building and local empowerment – is also the one to which those who regard pollution havens as irrelevant could subscribe to as it would help developing countries to overcome many more general problems in environmental policy-making.

Policy options and criteria of evaluation

Harmonization of environmental standards and minimum standards

An existing example for this on a regional level is the Treaty establishing the European Union (EU) (for a more detailed analysis, see Neumayer 2001b). Article 93 provides for the harmonization of indirect taxes. Article 95 has as its objective the adoption of 'measures for the approximation of the provisions laid down by law, regulation or administrative action in Member States which have as their object the establishment and functioning of the internal market' (Article 95:1). Article 175 has as its objective the harmonization of 'measures answering environmental protection requirements' (Article 174:2).

EU harmonized standards are in principle to be interpreted as setting minimum standards that can be exceeded by member states under certain conditions. Article 95:10 allows for harmonization measures to include, in appropriate cases, 'a safeguard clause authorising the Member State to take, for one or more of the non-economic reasons referred to in Article 30, provisional measures subject to a Community control procedure'. Article 95:4 allows EU member states, more generally, to maintain national provisions if it deems them necessary for the protection of the environment. Similarly, Article 176 proclaims that harmonization based on Article 175 'shall not prevent any Member State from maintaining or introducing more stringent protective measures'. Porter (1999) calls for a minimum standards agreement exclusively negotiated and concluded among developing countries.

Enforcement agreements

An existing example are Articles 3 and 5 of the North American Agreement on Environmental Cooperation, the environmental side agreement to NAFTA, which read as follows:

> *Recognizing the right of each Party to establish its own levels of domestic environmental protection and environmental development policies and priorities, and to adopt or modify accordingly its environmental laws and regulations, each Party shall ensure that its laws and regulations provide for high levels of environmental protection and shall strive to continue to improve those laws and regulations.* (Article 3.)

> *With the aim of achieving high levels of environmental protection and compliance with its environmental laws and regulations, each Party shall effectively enforce its environmental laws and regulations through appropriate governmental action...* (Article 5:1.)

> *Each party shall ensure that judicial, quasi-judicial or administrative enforcement proceedings are available under its law to sanction or remedy violations of its environmental laws and regulations.* (Article 5:2.)

Trade and capital restrictions

These encompass direct restrictions such as import bans as well as tariffs and quotas and 'voluntary' export restraints. The most popular form of these restrictions are so-called eco-tariffs which are imposed on foreign countries with lower than domestic environmental standards. Daly (1993, p26), for example, demands that 'whoever sells in a nation's market should play by that nation's rules or pay a tariff sufficient to remove the competitive advantages of lower standards' (similarly Kettlewell (1992)). Arden-Clarke

(1993, p81) from the WWF wants 'environmental leaders' to be able to 'take trade measures that "level the playing field" between environmentally sound and unsound goods'. The International Pollution Deterrence Act, unsuccessfully introduced into the 102nd US Congress as motion S.984 by Senator Boren (D-OK) called for countervailing duties equivalent to the cost that it would take a foreign firm to comply with US domestic environmental standards (OTA 1992, p92). In order to do so, a 'pollution control index' was supposed to be constructed for:

> *each of the top fifty countries identified by the Office of Trade and Investment of the Department of Commerce based on the value of exports to the United States from that country's attainment of pollution control standards in the areas of air, water, hazardous waste and solid waste as compared to the United States. The purpose of this index is to measure the level of compliance within each country with standards comparable to or greater than those in the United States. The Administrator shall analyze, in particular, the level of technology employed and actual costs incurred for pollution control in the major export sectors of each country formulating the index.* (cited in Hilton and Levinson 2000, pp19ff.)

Hilton and Levinson quote Senator Max Baucus (D-MT), one of the motion's supporters, as saying that one of its major goals was to 'level the playing field' with nations that have 'inadequate environmental protection' (ibid, p20).

Eco-labels

Existing examples include the German Blue Angel, the Nordic Swan, the EU eco-label award scheme, the Canadian environmental choice programme (OECD 1997a) and the Forest Stewardship Council's (FSC 2000) and Marine Stewardship Council's (MSC 2000) eco-labelling scheme.

Non-binding declarations

Existing examples include the OECD Guidelines on Multinational Enterprises (OECD 2000), the OECD statement of intent on officially supported export credits and the environment (OECD 1998h) and the International Chamber of Commerce's business charter for sustainable development (ICC 2000).

Assistance for political–institutional capacity-building and local empowerment

This encompasses first of all assistance aimed at building the capacity to formulate effective environmental policies with a long-term vision and strategy, and to implement, monitor and successfully manage these policies. Existing examples are the World Bank's assistance for National Environmental Action Plans, the Global Environment Facility, and the United Nations Environment Programme (UNEP) and the United Nations Conference on Trade and Development (UNCTAD) joint capacity-building task force for assisting developing countries in integrating their trade, environment and development policies (UNEP and UNCTAD 2000). Second, and equally important, is a strengthening of democratic citizenship and political accountability of policy-makers as well as improving the access of local communities to information about environmental pollution, to political decision making and to the legal system. There is ample evidence from developing countries that active and empowered citizens can play a significant role in improving local environmental conditions (Pargal and Mani 2000; World Bank 2000).

I would propose to apply the following set of criteria in assessing these options:[11]

- *Effective.* A policy option should achieve its objective of bringing environmental standards closer to their efficiency levels.
- *Politically realistic.* A policy option should be politically realistic, otherwise it has no chance of being realized.
- *Development friendly.* A policy option should be friendly towards the economic development prospects of developing countries. Given the huge inequalities between rich and poor countries, policies that come about at the expense of developing countries should be discouraged.
- *Closed to abuse.* A policy option should not be open to abuse by protectionist factions in countries with high standards under flimsy environmental pretexts.
- *Not unnecessarily restrictive.* A policy option should not restrict international flows of capital and trade beyond the necessary extent. It is this author's conviction that, *ceteris paribus*, a liberal capital and trade regime is desirable.

Effective

The harmonization of international environmental standards would be clearly ineffective. While it would raise inefficiently low environmental standards in developing countries, it would also either raise them to inefficiently high standards or would lower standards in developed countries below their efficiency level. The simple lesson is that one single standard does not fit them all, except perhaps for life-threatening toxics which should be banned everywhere (witness the negotiations on an international agreement banning persistent organic pollutants worldwide (see p166)).

Minimum standards fare somewhat better than the harmonization of standards as they do not imply a lowering of standards in developed countries below their efficiency level. There remains the danger, however, that minimum standards are set inefficiently high for developing countries. This danger is significantly less if minimum standards are set in an agreement exclusively concluded among developing countries. To be effective, harmonized as well as minimum standards would need to include certain monitoring and enforcement requirements.

Enforcement agreements address an important point in the pollution haven debate. A country that wants to attract foreign capital in setting inefficiently low de facto environmental standards might not even set low nominal standards. Instead, it might set standards that appear to be high on paper, with the understanding that they will not be enforced. Without ascribing the intention to attract foreign capital, it is often correctly pointed out that the former Communist countries in Eastern Europe often had environmental standards that looked strict on paper, but were virtually non-existent in reality (Ahlander 1994). In as far as an enforcement agreement could itself be enforced it could lead to an avoidance of this phenomenon. Of course, it could have the rather perverse consequence that pollution haven countries then lower their standards or at least fail to raise them in the future.

Trade and capital restrictions are very crude measures to aim for in order to raise environmental standards in developing countries, but they could be effective. If pollution havens are threatened with import bans or eco-tariffs against the products produced in their location, or find it hard to attract foreign investment due to capital restrictions, then those countries might very well abstain from setting inefficiently low, or failing to enforce, standards.

Eco-labels are unlikely to be effective in raising general environmental standards in developing countries. Past evidence of the effectiveness of eco-labels is usually confined to specific environmental aspects, such as whether tuna is caught with dolphin-safe nets, and whether forests and marine fish-stocks are managed and harvested sustainably. Otherwise it is most doubtful whether the various existent eco-labels had any significant effect so far (OECD 1997a).

Non-binding declarations would be ineffective if they were not backed up by some backdrop threat. It is a common experience that these declarations often create no more than hot air. If pollution havens exist they do so because of economic interests that do not simply vanish because of some non-binding declaration. Mabey and McNally (1999, p43) suggest that 'all OECD governments admit' that the OECD guidelines on multinational enterprises 'have not greatly influenced companies'. However, voluntary company codes can become somewhat more effective if they are linked to mandatory information disclosure rules in their country of origin, as proposed by Mabey and McNally (1999).

Whether assistance for political–institutional capacity-building and local empowerment would be effective depends on the factors that gave rise to pollution havens in the first instance. If they are due to bias against environmental preferences, then this option could be very effective in helping to overcome the political–institutional failures that prevent countries from setting efficient standards.

Politically realistic

The harmonization of international environmental standards is utterly unrealistic. There is no political support for such an option, especially among the developing countries, but also among the developed countries (ICTSD 1999a). The same is true to a large extent for the introduction of minimum standards as well, which would fail due to the resistance of developing countries. Even for an agreement to be exclusively concluded among developing countries, there currently seems to be no significant political momentum.

An enforcement agreement could be politically easier to realize, even though doubts remain about whether developing countries would consent. The reason is that they would feel stigmatized as countries in need of an international agreement to enforce their own laws and regulations. In this respect, it is pertinent to note that the enforcement clause in the North American Free Trade Agreement (NAFTA) had to be pushed through by the US and Canada against the explicit opposition of the Mexican government. It was one of the prices it had to pay to gain access to the North American markets.

Trade restrictions and eco-tariffs might find political support in developed countries among some protectionist factions and environmentalists, but they are not generally supported by their governments (OECD 1995). Furthermore, they prove to be unrealistic as the WTO currently puts such stringent conditions on the imposition of trade restrictions aimed at so-called process and production methods (PPMs) outside a country's jurisdiction that in practice they are quasi-prohibited (see p138). A reform of the GATT to allow these measures is utterly unrealistic as, according to Article X:3 of the Agreement Establishing the World Trade Organization (WTO), it would require a two-thirds majority and therefore the consent of developing countries which are strictly opposed to it (ICTSD 1999a).[12] Capital restrictions are not necessarily dependent on developing countries' consent as it is a rather one-sided game: developed countries invest in developing countries, but not to any significant extent vice versa (UNCTAD 1999a). However, it is doubtful whether there is significant support for capital restrictions in developed countries. The (failed) attempt to conclude a Multilateral Agreement on Investment (MAI), and the European Union's and Japan's insistence to include the liberalization of the international investment regime in any potential new round of WTO trade negotiations, shows that developed countries want to de-restrict rather than restrict capital flows. Also, capital restrictions could possibly clash with the bilateral investment agreements between developed and developing countries.

The establishment of eco-labels that relate to the environmental impacts of PPMs could find political support in developed countries, but they are generally resisted by the developing world (WTO 1996a). Whether such eco-labels would clash with the existing WTO rules has not been tested so far, and their legality or otherwise is not entirely clear (see p27). But if eco-labels became more than fringe measures to deal with international differences in environmental standards, one or the other developing country would surely start a dispute settlement under WTO rules. If the WTO panel and appellate body decided against the general use of eco-labels with respect to PPMs, as seems most likely, then their use would be dependent on WTO reform, which would face the same resistance from developing countries as the one referred to above concerning trade restrictions.

Non-binding declarations are politically realistic as they seem to be an easy option. At the time of writing, the OECD had just finished revising its Guidelines on Multinational Enterprises, with a somewhat strengthened environmental chapter that calls for environmental management systems and a precautionary approach towards environmental uncertainty (OECD 2000).

Assistance for political–institutional capacity-building and local empowerment is not particularly realistic as it would cost the developed countries money, and their willingness to provide aid has decreased over the last years (OECD 1999, Statistical Annex, Table 1). If capacity-building was to address effectively the inefficiently low environmental standard setting in developing countries, then developed countries would need to be much more willing to provide help either bilaterally or through inter-governmental institutions like the World Bank or WTO. In as far as developing country governments might resist local empowerment, developed countries would also need to use their political influence on those governments. This influence might be rather limited, however, and developed countries might be unwilling to use whatever influence they have.

Development friendly

Whether the harmonization of international environmental standards or international minimum standards would be development friendly depends on whether any assistance for developing countries to raise their standards was provided. The same holds true for an enforcement agreement. This is because the frequent failure of enforcement is likely to be caused not by a lack of will, but by the absence of an adequate political, legal and administrative infrastructure for enforcement. If assistance for developing countries was not given, as seems most likely, then these three options would be rather unfriendly to developing countries as they would have to shoulder all the burden alone. Trade and capital restrictions are clearly development unfriendly. They are inspired by a desire to punish developing countries for what is perceived as undesirable behaviour on their part. The same applies, but to a lesser extent, to eco-labels as well, at least if their imposition is not accompanied by assistance for developing countries to comply with the eco-labelling requirements. Non-binding declarations are relatively neutral with respect to development friendliness. Assistance for political–institutional capacity-building and local empowerment excels all other options on this criterion. To overcome the failures that gave rise to pollution havens would potentially help developing countries to rid themselves of other inefficiencies as well and would thus strengthen their overall developmental capacity.

Closed to abuse

The international harmonization of standards or the establishment of international minimum standards are unlikely to be open to abuse as they would need the consent of countries with lower environmental standards. The same holds true for an international enforcement agreement. Capital and trade restrictions clearly are open to abuse by protectionist factions in high standards countries under green disguise, given the fundamental uncertainty about whether or not existing environmental standards are efficient or not. The severe information difficulties – are standards inefficiently low and if so by how much? are standards not enforced and if so to what extent? – give countries imposing trade or capital restrictions substantial potential for abuse. Developing countries rightly fear an unholy alliance between 'baptists' (environmentalists) and 'bootleggers' (protectionists) in the trade arena (DeSombre 1995).[13] Eco-labels can represent barriers to market access for developing countries and are therefore open to abuse. Many developing countries fear that they do not have adequate information and capacity to comply with, for example, eco-labels which mainly affect goods such as textiles, leather, footwear, forestry and food products that developing countries have a comparative advantage in producing and exporting (WTO 1996a). Non-binding declarations can be abused in principle as well, but in general seem to be fairly neutral on this criterion. Assistance for political–institutional capacity-building clearly is the policy option least open to abuse.

Not unnecessarily restrictive

At first sight, the harmonization of international environmental standards or the establishment of international minimum standards do not appear to restrict international trade and capital flows. However, if developing countries' standards were to rise above their efficiency levels, these countries would face implicit restrictions towards their exports of goods and services and their import of capital. An international enforcement agreement would not be restrictive, as it would merely aspire to ensure that a country's laws and regulations have more bite than paper tigers. Trade and capital restrictions are by definition restrictive, and unnecessarily so in as much as their objective can be achieved with other less restrictive measures – for example, with assistance for political–institutional capacity-building and local empowerment or, if effective, with eco-labels and non-binding declarations.

Table 3.3 *Evaluation of policy options addressing the 'pollution haven' problem*

Policy options	Effective	Politically realistic	Development friendly	Closed to abuse	Not unnecessarily restrictive
		Criteria of evaluation			
Harmonization of standards	—	—	–	+	–
Minimum standards	+/–	—	–	+	+/–
Enforcement agreement	+	–	–	+	++
Trade and capital sanctions	++	—	—	—	—
Eco-labels	–	+/–	–	–	+
Non-binding declarations	–	++	+/–	+/–	+
Assistance for capacity-building and local empowerment	+	–	++	++	++

Key: ++ very good, + good, +/– neutral, – poor, — very poor

Summary of findings

Table 3.3 provides a summary of the findings on policy options. While no option fares unambiguously better than all others, assistance for political–institutional capacity-building and local empowerment seems to be the best option. It has only two drawbacks: it might not be very effective if pollution havens are not due to political–institutional failure but to other factors, and it is doubtful whether developed countries are ready to provide such assistance.

Conclusion

Developing countries might set low environmental standards for a number of reasons. Some, but by far not all, of these reasons will mean that their standards are not only low, but inefficiently so. In a world of imperfect information it is hard to detect when this is the case. The rather weak systematic evidence with respect to pollution havens implies that they represent a rather elusive phenomenon. Nevertheless, they might very well exist. Other factors might prevent inefficiently low or badly enforced environmental standards in developing countries from exerting a statistically traceable influence on the international allocation of investment flows, on the pollution intensity of developing countries' production and exports and on the extent to which pollution-intensive countries flee countries with high environmental standards. Given that specific policies addressing the pollution havens problem are not clearly necessary and that discrimination between efficiently low environmental standards and real pollution havens is rather difficult to achieve, the more important it becomes that policy options dealing with (potential) pollution havens are development friendly, closed to abuse and not unnecessarily restrictive – exactly the criteria on which assistance for political–institutional capacity-building and local empowerment fares best. This chapter therefore recommends assistance for political–institutional capacity-building and local empowerment as the best policy option to deal with potential problems connected to pollution havens.

In concluding this chapter, it is important to point out that even if the systematic evidence for pollution havens is rather weak, this does not contradict the more anecdotal evidence that purports to demonstrate that at times environmental conditions in developing countries can be abhorrent, that some TNCs abuse low environmental standards (especially in the mining and other resource-extraction sector, such as in Indonesia, Nigeria and Papua New Guinea) and that specific industries might migrate out of high standards countries into nearby low standard areas as, for example, into the so-called Maquiladora region along the US–Mexican border (for a good documentation and referencing, see Mabey and McNally 1999 and OTA 1992, Appendix E).

Furthermore, an important limitation of the analysis above is that I have looked at whether and under what conditions developing countries have incentives to set inefficiently low environmental standards. I have not analysed whether international capital mobility might deter particularly developed countries from setting higher environmental standards for fear of losing capital to their competitors. This hypothesized phenomenon is sometimes called 'regulatory chill' and is addressed in the next chapter.

4

Regulatory Chill: Do Developed Countries Fail to Raise Environmental Standards Because of Feared Capital Flight?

In the last chapter we focused on developing countries and examined whether they set inefficiently low environmental standards or fail to enforce standards to attract foreign capital. In this chapter we look at what effects the actual or imagined existence of inefficiently low or non-enforced environmental standards elsewhere might have on developed countries and their environmental standard setting. If policy-makers in these countries fear that high environmental standards will induce internationally mobile capital to move to countries with low standards, then they might themselves lower their standards to keep this capital or, perhaps more realistically, at least fail to raise environmental standards by as much as they would otherwise do over time. In the following I will refer to this, in accordance with much of the relevant literature, as the 'regulatory chill' hypothesis – that is, developed countries fail to raise standards over time because of feared capital flight (Esty 1994; Zarsky 1997; Mabey and McNally 1999; Greenpeace 1999; Porter 1999).

Some preliminary considerations

From the outset of this chapter the reader should note four important points:

1   For the 'regulatory chill' hypothesis to hold it does not matter whether pollution havens and consequently the danger of capital migration induced by inefficiently low environmental standards setting or weak standard enforcement in developing countries are real phenomena. It is sufficient that policy-makers in developed countries believe that pollution havens exist to scare them away from potentially raising

environmental standards – and in spite of its shaky evidence, they actually do seem to believe in pollution havens. It follows that 'regulatory chill' could still be a real and significant phenomenon even if pollution havens are not.

2   The hypothesis need not depend at all on pollution havens, whether real or imagined. It can hold true independently on how environmental standards are set in developing countries. Policy-makers in developed countries might see capital flight into other developed countries to be the much more relevant danger. Therefore they might fail to raise environmental standards if other developed countries do not also raise environmental standards simultaneously.

3   We would expect 'regulatory chill' to be more prevalent with respect to environmental standards concerning pollutants that affect the so-called global commons, such as the global climate, the ozone layer and biodiversity. We would expect it to be less significant for environmental standards concerning pollutants that affect the national environment only. This is because in the case of the global commons, the benefits of raising environmental standards have to be shared with all or at least many other countries as well. In as far as capital flight is perceived to be one of the costs of raising environmental standards, it will become relatively more important in this case, then, as the costs are balanced against dispersed benefits.

4   Because the hypothesis refers to the absence of something that would otherwise have happened (namely, the raising of environmental standards), it makes in effect a counter-factual claim for which systematic statistical evidence is, almost by definition, difficult, if not impossible, to gather. In the words of Mabey and McNally (1999, p38): 'That there is little statistical evidence of this "chilling effect" is unsurprising, because evidence is needed of what has not happened. This issue must be investigated by historians and political scientists, not econometricians.' It follows that anecdotal evidence needs to be examined to gauge the validity of the hypothesis.

Some anecdotal evidence

Esty and Geradin (1998, p19) believe that the fear of capital loss has a 'most significant impact ... on the environmental policy-making process'. They suggest that 'in almost every political debate over environmental policy in the United States, competitiveness concerns are cited as a reason not to move toward tougher standards' (ibid, p20). While this quote refers to 'competitiveness concerns' more generally, it is relevant for investment issues as well, as exit of its capital would be the ultimate effect of a jurisdiction's 'loss of competitiveness'. What Esty and Geradin suggest for the United States holds true for Germany as well. The Bundesverband der Deutschen Industrie (BDI) and other industrial associations have continuously warned policy-makers that further raising environmental standards, especially with respect to a so-called ecological tax reform, would damage the competitiveness of German industry and would lead to capital flight out of Germany (BDI 1998a, 1998b). The same holds true for the opposition against the UK climate change levy from British industrial groups. But do these concerns and threats really translate into 'regulatory chill'? Are policy-makers scared away from raising standards or do they regard these threats by industrial groups as cheap talk whose only function is to prevent policies that would raise costs to the industry and (potentially) lower its profits?

In the following I will concentrate on one issue for which I believe that we have sufficient evidence to show that the fear of capital loss has actually led to a 'regulatory chill'. The issue is how much developed countries should reduce air emissions, particularly greenhouse gas emissions, and, specifically, whether they should introduce a tax on fossil fuels to achieve reductions in these emissions. As concerns the United States, President Clinton's initial plan to introduce a 25.5 cents per million of British Thermal Units (BTUs) energy tax over a period of three years was defeated, not least by the massive resistance of the 'American Energy Alliance', behind which stood the National Association of Manufacturers and the Affordable Energy Alliance, as well as the American Petroleum Institute, behind which in turn stands the US oil industry (Erlandsson 1994). These lobby groups claimed that such a tax would reduce their 'competitiveness' with a consequent loss of jobs and might ultimately lead to a flight of capital out of the US.

Similarly, the United States' position in the Kyoto Protocol negotiations in 1997 was significantly influenced by the opposition of some of its industries which gathered in the so-called Global Climate Change Coalition (GCC), as well as the AFL-CIO, the major US trade union, which again warned that millions of jobs would be lost due to decreased competitiveness and capital flight if a climate change protocol did not encompass the major developing countries (BNA 1997; API 2000; Zarsky 1997, p36ff).[1] As a result, the US Senate voted 95–0, with five senators not voting, in favour of a motion that the US must not sign a treaty which does not mandate 'new specific scheduled commitments to limit or reduce greenhouse gas emissions for developing country parties within the same compliance period' or would result in 'serious harm to the economy of the United States' (BNA 1997) – 'where by "serious harm" the Senate meant, in the words of Senator Robert Byrd, a co-author of the resolution, capital flight and a loss of jobs in the United States' (Barrett 1998, p21). In the end, the US government signed the Kyoto Protocol which does not include any emissions reduction obligations for developing countries. But whether this signature will be followed by the necessary ratification through the US Senate is far from clear. Immediately after the US government's signature under the Kyoto Protocol, the GCC, the Competitive Enterprise Institute, as well as Republican Senator Chuck Nagel, co-sponsor of the above-mentioned motion, called for President

Clinton to bring the Protocol to the Senate floor so that it could be rejected (BNA 1998a). The Clinton administration wisely refused (ibid). With George Bush as President ratification of the Kyoto Protocol has become unthinkable.

As concerns the European Union (EU), its Commission had originally proposed a communitywide introduction of a tax on carbon dioxide emissions and energy in 1992 (European Commission 1992), which, among other things, would have raised the price of petrol by about US$10 per barrel in 2000. Nine years later, at the time of writing this book, this tax has still not materialized and it is highly unlikely that it ever will.[2] At least partly this failure is to be explained by opposition from business groups which did not leave policy makers, even those from environmental 'leaders' such as the Scandinavian countries and Germany, unimpressed. Maybe more importantly, however, the Commission's original proposal had the possibility for 'regulatory chill' already included. This is because in its Article 1 it conditioned the realization of the tax within the EU on the introduction 'by other member countries of the OECD of a similar tax or of measures having a financial impact equivalent to those provided for in this Directive'. In other words, the Commission was so much impressed by the threat of 'loss of competitiveness' and, ultimately, loss of capital, that it accepted that environmental standards would not be raised if other OECD countries did not follow suit. As the likelihood that this might happen, especially as concerns the US, was very small indeed, the EU's regulatory efforts were effectively chilled.

As concerns Germany, the ecological tax reform became realized after a Social Democrat–Green coalition took over power at the federal level in October 1998. However, the tax reform had to be downsized and had to include a number of exceptions for energy-intensive industries due to immense pressure from industrial lobby groups. Ironically, the Federal Environment Minister himself rushed to persuade industries and the public alike that with so many exceptions and rather low tax rates, capital flight out of Germany had been effectively prevented (BMU 2000).

Policy recommendations: a plea for standard harmonization and MEAs

Are policies that are trying to overcome 'regulatory chill' necessary? The conclusion from the anecdotal evidence is that the fear of 'loss of competitiveness' in general and of the loss of capital in particular, seems to have exerted some regulatory chilling effect on developed countries with respect to reducing greenhouse and other air emissions and, in particular, with respect to introducing taxes on fossil fuels. This chilling effect did not completely prevent the introduction of carbon abatement policies. After all, the United States and other developed countries did successfully sign the Kyoto Protocol (but have not yet ratified), Germany has entered into an

ecological tax reform, the Scandinavian countries had earlier already introduced carbon/energy taxes (Brack, Grubb and Windram 2000, pp59–70)
and a EU-wide carbon tax might still materialize. But it is also true that
policy makers in developed countries did not introduce abatement policies
as stringent as they would have otherwise done had they not been concerned
about 'loss of competitiveness' and loss of capital.

Whether this evidence in favour of the 'regulatory chill' hypothesis holds
true for other environmental issues as well is not fully clear. Few case studies
have been undertaken on this matter and there is a clear need for future
research. But greenhouse gas and other air emissions represent major
environmental problems, so that it is appropriate to move one step further
and evaluate policy options to deal with 'regulatory chill'. As was the case
with pollution havens, the necessity for policies dealing with 'regulatory
chill' has not been fully and convincingly established so far. But again, the
'regulatory chill' hypothesis cannot be dismissed, so we need to address the
question, 'Which policy option satisfies our evaluation criteria best?'

Policy options and criteria of evaluation

In this section, a number of policy options will be examined that deal with
the problem of 'regulatory chill'. Two were introduced in Chapter 3, namely:
harmonization of environmental standards and minimum standards; and
enforcement agreements.

In addition, three more policy options, multilateral trade restrictions,
border tax adjustments, and subsidies, will also be considered.

Multilateral trade restrictions. These play an important role in multilateral environmental agreements. Their purpose is to deter non-compliance by
parties to the agreement (internal free-riding), to encourage participation (to
deter external free-riding) and to prevent so-called emission leakage. Many
of the most important MEAs – the Montreal Protocol, the Basel and
Rotterdam Convention, the Convention on International Trade in
Endangered Species – contain substantial trade restrictions (see Chapter 9
for more detail).

Border tax adjustments (BTAs). These are defined as the imposition of a
domestic tax on an imported good which has been taxed either not at all or
at a level that is less than the domestic tax, and the remission of a domestic
tax on products to be exported.

Subsidies. These could be granted in the form of per unit of production
or lump-sum payments to 'footloose' (internationally mobile), pollution-
intensive or energy-intensive industries.

The following criteria will be applied in assessing these options:

- Effective. A policy option should achieve its objective of combating
  'regulatory chill'.
- Politically realistic. A policy option should be politically realistic, otherwise it has no chance of being realized.

- Closed to abuse. A policy option should not be open to abuse by protectionist factions in countries with high standards under flimsy environmental pretexts.
- Not unnecessarily restrictive. A policy option should not restrict international flows of capital and trade beyond the necessary extent.

Effective

The introduction of minimum standards in itself is likely to be ineffective. The essential problem of 'environmental chill' is that countries fail to raise standards above other countries' standards for fear of capital flight. This fear might be alleviated, but will not be overcome by setting a minimum standard, which will merely mean that those countries with the lowest environmental standards have to raise their standards to the minimum. A 'competitive disadvantage' can still be perceived relative to countries at the minimum standard. The same applies to countries above the minimum standard, but below the current or future raised standard of the country considering raising its standards. Minimum standards can be more effective if they themselves are raised continuously, because then the environmental frontrunners can trust that their advance will sooner or later be matched by proportional increases in the minimum standards faced by other countries.

Whether the harmonization of standards is an effective policy option depends on what kind of harmonization occurs. If harmonization is downward – that is, if countries with high environmental standards lower them considerably more than countries with low standards raise theirs in order to agree on a common, but relatively low, standard – then this option will be completely ineffective. Instead of overcoming the obstacles to raising environmental standards, these same standards are lowered. The situation can be different if harmonization is upward, however. In this case, countries with high standards will lower them considerably less than countries with low standards raise theirs. In the extreme case, they might not lower their standards at all. Because countries now agree on a common, but relatively high standard, advanced countries have less reason to fear that raising their standards further will lead to considerable loss of capital. However, countries with high standards might only induce countries with low standards to agree on upward harmonization if they commit to not raising their standards further or, more realistically, if they commit to not insisting on further rounds of upward harmonization in case they raised their standards after the initial upward harmonization. In other words, the upward harmonization of standards might only be achievable at the expense of excluding or at least making more difficult further upward harmonizations. In this case, 'regulatory chill' would only be alleviated once, but not permanently.

Enforcement agreements are likely to be ineffective in overcoming regulatory chill as they do nothing to raise standards, but merely attempt to enforce existing standards. They might even lead to the perverse effect of exacerbating the problem. This is because it might impose a further fear on a country contemplating a rise in environmental standards: that it would be obliged via international agreement to enforce these higher standards.

Trade restrictions can be effective if they are part of the instruments of a Multilateral Environmental Agreement (MEA) to ensure compliance with the treaty and deter free-riding. The idea is that instead of unilateral action a multitude of countries agree on raising their respective environmental standards. This collective action overcomes the prisoner's dilemma in which countries facing 'regulatory chill' are caught: countries would like to raise their environmental standards, but only if all other countries raise their respective standards as well, since otherwise the costs of the loss of capital are feared to outweigh the benefits from unilateral standard raising. But in order to be successful, this kind of collective action needs to ensure compliance of the participating countries (to deter internal free-riding). Also, it needs to ensure that as many countries as possible participate in the multilateral agreement – that is, external free-riding needs to be deterred. Trade restrictions can be an effective instrument to deter both internal as well as external free-riding (for more detail see Chapter 9). If they are effective, they can overcome 'regulatory chill'.

Subsidies to 'footloose' or pollution-intensive or energy-intensive industries can in principle be an effective policy option. If they compensate fully the industries for any cost increases due to higher environmental standards, there is no incentive for these industries to flee the country. However, depending on the way in which subsidies take place, the initial environmental objective can become partly defeated. If some industrial sectors receive an implicit subsidy in simply exempting them from the taxes or offering them a lower tax rate, then the environmental benefits will be lower than they would otherwise be.[3] Alternatively, the tax rates facing all non-exempted agents have to be raised to secure the achievement of the same level of environmental benefits. Also, exemption of certain industries from taxation leads to all sorts of intersectoral allocative inefficiencies. Furthermore, it will attract firms into the subsidized industries as it raises their relative profitability. If the 'footloose' industries are also pollution-intensive industries, this re-allocation of capital will again partly defeat the environmental objective. To avoid the negative effects of subsidization on the environmental benefits achieved, the full tax rate should apply equally to all industries and the 'footloose' industries should receive a lump-sum subsidy to compensate them for their total cost increases. It should be noted, however, that this option will still lead to allocative inefficiencies as subsidized industries become more profitable relative to non-subsidized ones.

BTAs can in principle be an effective policy option. If foreign competitors have to pay the differential in environmental compliance cost at the border and if domestic exporters are fully compensated for complying with higher environmental standards, there is no incentive for capital to flee the country. However, because compensating domestic exporters for cost differentials is equivalent to providing them with a subsidy, BTAs can face the same kinds of problems with allocative inefficiencies and defeat of the environmental objectives, as discussed with respect to subsidies above. The higher the share of domestic production that becomes exported, the more prevalent these problems will become.

Politically realistic

The introduction of minimum environmental standards as well as the harmonization of international standards or an enforcement agreement does not currently seem to be pursued with any great vigour by developed countries except within the EU, which represents a special case. However, should the developed countries decide to make such an agreement, there would be no hindrances by international trade rules as the WTO does not prohibit consensually agreed minimum or harmonized standards. The same is true with respect to an enforcement agreement.

Trade restrictions have become a common instrument in MEAs. Whether they could clash with WTO rules and if so what could be done for reconciliation is discussed in Chapter 9. What is of interest here is whether the MEAs themselves are politically realistic. Multilateral action with respect to the environment is often difficult to bring about, often takes a long time and is regarded by many environmentalists as insufficient since countries tend to agree on the lowest common denominator. The Kyoto Protocol represents a case in point: it took five years after the Rio Summit in 1992 to conclude a binding agreement. The past difficulties in bringing about this agreement are legendary as are, and even more so, the future difficulties of bringing the Protocol into force and of deciding on the many particularities left unaddressed. Indeed, one of the issues still to be addressed is whether and how trade restrictions should play a role in ensuring compliance and deterring free-riding. Finally, many environmentalists consider the Protocol as falling so much short of what they regard as necessary action that presumably they would regard it as further proof of 'regulatory chill' rather than as a significant step towards overcoming it.

BTAs are usually liked by domestic policy-makers, who are attracted to the notion that foreign competitors must face the same environmental compliance costs as domestic producers. However, BTAs can clash with international trade rules. WTO rules allow BTAs for taxes on environmentally damaging products, which are quite common. They also allow for BTAs for product-related environmental taxes, as can be seen by a WTO panel decision upholding a US tax on luxury cars and a gas-guzzler tax (WTO 1994a). BTAs for non-product related taxes, usually known as taxes on process and production method (PPM) are much less common, but there are two prominent examples: one is a BTA for chemicals manufactured using base chemicals as feedstock, which were subject to product taxation in the US. As this tax was part of the US Superfund Amendments and

Reauthorization Act of 1986, it is commonly referred to in the literature as the superfund tax. The other example is a BTA for ozone-depleting chemicals, which were subject to product taxation in the US as part of its effort to phase out the production and use of these substances. Whereas the BTA for the ozone tax was never challenged under the rules of the international trade regime, the BTA for the superfund tax was. In 1987 a GATT panel basically upheld the BTA for the superfund tax *because the taxed input was to some extent physically incorporated in the final product* (GATT 1987a). If, on the other hand, the taxed input is not physically incorporated in the final product, then the relevant WTO Agreement on Subsidies and Countervailing Measures does not seem to allow for a BTA.[4] As most environmentally relevant inputs into the production process do not become physically incorporated in the final product, the World Trade Organization's (WTO) rules would forbid the use of a BTA for most cases in which countries would want to apply them. Furthermore, WTO rules do not allow for BTAs for cost differences that follow implicitly from higher environmental standards if these higher standards are not realized via higher taxes or charges, but via command-and-control or other forms of regulation instead. That the relevant WTO rules could be reformed to allow for general PPM-related BTAs is highly unlikely. First, there does not seem to be strong support for such a reform, even among the developed countries. Brack, Grubb and Windram (2000, p86ff) cite a letter from a US Trade Representative official that refers to an informal (gentlemen's) agreement among developed countries to the effect that the Agreement on Subsidies and Countervailing Measures

> *was never intended to fundamentally expand the right of countries to apply border adjustment for a broad range of taxes on energy, especially in the developed world... We discussed the matter with other developed countries involved in the Subsidies Code negotiations. We are satisfied that they share our views on the purpose of the text as drafted and the importance of careful international examination before any broader policy conclusions should be drawn regarding border adjustment and energy taxes.*

Second, because a reform of WTO rules would need a two-thirds majority, according to Article X:3 of the Agreement Establishing the WTO, developing countries would need to consent as well. However, they are completely against such a reform as they rightly fear that they would be affected by BTAs as well (or even predominantly so), and not just developed countries.

Subsidies seem to be politically realistic as they might be considered an easy option that is less overtly intrusive into foreign countries' rights. However, as they might be regarded as giving domestic industries an unfair advantage, they might still be regarded as harmful to foreign countries and might therefore clash with international trade rules. The reader should recall that one of the types of subsidies excepted from the rules laid down in the

WTO Agreement on Subsidies and Countervailing Measures, and therefore non-actionable, is assistance to adapt existing industries to new environmental requirements (Article 8.2 (c)) (see p31). However, to qualify, such assistance must occur only once, not cover more than 20 per cent of the adaptation costs, and must be made available to all firms that can adopt the new equipment and processes. As most subsidies would not fall in this category and could well exceed 5 per cent ad valorem of benefited firms, subsidies to prevent capital flight might be challenged under WTO rules. This has not been tested yet as there has been no dispute over these kinds of subsidies so far, but it could well be that this policy option becomes partly barred and therefore rendered politically unrealistic.

Closed to abuse

Minimum standards as well as the harmonization of standards and an international enforcement agreement are relatively closed to abuse as they depend on the consent of all parties involved. The situation is different with trade restrictions, which are targeted partly towards non-participating and therefore non-consenting parties. These restrictions can be abused as participating countries (or a subset of them) might install restrictions against non-participants under the pretext of fulfilling their mandatory obligations according to an MEA, but with proper protectionist intentions instead. BTAs and subsidies are also open to abuse. They open a Pandora's Box in that all sorts of industries will lobby policy-makers to grant them protection from 'unfair' foreign competition. The incentive for protectionist abuse might be higher with BTAs relative to subsidies, as subsidies cost money to the domestic taxpayers, whereas in the case of BTAs the costs are borne partly by the foreign producers and partly, but much less visibly, by higher prices for domestic consumers.

Not unnecessarily restrictive

Minimum standards as well as the harmonization of standards are not very restrictive in the sense that once the standards have been established, capital as well as goods and services are allowed to cross borders without constraint. However, in so far as some countries' environmental standards might rise above their efficiency levels, these countries would be confronted implicitly with inefficient restrictions towards their exports of goods and services. An enforcement agreement is not restrictive at all as it merely aspires to ensure that a country's existing laws and regulations are actually enforced. Trade restrictions are restrictive by definition. However, if trade restrictions as an instrument of an MEA to ensure compliance and deter free-riding are fully effective, then ironically they will not be restrictive at all as there is no need to employ them. The best restrictions are the ones that will never come into force (see Chapter 9). BTAs can be restrictive. If they are applied in a protectionist or non-transparent manner, they will restrict the flow of capital and

Table 4.1 *Evaluation of policy options addressing the 'regulatory chill'-problem.*

	Minimum standards	Harmonization	Enforcement agreement	Multilateral restrictions	Border tax adjustments	Subsidies
Effective	–	+/–	—	++	++	++
Politically realistic	–	–	–	+/–	–	–
Closed to abuse	+	+	+	–	–	–
Not unnecessarily restrictive	+	+	++	+	+/–	+/–

Legend: ++ very good, + good, +/– neutral, – poor, — very poor

goods and services. Subsidies can be restrictive as well if they are applied in a protectionist manner. If they are, they will distort the comparative advantage of countries such that the non-subsidizing countries face implicit restrictions towards their exports of goods and services and their import of capital.

Conclusion

In a world of imperfect information about what constitutes efficient environmental standards, it is not easy to assess whether developed countries inefficiently fail to raise their standards or not. 'Regulatory chill' is a potentially serious, but difficult to detect, phenomenon. Because counterfactual claims are being examined, the researcher has to rely on anecdotal evidence, some of which has been presented in this chapter. It seems fair to say that 'regulatory chill' has not been proven, neither in general nor with respect to the case of reducing greenhouse gas emissions. But enough evidence is there to warrant an evaluation of policy options to address the (potential) problem of 'regulatory chill'.

Table 4.1 provides a summary of the findings on evaluating policy options. As can be seen, no option fares clearly better than all others. However, the harmonization of standards and multilateral trade restrictions do relatively well on our criteria so that they are recommended here as policy options to deal with potential 'regulatory chill' problems. The challenge with the harmonization of standards would be to strive for upward rather than downward harmonization to make it effective in overcoming 'regulatory chill' and to gather political support to make it more politically realistic than it currently seems to be. The challenge with multilateral trade restrictions would be to gather political support for fast and effective multilateral action on international and global environmental problems.

5

Roll-back: Do Foreign Investors Use Investor-to-State Dispute Settlement to Knock Down Environmental Regulations?

The third issue that we look at in the area of investment and the environment is a hypothesis which I will refer to as the 'roll-back' hypothesis. It consists of two related parts and goes as follows: first, companies use the investor-to-state dispute settlement to knock down environmental regulations. Second, companies use the possibility of investor-to-state dispute settlement to scare policy-makers away from raising environmental regulations. Scott Nova, Trade Campaign Executive Director of the Washington-based Citizens Trade Campaign group, for example, alleges that the investor-to-state dispute settlement allows companies to use 'NAFTA to blackmail an entire country into environmental submission' (Citizens Trade Campaign 1999).

The empirical cases, which are invoked by its supporters to claim the validity of the hypothesis, need to be examined in order to assess the roll-back hypothesis. To my knowledge, all these cases are linked to the investor-to-state dispute settlement within NAFTA, none of them to BITs. Let us therefore examine each of the most prominent cases in more detail.

Relevant investor-to-state investment disputes

Ethyl Corporation versus the Government of Canada

Ethyl Corporation versus the Government of Canada is an example of an investor-to-state dispute that is most often invoked to support the roll-back hypothesis. In April 1997 the Canadian parliament passed Bill C-29, based on an earlier bill introduced by then Environment Minister Sergio Marchi, which banned the import to Canada and the interprovincial trade, but not the use, of methylcyclopentadienyl manganese tricarbonyl (MMT). Ethyl Corporation was the sole producer of MMT, which is a fuel additive that enhances octane in petrol. The parliament justified this ban by citing the health risks posed by the manganese content of MMT. Ironically, Ethyl argued that the use of MMT is actually in the environmental interest as it would lead to the cleaner burning of fuel, thus reducing nitrogen oxide omissions, as well as allowing refiners to produce more petrol from a given barrel of crude oil (Ethyl Corp 1998a, 1998b).

Ethyl in turn filed a suit in the domestic Canadian legal system claiming that the act was unconstitutional and entered the investor-to-state dispute settlement mechanism according to Chapter 11 of the North American Free Trade Agreement (NAFTA), claiming US$347 million compensation for measures undertaken 'tantamount to expropriation' of its investment. Independently, the province of Alberta, supported by the provinces of Quebec, Nova Scotia and Saskatchewan, challenged the act as well, claiming that it violated Canada's Agreement on Internal Trade. Alberta, home to Canada's petroleum refinery industry, claimed that 'the cross-border ban is a blatant example of Ottawa favouring the Ontario-based car-makers over the refineries' (cited in Soloway 1999a, p79). The provinces succeeded and a panel decided that Bill C-29 established an obstacle to internal trade in Canada without addressing a valid environmental objective (Panel Report 1998). As concerns the Ethyl suit, on 20 July 1998 the Canadian government decided to avoid third-party arbitration and to agree on a settlement with Ethyl. In this it agreed to lift the ban on MMT and paid nearly US$13 million in compensation to the company.[1] For proponents of the roll-back hypothesis, this seemed to be a clear proof of their case.

However, on closer inspection this is not quite so. To start with, the scientific evidence demonstrating the health risks of MMT was everything but solid. On the one hand, MMT was banned as a fuel additive in the US by the Environmental Protection Agency (EPA) between 1977 and 1995. For the EPA there was 'a reasonable basis for concern regarding the potential adverse effects on public health which could result from the emissions of manganese particulates associated with MMT use' (cited in Soloway 1999a, p64). Also, many environmental groups both in Canada and the US actively promoted an outright ban of MMT. On the other hand, on the day of the settlement with Ethyl, the Canadian government embarrassed itself in issuing a statement that 'there is no new scientific evidence to modify the conclusions drawn by Health Canada in 1994 that MMT poses no health risk' (cited in Ethyl Corp 1998a). That the environmental justification for banning MMT was rather weak from the start can also be seen by the fact that the Canadian government could not ban the use of MMT under the Canadian Environmental Protection Act (CEPA) – which, to be fair, is rather strict, as it requires unambiguous evidence for a product to be considered as a toxic substance and consequently banned (Soloway 1999a, p68).

Instead of serving valid environmental objectives, it seems that the ban came largely about because of lobby pressure by two groups: first, the car manufacturers who asserted that MMT would damage the emissions diagnostics and control equipments in cars. This impression is supported by an independent panel ruling from June 1998 on the suit put forward by the province of Alberta, which came to the conclusion that 'it was the automobile manufacturers who were the driving force behind the elimination of MMT' (Agreement on Internal Trade Panel 1998, p7). After lifting the ban on MMT, the Canadian government admitted that 'the current scientific information fails to demonstrate that MMT impairs the proper functioning of OBDs [motor car on-board diagnostic systems, EN]' (Environment Canada 1998). Second, agricultural lobby groups had an interest in getting MMT banned as this would boost the use of ethanol as a fuel additive substitute which is primarily produced from corn (Soloway 1999a, p70ff).

Methanex Corporation versus the Government of the United States of America

On 14 June 1999, the Vancouver-based Methanex Corporation notified its 'intent to file' a US$970 million claim against the the United States government. Methanex sought compensation for a ban imposed by the government of the state of California on MTBE (methyl tertiary butyl ether, manufactured from methanol and isobutylene), Methanex's sole product.[2] On 25 March 1999 California had decided to phase out the use of MTBE, with an effective ban by 2002. Methanex regarded this decision as unjustified and as amounting to an expropriation of its business without compensation.

Methanex and Ethyl are similar cases. Both MMT and MTBE are fuel additives whose objective is octane-enhancing and a cleaner burning of fuel, and both the Canadian government and the state government of California justified their ban on these additives by citing health reasons. The Californian government claimed that MTBE, regarded by the US EPA as a potential human carcinogen, is responsible for groundwater contamination. As Ethyl disputed the Canadian government's reasons for banning MMT, so Methanex disputes that MTBE should be considered a human carcinogen, citing among other things a 1998 International Agency for Research on Cancer study and a report to Congress by the National Toxicology Program (Methanex 1999a, p5). It does not claim that MTBE poses no hazards, but maintains that, if properly used, it does not have 'any adverse impact on human health at reasonably expected exposure levels' (ibid, p4). It argues that studies used by the Californian government for justifying its ban were fundamentally flawed (Scoffield and Chase 1999). As Ethyl argued its case for the environmentally benign use of MMT, so Methanex also argues that the use of MTBE is actually in the environmental interest as it would lead to a cleaner burning of fuel and would dilute 'harmful gasoline components like benzene, a known human carcinogen' (Methanex 1999b, p1).

Indeed, Methanex claims that the Californian government itself is to be blamed for failing to enforce properly state legislation on underground storage tanks to avoid the leakage of petrol containing MTBE into the groundwater system. Methanex alleges that in December 1998,

> *the California State Auditor presented a highly critical report to Governor Gray Davis detailing the state's poor record of environmental law enforcement related to underground storage tanks, which are the major source of gasoline release to the environment. In addition to the Auditor's criticisms, many underground storage tanks are not even regulated* (Methanex 1999c).

In a strategically clever move, Methanex therefore also complained to NAFTA's Commission for Environmental Cooperation (CEC) that the Californian government had violated its duty to enforce its own environmental protection legislation, which it is obliged to do under the North American Agreement on Environmental Cooperation (NAAEC), the environmental side agreement to NAFTA. However, in July 2000 the CEC dismissed the Methanex complaint, agreeing with the US government that the company had brought the complaint with the intention of furthering its dispute with the US government under NAFTA's Chapter 11 provisions, so that the issue was already the subject of ongoing international arbitration and could not be considered simultaneously by the CEC (BNA 2000b).

In another attempt to portray the company as a promoter of environmental standards, Pierre Choquette, President and Chief Executive Officer of Methanex, offered the Californian government support in protecting the health of its citizens should it decide to lift the ban on MTBE:

> *We promote alternative measures such as improved gasoline infrastructure management (especially underground storage tanks), more stringent boat engine emission standards and managed recreational use of lakes and reservoirs. These preventive measures would address the root cause of the issue by substantially reducing gasoline release to the environment.* (Methanex 1999d).

Methanex left no doubt that its 'intent to file' a suit against the United States government was meant to scare other states away from enacting similar bans. According to Scoffield and Chase (1999), Michael Macdonald, spokesman of Methanex, said that 'Methanex felt this was an "appropriate" time to react to California's ban because Maine is considering a similar motion, and legislation is also in the works at the US federal level'. Several US states have now passed or are in the process of passing similar laws. As was the case with the ban on Ethyl's MMT, so with Methanex, justifications to ban MTBE on health grounds intermix with the protectionist interests of the Ethanol lobbying group. As Leon Corzine, president of the Illinois Corn Growers Association, has put it: 'Illinois corn growers welcome this action by the City of Chicago to restrict the use of MTBE because it's the right thing to do for the state's economy, consumer health, and the environment' (quoted in BNA 1999f).

At the time of writing, there has been no decision on this case.

Pope & Talbot Inc. versus the Government of Canada

On 25 March 1999 the Portland-based forestry company Pope & Talbot Inc. filed a claim of over approximately US$500 million against the Government of Canada. While Pope & Talbot is at pains to stress that it does not challenge the validity of the Canada–US Softwood Lumber Agreement from 1996, it does claim that the Canadian government implemented this agreement in an unfair manner. In particular, Pope & Talbot claims that while the overall amount of quotas stayed constant, the Canadian government reduced its duty-free quota for exporting lumber to the US (Appleton 1999). Furthermore, it claims that the Canadian government did so without fully informing the company, providing adequate reasons or granting a fair hearing to the company. The company alleges that the Canadian government has violated the national treatment, most favoured nation, minimum standard of treatment and performance requirements provisions of NAFTA.

In June 2000 an arbitral tribunal rejected the investor's claims in an interim award. While stating that 'regulations can indeed be exercised in a way that would constitute creeping expropriation' (Arbitral Tribunal 2000a, p35), the tribunal came to the conclusion that the 'degree of interference with the Investment's operations' caused by the incriminated regulatory measures 'does not rise to an expropriation (creeping or otherwise) within the meaning of Article 1110' (ibid, p37), as the investor could merely claim a reduction in profits, while continuing 'to export substantial quantities of softwood lumber to the US and to earn substantial profits on those sales' (ibid, p36).

Of more general significance is another aspect of the tribunal's ruling concerning the scope of the 'tantamount to nationalization or expropriation' clause in NAFTA's Article 1110. The tribunal stated that it does not believe that this phrase 'broadens the ordinary concept of expropriation under international law to require compensation for measures affecting property interests without regard to the magnitude or severity of that effect' (ibid, p34). It rejected the investor's claim that the phrase 'tantamount to expropriation' would somehow imply that NAFTA goes beyond the ordinary meaning of expropriation to include 'measures of general application which have the effect of substantially interfering with the investments of investors of NAFTA Parties' (ibid, p37), stating that '"tantamount" means nothing more than equivalent' and that 'something that is equivalent to something else cannot logically encompass more' (ibid, p38).

Metalclad Corp versus Government of Mexico

On 30 July 1997 Metalclad Corp, a hazardous and toxic waste-management company based in Newport Beach, California, filed a claim against the Government of Mexico seeking US$96 million in damages (BNA 1999b). Metalclad had bought Coterin, a Mexican company which operated a site for the transfer of industrial waste in Guadalcazar, in the state of San Luis Potosi. The transfer site was formerly closed down by the Mexican government because of the illegal storage of 20,000 tons of hazardous waste. At the time of purchase, Metalclad had the support of the Mexican government to clean up the illegal waste and transform the unit into a hazardous waste-confinement unit. The local government, however, refused to grant a building permit and other authorizations. When Metalclad built the site at a cost of US$22 million nevertheless, the site was seized by the state government in late 1995, which the corporation regarded as expropriation without compensation.

The Mexican government in turn argues that the seizure is due to Metalclad's own failure to clean up the site to the level desired by the state and local community. (Metalclad had decided merely to contain the pollution at the site.) Martin Diaz Diaz, Legal Director for Mexico's Secretariat of the Environment, Natural Resources and Fisheries, said that if Metalclad had provided the desired clean-up 'it could have gained a lot of goodwill in the community' (quoted in ibid). Furthermore, Mexico's Environment Secretary Julia Carabias accused Metalclad of attempted bribery.

On 31 March 1999 Metalclad announced its intention to discontinue all its operations in Mexico. This decision was regarded as a blow by market observers to the Mexican government's plans to attract foreign investment into its hugely inadequate hazardous waste recycling and confinement facilities (ibid). In August 2000 the tribunal ordered the Mexican government to pay almost US$17 million in compensation to Metalclad (*Financial Times* 2000).

The tribunal justified its decision by saying that Mexico had not ensured that 'all relevant legal requirements for the purpose of initiating, completing and successfully operating investments' were capable to being readily known by Metalclad, thus violating the 'transparency' requirement contained in NAFTA Article 102(1) (Arbitral Tribunal 2000c, paragraph 76). In particular, Metalclad could not have known, according to the tribunal, that a permit from the municipality was needed: 'Metalclad was led to believe, and did believe, that the federal and state permits allowed for the construction and operation of the landfill' (ibid, paragraph 85). Since Metalclad had all but finished constructing its hazardous waste confinement unit when it became clear that it would never be allowed to operate it, the tribunal ruled that 'Mexico must be held to have taken a measure tantamount to expropriation in violation of NAFTA Article 1110(1)' (ibid, paragraph 104).

While welcoming the tribunal's decision, Metalclad was thoroughly disappointed by the amount of compensation granted. Its President, Grant Kessler, called the ruling 'a completely hollow victory for us' (quoted in ibid). As mentioned above, Metalclad had sued for US$96 million, but was only awarded approximately the actual cost of the investment itself. Mexico has appealed the tribunal's ruling (ICTSD 2001a).

S D Myers Inc. versus Government of Canada

On 22 July 1998, S D Myers Inc., an Ohio-based US company specializing in the shipment and disposition of hazardous waste contaminated with polychlorinated biphenyl (PCB), notified the Government of Canada of its intent to submit a claim to arbitration. The company is seeking compensation for alleged losses following a temporary export prohibition of PCB waste to the US (Appleton 1998). S D Myers alleges that officials from Environment Canada have admitted in internal briefing notes that this trade ban was enacted purely to protect Canada's domestic PCB destruction company (Chem-Securities of Swan Hills, Alberta) (ibid). In the words of its legal representative, Barry Appleton: 'This isn't about environmental protection. It's about protectionism. Myers' only crime is that it's American' (Anonymous 1999).

In response, the Government of Canada is arguing that S D Myers never had an 'investment' in Canada (Government of Canada 1999). Therefore, the import ban could not be regarded as 'relating to' 'investors' or 'investment' in the NAFTA sense and that consequently Myers has no right to challenge Canada via the investor-to-state dispute settlement.

On 13 November 2000 the arbitral tribunal decided in favour of SD Myers. It ruled that the export ban was 'intended primarily to protect the Canadian PCB disposal industry from US competition' (Arbitral Tribunal 2000b, paragraph 194) and found that 'there was no legitimate environmental reason for introducing the ban' (ibid, paragraph 195). According to the tribunal, the Government of Canada had failed to afford S D Myers the treatment it affords its own nationals 'in like circumstances', thereby violating Article 1102 of NAFTA. While stressing the right of states 'to establish high levels of environmental protection' (ibid, paragraph 247) it noted that the Government of Canada had many ways open to it other than a complete export ban in order to ensure that the Canadian PCB disposal industry maintains its ability to process PCB in the future (ibid, paragraph 255). As legitimate alternative measures it suggested the sourcing of all government requirements from the Canadian PCB disposal industry and the granting of subsidies to it.

The tribunal decided against the investor in one important aspect, however. S D Myers had claimed that the export ban would amount to a measure that is 'tantamount to expropriation' in accordance with Article 1110 of NAFTA. The tribunal fully rejected this claim. Noting that the primary meaning of the word 'tantamount' given by the *Oxford English Dictionary* is 'equivalent', it sided with the arbitral tribunal in the Pope & Talbot case (see above) by saying that 'something that is "equivalent" to something else cannot logically encompass more' (ibid, paragraph 286). It further stated that the 'drafters of the NAFTA intended the word "tantamount" to embrace the concept of so-called "creeping expropriation", rather than to expand the internationally accepted scope of the term expropriation' (ibid). Since the export ban clearly did not amount to 'creeping expropriation' the tribunal simply concluded 'that this is not an "expropriation" case' (ibid, paragraph 288).

The Canadian Government has appealed against the tribunal's ruling before the Federal Court of Canada. Canada's International Trade Minister Pierre Pettigrew justified this move in saying that 'we are seeking this review because we believe the tribunal exceeded its jurisdiction in several key elements of the award' (quoted in ICTSD 2001a). It also announced its support for Mexico's appeal against the arbitral tribunal's ruling in the Metalclad case (see above).

Other cases

At the time of writing, a number of other cases are either pending or have been declined, not all of which are related to environmental regulations. Because of the secretive character of investor-to-state dispute settlements – claims do not need to be published, tribunal hearings are not open to the public – it is sometimes very difficult to get hold of information about these cases:

- Waste Management Inc., formerly known as USA Waste Services Inc., based in Houston, against the Government of Mexico, seeking US$60 million in damages for non-payment for waste collection and disposal services in the area of Acapulco (BNA 1998b). In June 2000 the arbitral tribunal decided that it lacks jurisdiction to decide the dispute as the claimant has failed to waive its right to initiate or continue proceedings before any other court or tribunal on the same matter (ICSID 2000).
- Loewen Group Inc., a Canadian funeral homes and related business company, against the US Government, seeking US$725 million for alleged excessively biased court proceedings and lack of due process in a civil case against the company (BNA 1999e). There is no environmental connotation in this case.
- Sun Belt Water Inc., a Santa Barbara-based water exports company, against the Government of Canada, seeking US$220 million in compensation for alleged biased treatment by the Government of British Columbia concerning a joint venture. The government had first allowed, but then put a temporary and later permanent moratorium on freshwater exports from British Columbia to the US without compensating

the company, whereas its joint venture partner Sun Belt was compensated (BNA 1998c).

- Marvin Feldman, exclusive stock owner of Corporacion dc Exportaciones Mexicanas S A de C V (CEMSA), against the Government of Mexico, seeking US$50 million for alleged losses following the denial of excise tax rebates on cigarette exports, the loss of goodwill and violation of due process and the rule of law (BNA 1999d). No environmental connotation exists.
- United Parcel Services of America Inc. (UPS) has filed a statement of claim against the Government of Canada as a first step of entering the investor-to-state dispute settlement. UPS alleges that Canada has failed to regulate properly the monopoly of Canada Post Corporation over postal delivery in Canada. There is no environmental connotation in this case (BNA 2000e).

Another case, the first ever to be decided, ended with the Government of Mexico prevailing against three US shareholders of Desechos Solidos de Naucalpan S A de C V (DESONA) (ICSID 1999b; BNA 1999a). They had sought compensation for the annulment of a concession contract related to waste disposal by the city of Naucalpan, an important and heavily industrialized suburb of Mexico City. The tribunal had found no violations of NAFTA articles on the Mexican side, saying that the claimants 'have not even attempted to demonstrate that the Mexican court decisions constituted a fundamental departure from established principles of Mexican law' (ibid, p33).

'Regulatory chill' due to a potential dispute challenge?

So far we have dealt only with cases where companies allegedly use the investor-to-state dispute settlement to knock down existing environmental regulations. Hardly any concrete evidence is available on whether states might be scared away from enacting stringent environmental standards due to the threat of a potential dispute challenge. Indeed, to my knowledge there is just one concrete case: Eastman (1999, p117) suggests that the Canadian government might be cautious about restricting the sale of genetically modified products due to the fear of being sued by the US company Monsanto.

Of course, it could well be that the threat of a potential dispute challenge has a far greater 'chilling' effect than would be suggested by this very limited evidence. It lies in the nature of such an effect that it can be very difficult to detect. It might as well be, however, that the challenges of companies towards existing regulations have been too recent to exert a significant 'chilling effect' on future regulation.

Reforming NAFTA's investor-to-state dispute settlement process?

Restricting the scope of 'tantamount to expropriation' in Chapter 11?

Mann and von Moltke (1999) as well as the Canadian government have called for an 'interpretative statement' by the NAFTA partners that would restrict the scope of investors to challenge environmental regulations on the grounds of Chapter 11 provisions. In particular, both want to put restrictions on what constitutes 'a measure tantamount to expropriation' in Article 1110 of NAFTA, such that 'the clause could not be used to challenge legitimate government regulatory activity' (ICTSD 1999c). Interestingly, Canada wants its proposal to be enacted retroactively as well, such that 'many Chapter Eleven claims currently pending would, in effect, be dismissed' (Eastman 1999, p116).

At a trilateral ministerial meeting of NAFTA's CEC, Canada's proposal has been rejected by Mexico, even though Mexico itself has been sued for compensation by investors as discussed above. Mexico is keen to keep Chapter 11 as it is because doing so helps the country, which has an underdeveloped domestic judiciary system relative to the ones in the US and Canada, to signal to foreign investors that Mexico is credibly committed to grant them full protection of their investment. Amending Chapter 11, and be it only via an interpretative statement, could provide foreign investors with the signal that, if need comes, any of its provisions are subject to alteration and reinterpretation (Soloway 1999b, pp14ff). The US Administration is split over whether to support an interpretative statement: whereas the EPA and the Justice Department are generally in favour of such a proposal, the Treasury Department, the Department of Commerce, the State Department and the US Trade Representative tend to object as they are more concerned about the level of protection granted to US investment abroad (ibid, p14). At the trilateral meeting, ministers therefore merely recognized 'the sovereign right of governments to legislate in the area of the environment' and decided to continue talks on 'a range of substantive issues, including certain provisions in Chapter Eleven' (CEC 1999).

In my view, Canada's proposal fails to pass the initial necessity test. So far, merely five cases have come to a conclusion. Other cases are still pending and before one can assess the outcomes of these cases and the arguments of the arbitral tribunals, it seems premature to call for amendments or interpretative statements. Certainly, the NAFTA partners never intended that Chapter 11 would be abused by foreign investors to prevent them from enacting new environmental regulations or rolling back existing regulation. But it is also true that Chapter 11 was intended to protect foreign investors from arbitrary discrimination and uncompensated expropriation. There has to be a fair and equitable compromise between the sovereign right of nation states to enact regulation and the protection granted to foreign investors. There is no reason to presume that the arbitral tribunals in the pending cases cannot find this fair compromise and they should be given the benefit of the doubt until proven wrong.

Certainly the cases decided so far do not demonstrate any necessity to reformulate Chapter 11 of NAFTA. The tribunal in the case 'DESONA versus Government of Mexico' dismissed the investor's claim as lacking any sound foundation. The arbitral tribunal in the case 'Pope & Talbot Inc. versus Government of Canada' came to the right decision and rejected the investor's claim that a mere exercise of regulatory power amounts to measures that are tantamount to expropriation. Similarly, the tribunal in the case 'S D Myers Inc. versus Government of Canada', while finding reason to decide in the investor's favour on grounds of failure to provide national treatment on the part of the Canadian Government, rejected the investor's claim that the PCB export ban would amount to a measure 'tantamount to expropriation'. The tribunal in 'Metalclad versus Government of Mexico' was the only one so far to award compensation for a measure 'tantamount to expropriation'. It remains to be seen whether it will withstand Mexico's appeal against the tribunal's decision. While a detailed argumentation is impossible here as it would imply a lengthy presentation of detailed aspects of the dispute, certain passages in the tribunal's decision appear to be biased towards the investor's rights without due regard to the leeway sovereign states must have in enacting and changing investment-relevant environmental regulation.

An assessment of the Ethyl case, where the investor in some sense also won the case even though it never went to arbitration, also does not warrant changing the provisions in NAFTA's Chapter 11. Because the environmental justification for the trade ban of MMT was rather weak, Ethyl's claim that Bill C-29 de facto expropriated its business in Canada does not seem a priori unjustified. Apparently, the Canadian Government realized this and preferred to settle with Ethyl before the company would be awarded a potentially much higher compensation by an arbitral tribunal. The case of Ethyl Corporation versus Government of Canada does not prove therefore that governments cannot enact comprehensive environmental regulation. Neither does it prove that companies use the investor-to-state dispute settlement to knock down environmental standards. What it does demonstrate, however, is that discriminatory trade measures can be successfully challenged under the investor-to-state dispute settlement provisions if they are justified with dubious reasons, environmental or not.

Making the dispute settlement process open and transparent

There is another aspect of the Canadian proposal that has more merit. It wants to make the investor-to-state dispute settlement process more open and transparent. In my view, the secretive character of this process is partly to be blamed for the suspicion it encounters. Parties to the settlement process should therefore be required to publish their statements of claim and defence, hearings should be open to the public, all decisions should be published, and environmental and other stakeholder groups with a valid interest in the subject matter should be allowed to send so-called amicus curiae briefs to the tribunals.[3] The WTO dispute settlement process has recently made much progress in this direction. It still needs some way to go to become a fully open and transparent process (see p144). But in comparison to NAFTA's investor-to-state settlement process it is much advanced.

It might be argued that private investors have no interest in disclosing sensitive information and that it would be unfair to require them to have an open and transparent dispute settlement process. This is not the case, however. First, many investors are proactive in giving public access to their claims (this is true, for example, for Ethyl, Methanex, Pope & Talbot, S D Myers). Attorneys of Marvin Feldman in his claim against the Government of Mexico have proposed opening every aspect of the proceeding to the public including the hearings, a proposal that the Mexican government immediately rejected (BNA 2000c). Second, if an investor challenges a regulation enacted by publicly elected policy-makers, the public should have the right to gain access to all relevant information. Highly sensitive private information could still be excluded from publication on a case-by-case basis. But there is no justification for a highly secretive process when democratically enacted regulations are in dispute – after all, democracy lives from openness and transparency.

On the aspect of amicus curiae briefs, the tribunal in the case 'Methanex Corporation versus United States of America' announced its willingness to consider in principle such briefs on 15 January 2001 (Arbitral Tribunal 2001). While this represents an important step towards a more open and transparent arbitration process, there is still a long way to go. Also, significant change is only feasible if the relevant NAFTA rules become changed by the parties themselves. Expansive, but discretionary and ad hoc interpretation of existing NAFTA rules by tribunals will not carry the process much towards transparency and openness. Unfortunately, a change of NAFTA rules is rendered unlikely by the opposition of Mexico to such change. Mirroring the resistance of developing countries towards a more open and transparent dispute settlement at the WTO level (see p144), Mexico is the only NAFTA party opposing the tribunal's decision in the Methanex case to consider amicus curiae briefs and indeed opposing any further-reaching proposals concerning transparency and openness.

A Case Study: The Failed Attempt to Conclude a Multilateral Agreement on Investment

The failed attempt to conclude a Multilateral Agreement on Investment (MAI) can serve as a case study because much of the radical critique raised by non-governmental organizations (NGOs) and trade unionists, as well as the more qualified critique by parliaments and subnational governments, echoes the fears that we have assessed in previous chapters concerning the alleged existence of pollution havens in developing countries, 'regulatory chill' in developed countries and the roll-back of environmental regulation through companies via the investor-to-state dispute settlement. From the perspective of the critics, the MAI would have made things much worse had it become reality. Building on the analysis in earlier chapters of Part II, I will argue, however, that this critique is based on a number of common misperceptions. Even so, the draft MAI did indeed suffer from a number of shortcomings which are summarized briefly at the end of this chapter.

Radical opposition: The critique by NGOs and trade unionists

Environmental, developmental and other NGOs, as well as trade unionists, opposed virtually every substantial aspect of the draft MAI and have pledged to oppose with quite the same fervour any future agreement with similar provisions as well. The major aspects of their critique can be summarized as follows:

*   Because investors were supposed to gain a general right of entry, governments could no longer ban FDI from investors with a bad record on environmental and labour issues (for example, Valliantos 1997; Sforza 1998a and Ad Hoc Working Group on the MAI 1998). Also, investment in certain sectors of the economy could no longer be banned.

- Similarly, national and most favoured nation treatment would disable governments and local communities to punish foreign investors for atrocities they supposedly undertake somewhere else with respect to either the environment, labour standards or human rights (for example, Vallianos and Durbin 1997).
- Because of the general prohibition of performance requirements, governments would no longer be able to favour local industries or require foreign investors to employ local workers or use local production inputs (for example, Vallianos 1997 and Sforza 1998a).
- The liberalization of investment regimes would allow companies to relocate to the lowest cost production sites. The MAI would have preempted 'strategies for restricting corporate flight to low-wage areas – a major cause for job loss and income stagnation in the industrialized world' (Nova and Sforza-Roderick 1997; similarly, Ad Hoc Working Group on the MAI 1998). The protectionist and nationalist tune was also and in particular played by trade unionists (see, for example, AFL-CIO 1998 and White 1998).[1] Not surprisingly, the US trade union AFL-CIO (1998) also opposed the immigration clause of the draft MAI which allowed key personnel the temporary right to enter and stay inside the host country.
- The threat of relocation would already suffice to undermine the bargaining power of trade unions (for example, Nova and Sforza-Roderick 1997). Similarly, the broad definition of expropriation, together with the compensation requirement and the possibility for investors to sue states before an international arbitration panel for dispute settlement, was regarded as sufficient to scare policy-makers away from passing stringent environmental and social regulation (for example, Oxfam 1997).
- More generally, the MAI would severely undermine the sovereignty of nation states to formulate whatever policy they perceive to be in their interest. The MAI was regarded as an agreement that privileges profits above everything else, puts democracy at risk and would 'radically limit our ability to promote social, economic and environmental justice' (Ad Hoc Working Group on the MAI 1998).

Qualified opposition: The critique by parliaments and subnational governmental institutions

Partly in response to the vigorous criticism of NGOs and other groups opposed to the MAI draft, there have been a number of parliamentary enquiries and a position paper of the US Western Governors' Association on the subject matter. These enquiries have found reason to object to both the substance of the draft treaty text and the way the negotiations were undertaken. In general, however, the critique put forward by these elected assemblies and subnational governmental institutions has been more qualified and less fundamental than the one advanced by NGOs.

The US Western Governors' Association (1997), for example, welcomed in principle a multilateral agreement on investment which it expected would 'encourage foreign investment and improve the economy in their states'. At the same time, however, the Association spoke out against the national treatment provision in the draft MAI that would prohibit them from discriminating in favour of state residents and against a large-scale banning of performance requirements and investment incentives. It urged US negotiators to include sufficient reservations and exemptions in a potential MAI in order to protect fully the sovereignty and authority of the states they represent.

In one of the first parliamentary enquiries, the Canadian Parliament Sub-Committee on International Trade, Trade Disputes and Investment (1997) called for the expropriation clause of the draft MAI to be narrowly defined so that governments would not run the risk of having to compensate investors for the mere exercise of their normal regulatory power and for open, accessible and transparent procedures for dispute settlement, which it saw violated by the fact that arbitration could take place behind closed doors if the investor so wishes. It also demanded to be kept permanently informed by the Canadian government about the state of the negotiations that it wanted to take place in an open and transparent process. This latter point is echoed by the UK House of Commons Environmental Audit Committee (1999) and the Australian Parliament Joint Standing Committee on Treaties (1999). All these enquiries shared the concern of the NGO community that the negotiating parties, whether by intention or not, did not adequately inform the parliaments or the wider public about a subject that they regarded as extremely relevant to both parliamentarians and the general public alike. In a resolution to the European Commission, which also took part in the MAI negotiations, the European Parliament (1998) went as far as claiming that negotiations were undertaken 'in utmost secrecy', which gave some support to the claim made by many NGOs that they were confronted with a conspiracy (see, for example, Ad Hoc Working Group on the MAI 1998). The European Parliament, too, demanded a narrowing of the expropriation clause, expressed concern about the dispute settlement procedures, and called for an inclusion of duties and obligations for foreign investors in the draft MAI so that, according to the Parliament's view, a better balance between investors' rights and obligations was achieved.

The most fundamental critique was raised in the so-called Lalumière report (Lalumière and Landau 1998), however. In 1998 the French government, which from the start had been rather sceptical about many of the draft MAI provisions, had commissioned a report to advise it on how to proceed with the then still ongoing negotiations at OECD level. Member of European Parliament Catherine Lalumière and Inspector General of Finance Jean-Pierre Landau provided an intermediary report in September 1998 which condemns the draft MAI as fundamentally flawed. It demanded that any future agreement on investment should apply a narrow definition of investment, excluding all portfolio investments and financial market operations, that the dispute settlement mechanism should only apply to sovereign nation states so that private investors would be excluded, that the definition of expropriation should be narrow and exclude indirect expropriation, that only those performance requirements should be prohibited that are already forbidden under the WTO, and finally that because developing countries are expected to become signatories to a potential agreement, the OECD was the wrong forum and negotiations should be undertaken at the WTO instead. This report prompted the French government to pull out of the negotiations in October 1998, which in turn led to their breakdown in early December 1998 since the EU itself would have had to sign any MAI in addition to the member states, and could only have done so had all the member states been supportive (UK Department of Trade and Industry 1999).

Common misperceptions

The Lalumière report stated that the NGO activists who opposed the MAI 'seemed to us perfectly well informed, and their criticisms well argued on a legal level' (Lalumière and Landau 1998, p3). This is only partly true as they shared a number of substantial misperceptions about the actual effects of an MAI in reality and about how novel many of the draft MAI provisions were. Indeed, some of these misperceptions were not confined to the NGO community, but appeared in some parliamentary statements as well. The most common misperceptions were as follows:

- The provision for dispute settlement was often portrayed as innovative, granting 'new rights in international law which are solely to the benefit of foreign investors' (Lalumière and Landau 1998, p3). This is simply incorrect. As seen in Chapter 2, that investors have access to binding dispute settlement procedures via third party arbitration has been a characteristic of many BITs and NAFTA long before negotiations on the MAI began.
- Similarly, the supposition that the investor-to-state dispute settlement provisions put foreign investors in a privileged position (for example, Sierra Club of Canada 1997) needs to be qualified at least. The governments of host countries can always use their own legal system to challenge foreign investors. That foreign investors have access to binding third-party arbitration can be justified by the fact that many investors, rightly or wrongly, do not have much confidence and trust in the often underdeveloped and corrupt legal system of many poor countries.
- Withdrawing from the MAI was supposed to be a lengthy process according to the draft treaty. A country needed to file its intent of withdrawal 5 years in advance and after this period existing investments would still enjoy the protection of the agreement for another 15 years. This provision is often portrayed as a revolutionary device and a mean

attempt to lock signatory countries into rules that are friendly towards foreign investment (for example, Sforza 1998a). But, again, this provision is simply taken over from BITs, which mostly also give substantial temporary protection to existing investment.

- That countries which accede to the MAI could no longer ban investment in certain sectors, put limits on mineral resource extraction or set up zoning regulations is an unjustified inference (see, for example, Valliantos 1997 and Sforza 1998b). This is because all countries were allowed to set up country-specific exceptions (OECD 1998a, p103).

- That negotiations were undertaken in secrecy, and by malicious intention so, is an accusation that needs to be qualified at least. While it is true that the draft MAI treaty text was not publicly available until it was leaked to an NGO in February 1997 and subsequently published on the internet, the Organisation for Economic Co-operation and Development (OECD) has since then installed its own official MAI web page. It must also be taken into account that a certain extent of reluctance to make public the ongoing disputes about highly contested issues is not unusual for international negotiations concerning similar issues (for example, international trade rounds under World Trade Organization (WTO) or formerly the General Agreement on Tariffs and trade (GATT)). On the other hand, both the OECD and the participating countries could have done more to inform the public and especially the democratically elected members of parliament. When in late April 1998 ministers from OECD countries at their annual meeting pledged commitment 'to a transparent negotiating process and to active public discussion on the issues at stake in the negotiations' (OECD 1998b), and both the OECD and governments from member countries started to invite groups from civil society for hearings and informal seminars, it was already too late to get rid of the conspiracy theories.

- The expropriation clause was initially drafted in a way that did not clearly rule out an interpretation that every and any public policy that diminished current or future profits could potentially be included under this clause. Such an interpretation, together with the possibility of foreign investors to enforce their compensation claims via dispute settlement procedures, prompted many critics to fear that the MAI would have undermined the ability of governments to exercise their normal regulatory control, especially over environmental matters. Either they would be scared away from enacting such policies or they would have to face multimillion dollar compensatory claims in arbitration courts. In Chapter 4 we saw, however, that there is no convincing evidence that companies abuse these dispute settlement procedures to roll back existing or to deter future environmental regulations. As Witherell (1998), Director of the OECD's Financial Fiscal and Enterprise Affairs unit, has put it, the *strength of these concerns frankly came as a surprise as there has been complete agreement among the negotiators from the beginning that the MAI should not infringe on normal regulatory powers of Governments which are exercised in a non-discriminatory manner and that the MAI should be fully compatible with the pursuit of high environmental standards both in a national context and via international environmental agreements.*

To soothe these concerns somewhat, the chairman of the negotiations proposed to include a 'specific affirmation that the MAI does not inhibit normal non-discriminatory government regulatory activity' and 'that the exercise of such powers will not amount to expropriation' (OECD 1998c). Furthermore, he proposed either to include a general environmental exception to the MAI similar to GATT's Article XX or to allow specifically performance requirements that are necessary to achieve environmental goals. In order to meet the concerns that potential host countries would lower their environmental or other standards in order to attract FDI, a 'not lower measures' clause similar to NAFTA's Article 1114:2 was to be included in the draft MAI text to ensure that a

Contracting Party shall not waive or otherwise derogate from, or offer to waive or otherwise derogate from, its domestic health, safety, environmental, or labour measures, as an encouragement to the establishment, acquisition, expansion, operation, management, maintenance, use, enjoyment and sale or other disposition of an investment of an investor (ibid).[2]

Some real problems with the draft MAI

The draft MAI suffered, however, from a number of severe substantive and procedural problems.

• To start with, the negotiating countries have not made it sufficiently clear why there was a need for such an agreement at all. On the one hand, the economic, political and legal circumstances can provide a justification for the need for an MAI. The increasing importance of private investment flows renders a potential MAI more significant. Whereas in former times one could have argued that investment flows were minor relative to international trade flows so that there was no need for a special agreement, the sheer size of the increase of the flows invalidates such an argument. Similarly, the manifold, but rather uncoordinated steps towards a more liberal and investment-friendly environment can provide a justification to make these policy changes more systematic and to make them irreversible by locking them into an international agreement. The socially wasteful increase in investment incentives calls for putting disciplines on potential host countries. Furthermore, an MAI could make the widespread, but rather chaotic, system of BITs more transparent and render unnecessary the establishment of new BITs, and could make the legal framework in which investment flows operate more certain. On the other hand, the very same factors that can provide a justification for an MAI can also be invoked to dispute its necessity. The very fact that investment flows have increased tremendously without an MAI puts into doubt that such an agreement is necessary to sustain these flows or to enable further future increases. Similarly, why should nation states want an MAI to lock in the liberalization of investment policies? If countries regard an investment-friendly environment to be in their interest, they will continue liberalizing their regulatory system. If they do not, they will reverse the policy changes they have undertaken. With respect to the legal framework, it could be argued that an MAI is undesirable as, by definition, it cannot fit the special circumstances of the contracting parties as well as a BIT can and is unnecessary as hundreds of BITs already exist. Furthermore, empirical studies show that investment treaties have virtually no influence on where FDI, the most desired form of investment, flows to (UNCTAD 1998b, p122). Many countries actually exist that have signed no or very few BITs, but receive massive inflows of FDI. Given that the economic, political and legal background can be invoked both for the necessity of an MAI and its irrelevance, it is not entirely clear why the world is in need of a multilateral agreement on investment in whatever form.

- On a procedural level, it was a mistake from the start that negotiations took place at the OECD level. While a number of developing countries and economies in transition, such as Argentina, Brazil, Hong Kong and the Baltic countries, were allowed to sit at the table as observers, negotiations should have taken place under the auspices of either the WTO or the United Nations Conference on Trade and Development (UNCTAD), where developing countries take part fully. This is because it was quite clear from the beginning that developing countries were expected to accede to the MAI once negotiations were finished among the OECD countries. The draft treaty, for example, included a footnote to the relevant clause that sent out a 'strong political message' to developing countries that accession to the treaty is 'welcome' (OECD 1998a, p103).[3] In this respect, the assertion by FitzGerald et al (1998, p39) that the MAI merely 'represents the rationalization of existing arrangements between OECD members – many of them bilateral in nature – with voluntary accession for other countries' is simply wrong, as the vast majority of BITs are not concluded between OECD members, but between them and developing countries (UNCTAD 1998b, pp11–14). There is something fundamentally wrong with procedural fairness when an international treaty is negotiated in an exclusive club of members and afterwards the excluded are persuaded to accede. It cannot come as a great surprise, then, that the draft MAI has prompted suspicions from the developing world. A V Ganesan (1998, p2), former Commerce Secretary of India, for example, suggests that 'the main motive of the industrialized countries behind a MAI is the gaining and consolidation of market access opportunities for their business enterprises around the world'. Similarly, Bhagirath Lal Das (1997), former Director of UNCTAD's Trade Programme, suspects that the OECD countries wanted to 'eliminate or, at least, constrict the powers of host governments regarding the choice of the priority sectors for FDI and imposition of conditions on such investments, so that foreign investors are able to operate unencumbered by such constraints'.

- Connected to this point, the draft MAI did not include any clauses for the special needs of developing countries. To give one example: most developing countries use performance requirements in order to gain as much as possible from foreign investment. If the OECD (1998e) is correct in stating that 'foreign investment brings higher wages, and is a major source of technology transfer and managerial skills in host developing countries', then why should these countries not be allowed to use local employment requirements to enhance this transfer? Similarly, why should they not be allowed to require a certain amount of local content for production inputs when there is no evidence that such requirements distort the efficient allocation of resources, and TNCs otherwise use mainly imported inputs (Balasubramanyam 1998, p10 and p15)? Also, the draft MAI did not include any clauses for the protection of the most vulnerable of developing countries. Many TNCs have higher sales than the GNP of a great many of these poor countries, so that they are at a comparative disadvantage relative to foreign investors and it is they who need protection from an international agreement rather than the investors.

- The biggest substantial problem of the draft MAI is to be found in two failures. The first is a failure to curb the socially wasteful investment incentives that are provided by competing host countries. The draft treaty text did practically nothing in that respect and Kodama's (1998, p34) assertion that 'the MAI's main purpose is to establish a stronger discipline on investment at the multilateral level' is only partially correct. The OECD negotiating parties did everything to establish disciplines on potential host countries with respect to measures that those could use to seize some of the profits of foreign investors. They did hardly anything, however, to establish disciplines on potential host countries to provide incentives to potential investors as the major beneficiaries of these incentives are the TNCs and their shareholders in developed countries.

- Another important shortcoming was the failure to ensure full investment neutrality. The draft MAI aspired to ensure that foreign investment is not discriminated *against*, but it did not ensure that host countries cannot discriminate *in favour* of foreign investment. In establishing absolute rights for foreign investors that need not be granted to domestic investors, a bias towards foreign investment was allowed and the principle of investment neutrality was violated. Again, it seems that the draft treaty failed to put these kinds of disciplines on host countries because their TNCs would benefit from favourable discrimination.

Conclusion

Without having taken part, developing countries have already won the first round of negotiations on a potential future multilateral agreement on investment. Their bargaining power at either the WTO or United Nations Conference on Trade and Development (UNCTAD) is naturally much higher than at the OECD. Here they can demand concessions from the developed world in terms of increased trade access to their markets, or increased financial, technical or institutional aid in exchange for granting substantially new rights for developed countries' foreign investors. Such a linking will also make more overall sense for two reasons. First, trade and investment are obviously connected – for example, instead of directly investing in a country, a foreign company can also subcontract certain parts of its production process and import these goods and services. From the beginning, the OECD was the wrong forum for negotiations on multilateral investment rules, not least because no linkage to trade issues could be undertaken. Second, assistance will be necessary for those developing countries that only receive marginal inflows of investment so far to help them gain from the beneficial aspects of foreign investment. Virtually all empirical studies confirm that FDI enhances a host country's growth prospects, but most of them also demonstrate that in order to really gain from foreign investment a country needs to have already a minimum level of development together with the accompanying stock of human capital (see, for example, Borensztein et al 1998; Olofsdotter 1998; de Mello 1997, 1999), and also needs an export orientation together with the possibility of actually exporting the goods it produces (for example, Balasubramanyam et al 1996).

Part Three

Trade

Environmentalists are mainly concerned about three distinct but related points with respect to the links between trade and the environment. The first is that for a number of reasons trade liberalization might lead to an increase in environmental degradation if strong environmental policies are not in place. The second is that the multilateral trade regime is, in their perspective at least, insensitive to environmental concerns and makes the enactment of strong environmental policies impossible as they would clash with countries' obligations under the multilateral trade regime. Environmentalists see evidence for this in the relevant decisions that the General Agreement on Tariffs and Trade (GATT) and the World Trade Organization (WTO) panels and appellate bodies have taken in disputes where environmental interests seemingly clashed with free trade interests. The third point is that trade measures or substantive provisions contained in Multilateral Environmental Agreements (MEAs) might clash with WTO rules. They might therefore be the object of a potential future WTO dispute and might be judged inconsistent with a country's trade obligations. Also, the fear of such a future trade dispute might have a deterrent effect on ongoing and future negotiations of MEAs to introduce trade measures or certain substantive provisions if these are at risk of being found inconsistent with WTO rules.

Part Three will therefore proceed in three steps: Chapter 7 examines the theoretical considerations and empirical evidence of the environmental consequences of trade liberalization. Chapter 8 inquires whether the relevant GATT/WTO panels and appellate bodies have really rendered strong environmental policies impossible. Chapter 9 analyses whether trade measures and other provisions of MEAs clash with WTO rules and, if so, what can be done for reconciliation.

As this book focuses on assessing options for reforming the multilateral investment and trade regimes, the emphasis of Part Three is on Chapters 8 and 9. Chapter 7 merely provides a brief survey of how trade liberalization might harm or benefit the environment. The reader should note that issues related to the pollution haven debate – for example, the issues of eco-dumping and strategic environmental policy to attract foreign investment – have been dealt with in Chapter 3 and will not be repeated here. This is in spite of the fact that trade liberalization has an important role to play in facilitating environmental degradation in these cases because a freer trade regime allows the exportation of goods and services from countries with low environmental standards to countries with higher standards.

Trade Liberalization and the Environment

How trade liberalization might benefit the environment

A more efficient allocation of resources

That countries gain in terms of welfare from trade liberalization is one of the oldest propositions of economics, dating back to at least the English economist David Ricardo (1817), the inventor of the concept of comparative advantage. The idea is that after trade liberalization countries will specialize in the production of goods and services in which they have a comparative productivity advantage or, in its more modern version enshrined in the so-called Heckscher-Ohlin theorem, will specialize in goods and services that use intensively factors of production that are abundant in a country. In other words, countries will specialize in the production of goods and services in which they have a comparative advantage and will therefore export these goods; in exchange they will import goods in which they have a comparative disadvantage.[1] If trade is free, then goods and services will be produced where the comparative costs of production are lowest. The beneficial environmental implications of production following international differences in comparative advantage are often not explicated, but they are rather obvious: if goods and services are produced according to comparative advantage, then scarce resources are not wasted and no environmental pollution is *unnecessarily* created. If countries, because of trade restrictions, produce goods in which they do not have a comparative advantage, then the same amount of goods and services could be produced with less natural resource input and environmental pollution output.

It is sometimes asserted by critics of free trade – for example, Daly (1993) – that comparative advantage has been rendered irrelevant with the emergence of the international mobility of capital. (In its original formulation the comparative advantage trade theory assumed that capital and labour – that is, the factors of production – are immobile and the only things that can cross national borders are the produced goods.) While it is true that capital and labour (the latter much less so) can be quite mobile, there are still many restrictions on their mobility, and the international production patterns between substantially differently endowed countries still roughly follow comparative advantage considerations:[2] resource-abundant countries export resources and resource-intensive goods, labour-abundant developing countries export labour-intensive goods, and capital-abundant developed countries export capital-intensive goods. Besides, neither the concept of comparative advantage nor gains from trade depend more generally on the immobility of the factors of production in modern trade theory (Keuschnigg 1999).

A more rapid introduction of modern technology

The second route through which trade liberalization might be beneficial for the environment is the effects it might have on the kind of technology employed by domestic producers. The idea is that in countries that are shielded from foreign competition via trade barriers the technology employed will tend to be old as firms have less incentive to employ the newest technology than if they are constantly under pressure to compete with the latest technological advances that foreign firms might introduce to gain a higher share in world markets. Trade liberalization is like a whip that forces a country's producers to stay abreast of the latest technological advances. In as much as modern technology is less resource and pollution intensive (that is, fewer resources are consumed and less pollution is generated for producing the same amount of goods and services), trade liberalization will be beneficial for the environment. Especially transnational corporations (TNCs), often blamed for exploiting inefficiently low environmental standards in developing countries (a case for which little statistical evidence was found in Chapter 3), can promote the environmental interest in diffusing modern technology worldwide. Often the plants set up by TNCs have the most environmentally benign technology operating, whereas older domestic factories are the biggest polluters.

There is considerable casual evidence for this hypothesis. In South America, for example, where many countries shielded domestic producers behind high walls of protection until the early 1990s, the employed technology was (and sometimes still is) decades behind and much more resource and pollution intensive than in many – for example, South East Asian – developing countries at roughly the same level of economic development. Maybe surprisingly, there is little systematic statistical evidence in favour of the hypothesis, however. But what there is speaks clearly in its favour. Wheeler and Martin (1992) demonstrate for the wood-pulp industry that countries that are trade-oriented are more likely to adopt and diffuse cleaner technologies than protectionist countries. Reppelin-Hill (1999) comes to similar results in an examination of the steel industry. Countries with regimes that are more open towards trade tended to diffuse more quickly a cleaner steel production technology named the electric arc furnace.

Economic growth might benefit the environment

A third reason why trade liberalization might benefit the environment is through economic growth, which is usually assumed to be fuelled via trade liberalization. Harrison, Rutherford and Tarr (1996), for example, estimate that world gross product will be between 96 and 171 billion US$ higher due to the Uruguay Round agreements.

The idea is that for a number of reasons economic growth might lead to increases in environmental protection that more than fully compensate any adverse effects that economic growth – the increase in the value of goods and services produced – might have on the environment. There are many reasons why this might be the case (see Neumayer 1999c, pp77–79 for more detail), but the two most important ones are as follows. First, with rising incomes individuals might demand more and more environmental protection, whereas poor people worry about other things than the environment. If demand for environmental protection rises more than proportionally with rising incomes, economists say that the environment is a 'luxury good'. Second, countries with higher income levels might also have the better capacities to supply this demand as they might have the more advanced political, legal and administrative infrastructure that is necessary for the design and enforcement of strong environmental policies.

The hypothesis that trade liberalization induced economic growth might benefit the environment is, as often argued, not only the most important, but also the most contested one. Its more general evidence is discussed briefly below on how economic growth might actually harm the environment.

Other factors

There exist a number of other factors why trade liberalization might benefit the environment. One is that trade liberalization usually leads to a more open society with freer flows of information, where environmental abuses cannot be covered up easily. Another is that trade liberalization facilitates international cooperation among policy-makers from different countries. In this respect it can create the right climate for international cooperation efforts on regional or global environmental protection efforts to succeed.

Yet another aspect is that trade liberalization might allow for the spatial separation of incompatible industries. For example, air pollution from heavy industries damages agricultural production. Trade liberalization allows some countries to specialize in heavy industries, others in agriculture, thus spatially separating the two and avoiding the damage. Similarly, trade liberalization allows the concentration of pollution-intensive production to concentrate in countries with resilient environments and clean production in countries with vulnerable environments (for a formal model see Copeland and Taylor 1999).[3]

A final aspect worth mentioning here is a phenomenon which Vogel (1995, 2000) has coined 'trading up': high environmental product standards in some countries will induce companies and possibly also the countries in which they reside to trade up their environmental product standards in order to be able to sell their products in these markets with high standards.[4] A limiting factor is, of course, that this trading up is only relevant for standards connected to a product's contents or characteristics. Arguably, the most important environmental effects are due to the process and production methods of a product, however. For these methods high environmental standards in one country have no spill-over effect as products can successfully compete in countries with high standards whether or not they themselves employ these high standards.[5]

How trade liberalization might harm the environment

So far some of the reasons why trade liberalization might benefit the environment have been presented. From an outside perspective, it might seem at times as if economists and free-trade proponents unreservedly subscribed to the view that trade liberalization is always in harmony with the environment. Such a perspective would be fundamentally wrong, however. A basic distinction needs to be drawn between cases in which environmental degradation occurs in spite of what economists call the efficient allocation of resources and the optimal management of the environment on the one hand, and cases in which environmental degradation is the result of inefficient resource allocation and suboptimal management of the environment on the other hand.

Environmental degradation in spite of efficient resource allocation

Effects due to specialization

Trade liberalization might harm the environment even if resources are efficiently allocated and the environment is optimally managed. The former means that resources cannot be reallocated in a way that more goods and services could be produced with the same amount of resources (the term 'resources' is to be interpreted widely here, not only encompassing natural resources, but also labour and capital factor inputs). The latter means that property rights over resources are clearly defined so that there is no open access to the resource, and that environmental externalities are internalized so that all economic activities bear their full cost.

How could trade liberalization harm the environment in this case? At the most fundamental level, it is uncontested that if a country specializes in the production of pollution-intensive goods after an opening up towards trade, its emissions will rise and its environment will suffer. On the other hand, other countries will become cleaner and their environment will benefit as they can satisfy their demand for pollution-intensive goods via increased imports (Rauscher 1991, p20ff) so that the overall amount of pollution need not increase.

In other models, however, a global increase in pollution follows from trade liberalization. In the two regions model of Copeland and Taylor (1994), for example, worldwide pollution increases even though emissions in the North decrease, because Southern emissions increase even more. Behind this result stands the assumption, widely shared among economists, that the environment is a normal good (if not a luxury good). This means that demand for environmental protection increases with income growth (and more than proportionally for a luxury good). It follows that trade liberalization which shifts the production of pollution-intensive goods towards the low-income, high-polluting South increases global pollution as the decrease in Northern emissions is insufficient at the margin to compensate for the increase in Southern emissions.[6] Note that this can occur despite the fact that environmental standards are at their efficiency levels both in the North and the South.

Economic growth might harm the environment

Trade liberalization induces economic growth. Critics argue that this increase in economic activity represents one of the major causes of environmental degradation. If the resource and pollution intensity of producing goods and services does not fall faster than the amount of goods and services produced rises, then increased economic activity will lead to increased environmental degradation.

This directly clashes with the optimistic notion that trade-induced economic growth might benefit the environment. What does the evidence reveal? It is very mixed: while some aspects of the environment, such as access to sanitation, unambiguously improve with economic growth, and some aspects, such as emissions of carbon dioxide, unambiguously become worse with economic growth, the most prominent case is represented by the metaphor of the so-called 'Environmental Kuznets Curve' (EKC).[7] Emissions of, for example, suspended particulate matter, sulphur oxides, faecal coliform, etc first become worse with rising incomes and tend to improve only after a certain income level has been reached (see Neumayer 1999c, pp82–86, for more detail). For the case of Mexico, Grossman and Krueger (1993) have concluded from an extrapolation of cross-country estimates on the relationship between economic growth and some forms of air pollution that the income growth spurred by the North American Free Trade Agreement (NAFTA) will actually lead to an improvement of its environment, as Mexico was just at the estimated turning point. However, most countries are still far short of the turning point for various pollutants, so that trade-induced economic growth is likely to lead in many aspects to increased environmental degradation.

Beghin and Potier (1997) survey the empirical evidence and conclude that increased economic activity in the manufacturing sector is likely to lead to increased environmental degradation if it is not accompanied by strong environmental regulation inducing innovation and the adoption of cleaner technology. The empirical study by Cole, Rayner and Bates (1998) tries to estimate the environmental effects of the Uruguay Round. It distinguishes between a scale (increased economic activity), composition (sectoral composition of the economy), and technique (pollution intensity of the technology employed) effect. It uses prior estimates of income increases due to the liberalization of trade of the Uruguay Round, together with estimates of EKCs to predict the likely environmental effects ensuing. While many local air pollutants, water pollutants, chlorofluorocarbons (CFCs) and other environmental indicators are not taken into account, the study does demonstrate that global emissions of nitrogen dioxide (NO_2), sulphur dioxide (SO_2), carbon monoxide (CO), suspended particulate matter and carbon dioxide (CO_2) are likely to have increased. This is because emission increases in the developing South overcompensate for possible emission decreases in the developed North.[8]

Environmental degradation due to increased transportation

Transport can be another important channel through which trade liberalization might harm the environment. The OECD (1997b) estimates that international transport is bound to increase by 4–5 per cent due to the increase in trade in the wake of the Uruguay Round. Transportation causes noise and the emission of many air pollutants such as CO_2 and CO, nitrogen oxides (NO_x), sulphur oxides (SO_x), hydrocarbons, particulate matters and, still in many developing countries, lead. Transportation usually is a sector that does not cover its full cost, and is therefore prone to environmental and other externalities – an aspect to which we will return in the next section. But it needs to be stressed here that even if transportation covered its full cost, the trade-induced increases in transportation might still harm the environment (for a good overview, see Quinet 1994).

Environmental degradation as a result of inefficient resource allocation

So far we have seen how trade liberalization might harm the environment even if resources are allocated efficiently and the environment is optimally managed. Trade liberalization will harm the environment even more if these conditions do not hold – for example, if significant environmental externalities exist. If these externalities are not internalized via taxes, tradable permits or command-and-control regulation, then free trade will worsen the negative effects on the environment. In these circumstances, trade liberalization can be like a fresh breeze of wind on a house that is already set on fire. Even the WTO (1997, p1) readily admits that for the benefits of trade liberalization to be realized and 'for trade-induced growth to be sustainable, appropriate environmental policies determined at the national level need to be put in place'. What is more, if an economy that is faced with trade liberalization suffers to a great extent from more general ineffiencies in resource allocation within its economy, an increase in trade can very well harm the country's overall welfare, not just its environmental quality (Markandya 1994, p10).

The negative environmental effects of trade liberalization due to the existence of externalities become exacerbated if one of two conditions hold: first, pollution is transboundary or global in nature, and second, property rights over resources are badly defined. In the first case, incentives to internalize the environmental externality are low, as the costs are borne by foreigners or the rest of the world. The most conspicuous example is greenhouse gases. In the second case, trade liberalization can lead to the export of the resource misallocation to other countries and thereby to a deterioration in environmental quality – for example, Chichilnisky's (1994) influential two regions model in which ill-defined property rights over natural resources in the South lead to the overproduction of environmentally intensive goods. The South has a comparative advantage in the production of this good – an advantage that is only apparent, however. Trade liberalization 'makes things worse, in the sense that the overuse of the resource increases as the South moves from autarky to trade' (ibid, p859). In a similar model with similar results, Brander and Taylor (1998) show that the resource-exporting countries not only experience excessive deterioration of their environments, but they can also lose in terms of welfare.

A final aspect of how trade liberalization can harm the environment as a consequence of suboptimal environmental management is via the increase in transportation. If transportation does not cover its full environmental costs, the increases in international transportation, which will be the inevitable consequence of trade liberalization, will harm the environment excessively, where excessively means in excess of how much transportation increases would harm the environment if transportation covered its full environmental costs.

Conclusion

To sum up, both theoretical reasoning and empirical evidence show that trade liberalization can lead to a global increase in resource depletion and to a global increase in environmental pollution. These effects are more likely to occur and to be stronger if property rights over resources are ill defined and if the environment is not managed optimally. There is ample evidence that, especially in many developing, but also in developed countries, environmental management is non-optimal and property rights over natural resources are ill-defined (see, for example, World Bank 1992). As concerns the so-called global commons – for example, the climate – property rights are practically non-existent and open access prevails, leading to excessive resource depletion and pollution. The first concern of environmentalists is therefore well supported by theoretical models and empirical evidence: trade liberalization can indeed exacerbate the existing high levels of environmental degradation.

This finding does not imply that overall welfare must fall if environmental degradation increases. The already mentioned study by Cole, Rayner and Bates (1998), which demonstrates that trade liberalization in the wake of the Uruguay Round agreements is likely to have caused increases in global emissions for many pollutants, also suggests that the monetary value of the increased environmental damage is likely to be drastically lower than the welfare gain due to the other beneficial effects of trade liberalization. This result echoes the theoretical finding of Anderson (1992, p29) that overall welfare is unambiguously higher with trade if environmental policy is not too far from its optimum, 'despite the fact that the environment is more polluted'.

Overall welfare can therefore well increase in spite of increased environmental degradation, if environmental management and resource depletion are not too far from their optimum. Two important observations follow. First, because trade liberalization can lead to both overall welfare improvements and a deterioration of environmental quality, a fundamental clash can arise between free trade proponents and environmentalists. While the former can refer to the overall increase in welfare in justification for their calls for trade liberalization, the environmentalists are likely to refer to increased resource depletion and environmental degradation in justification for their concern about or opposition to trade liberalization. This clash is often not clearly recognized and it is not easily ameliorated. Second, the increase in environmental degradation could in principle overcompensate any other beneficial effect of trade liberalization – in other words, a situation in which environmental degradation increases so much that overall welfare decreases cannot be ruled out per se. It is largely an empirical matter and would call for a careful assessment of the environmental consequences of trade liberalization (see the next section). Only after such an assessment has been done can the necessary macroeconomic and environmental management policies be undertaken to mitigate, if not avoid, the negative environmental effects.

If trade liberalization might harm the environment – especially in interaction with mis-specified property rights over resources and existent environmental externalities – then the question is whether trade restriction is the best way to address this problem. The answer is, in general, no. Rather, policies should be enacted that directly address the environmental problem. Environmental externalities need to become internalized, and property rights need to become clearly defined and enforced to avoid open access. If transportation, for example, causes excessive environmental degradation, the best way to deal with this problem is to internalize the environmental (and other) externalities caused by transportation, not to reject trade liberalization because of the increase in transportation needs that it would bring about. If, as another example, the global atmosphere is excessively polluted with greenhouse gases, chlorofluorocarbons (CFCs) and other emissions because of open access, then countries need to come together and negotiate an MEA that implicitly defines property rights in restricting emissions of these pollutants.

Unfortunately, most of these policies lie outside the reach of multilateral trade negotiations and environmentalists correctly complain that countries do not give as much political attention and support to a solution of these environmental problems as they give to trade matters. However, the great attention that countries tend to give to trade matters could be exploited for the benefit of the environment because, as the many policy recommendations contained in this book show, the multilateral trade (and investment) regimes can be reformed such that the enactment of stronger environmental policies is facilitated.

The international forest regime is a good example to illustrate how trade liberalization must go hand in hand with the enactment of strong environmental policies, namely forest protection policies and the reduction of logging subsidies (see, more generally, Tarasofsky 1999). Otherwise the tariff eliminations in forest products, envisioned by some members of the Asia-Pacific Economic Cooperation (APEC) for the WTO, could lead potentially to negative effects on deforestation and on the influx of pests, insects and diseases into formerly healthy forest ecosystems (Goldman and Scott 1999; Sizer, Downes and Kaimowitz 1999; for an attempt to disperse these concerns see USTR 1999). On the latter point, the full incorporation of the precautionary principle, recommended in Chapter 8, can play an important role in helping countries to design adequate forest protection policies.

Policy recommendations

Assessment of environmental impacts

Maybe surprisingly, comprehensive assessments of the environmental consequences of past, ongoing or future trade liberalizations are hardly existent so far. It is only now that, for example, the US, Canada and the EU have followed earlier suggestions by environmental NGOs – for example, WWF (1999b) – and have committed to conduct comprehensive environmental (or broader sustainability) assessments of a new round of trade negotiations (White House 1999; US Trade Representative 2000; Canada 1999c; European Communities 2000a). The US has issued a Federal Register Notice seeking public comments on the implementation of the Executive Order 13141 which commits the US to 'a policy of careful assessment and consideration of the environmental impacts of trade agreements' accomplished 'through a process of ongoing assessment and evaluation, and, in certain instances, written environmental reviews' (White House 1999). The US WWF has welcomed the order and has made several suggestions for its implementation to the effect that, for example, environmental considerations are fully integrated into trade policy decision-making and outcomes, that successive stages of environmental assessment and review should be undertaken at each significant step in trade negotiations, and that the public should be involved at each step of the process (WWF 2000).

The European Commission has already commissioned a pilot sustainability impact assessment study of a potentially enacted new round of trade negotiations. Environmental NGOs have cautiously welcomed the study and have put forward a constructive critique (for more detail see WWF et al 2000). Some of their major points of critique are that, in their view at least, the study's analysis is relatively underdeveloped and lacks a sense of priorities, that a pro-liberalization bias is built into the analysis, that no rigorous process is offered on how to link impacts of trade-induced change to indicators of sustainability, that no baseline data are provided against which to judge the effects of further trade liberalization, and that the assessment of impacts is overly simplified and is unclear on how judgements are made and on how to determine the intensity of an impact. On more fundamental terms, the environmental NGOs allege that 'from the outset, the study ignores the fact that there are limits to sustainability, in some cases effects are irreversible, and in some instances policy intervention is urgent' (ibid, p4).

Without assistance for institutional capacity-building, developing countries will hardly be able to perform their own environmental or sustainability assessments (OECD 1999c), even though such assessments will be equally, if not more, important to them. The policy to be recommended is therefore to initiate comprehensive, transparent and open assessments of the environmental consequences of trade liberalization, and for developed countries and multilateral institutions such as the World Bank or the WTO to provide assistance for developing countries to undertake such assessments on their own.

Establishing a special environmental negotiation group

This section contains many recommendations on how to 'green' the multilateral trade regime. But how is it possible to achieve these recommendations? On a procedural level it will be important to establish a special negotiation group on environmental issues in future trade negotiations to facilitate realizing these or similar recommendations. Such a negotiation group should have the competence to put forward proposals that cut across traditional areas of negotiation. It should consist of officials from national environmental institutions and, where relevant, representatives from MEA secretariats to facilitate coordination with ongoing or future international environmental negotiations. Such a negotiation group should also include representatives from ministries other than the environment, however. Doing so will boost the political significance of such a negotiation group and will minimize tensions and potential inconsistencies with other negotiation groups.

The special negotiation group proposed here is more far-reaching than the proposal for a 'Standing Conference on Trade and Environment' put forward by the International Institute for Sustainable Development and the World Conservation Union (IISD and IUCN 1999). While this conference would gather key environmental actors with an interest in trade policy in order to 'formulate practical recommendations, which could be introduced to the WTO and other policy forums' (ibid, p1), the special negotiation group would go one step further in making decisions and cutting deals rather than merely formulating recommendations.

Seeking NGO participation[9]

The negotiation group on environmental issues described in the last section should also be open, at least for specific aspects, towards selected NGOs in the form of granting them observer status, together with the right to introduce proposals and comment in a written form on member countries' proposals. This is for three reasons. First, trade negotiators can benefit from their specialized information and knowledge, alternative perspectives and their constructive critique. Second, the inclusion of NGOs will help to disperse the distrust and outright hostility that many environmentalists have with respect to trade liberalization in general and the WTO in particular that became so clearly visible in the street protests in Seattle. The negotiators for the failed attempt to conclude an MAI have learned the hard way that it can be deadly to ignore the mounting criticism raised against efforts to liberalize the multilateral investment or trade regimes (see Chapter 6). While it is true that some NGOs are radically opposed to the very principles of free trade and would not give up their fundamental opposition merely because trade negotiators reversed their exclusion, it is also true that the vast majority of established developmental, environmental and other NGOs, such as the International Institute for Sustainable Development (IISD), the International Union for the Conservation of Nature (IUCN), Oxfam and WWF, are interested in seeing some of their constructive critiques come true. As a model example can serve the negotiations leading to the North American Free Trade Agreement and its environmental side agreement: Because NGOs were allowed significant participation in the negotiations, some of them turned their opposition into eventual support for the agreements. Third, the inclusion of NGOs represents 'an important mechanism by which the WTO can reach out to citizens and build the requisite bridge to global civil society' (Esty 2000, p99) which will provide decisions made under the auspices of the WTO with a greater democratic legitimacy.

Negotiators of MEAs have made good experience with the inclusion of NGOs. For the WTO, however, NGO participation in such a special environmental negotiation group would represent a drastic step. At the moment, it does not even grant observer status to NGOs at the sessions of its various councils and committees. To be sure, the WTO has installed regular symposia with NGOs and has provided them with space on its web page. Some countries such as the Netherlands have included representatives from

NGOs in their negotiation teams. However, such rather sporadic attempts at the inclusion of NGOs are no alternative to systematic inclusion where it really matters – in the trade negotiations themselves. Symposia represent a nice gesture by the WTO, but in the end do not produce much more than hot air. NGOs are sometimes reluctant to become included if they have to fear that their inclusion is merely superficial and undertaken only with the objective of improving the public image of the WTO. Inclusion in the negotiation group will ensure that these fears are dispersed.

Without doubt the arguments made above for the inclusion of NGOs on environment related matters would be similarly valid for other matters related to, say, agriculture, development or consumers' and workers' rights.[10] There are some arguments pointing at the problems and dangers of a wider participation of NGOs (see Esty (1998, 2000) and Scholte, O'Brien and Williams (1998) for a critical discussion). Most centre upon two concerns: first, lack of representativity and second, lack of accountability. The first concern is that the NGOs selected by the WTO for inclusion might not be (fully) representative in terms of covering comprehensively all 'the various constituencies with a stake in the global trade regime' (Scholte, O'Brien and Williams 1998, p7), as well as covering the different interests from the various regions of the world, especially those from the developing world. A related concern is that NGOs tend to represent minority views in the sense that they have their specialist agenda which might not be in concordance with the will of the majority of people affected. This is closely linked to the second concern, which states that whereas governments are accountable to their parliaments and their people, NGOs are not accountable to anyone and can therefore advance particularist, elitist and fringe interests.

The concern relating to the lack of representativity is largely exaggerated and can be alleviated to some extent. First, it does not matter that NGOs tend to represent minority and specialist points of view. To the contrary, this should be one of the reasons for their inclusion, as government representatives are then forced to deal with alternative and competing perspectives and proposals which have not (yet) made it into majority thinking. Also, as Esty (1998, p4) points out: 'Adding a variety of environmental perspectives to the WTO's internal debates would help to counteract the influence of (often protectionist) business interests and therefore reduce, not increase, the risk of special-interest-driven policies.' Contrary to the demand from, for example, the US Council for International Business, there is no justification for providing the business community with a unique role in trade negotiations (USCIB 1998). Furthermore, if a country feels that NGO participation is non-representative, it can always encourage different NGOs to apply for accreditation. Funds could be made available to facilitate NGO participation from the developing world (Esty 1998, p6). Accreditation should be permanent and require the consensus of WTO member countries. The consensus requirement will make it easier for developing countries to accept NGO inclusion in the first place. Rightly or wrongly, governments from developing countries often feel threatened by NGO inclusion. Partly this might be because some of these governments have no experience with or sympathy for a pluralistic society, of which a healthy variety of NGOs is symptomatic.

The concern relating to the lack of accountability makes a valid point, even though the extent of the accountability of many a WTO member country's government is questionable as well. However, it seems that this lack of accountability matters little after all. In the end, it will still be the WTO member countries that have to make, and in some cases ratify, decisions. Hence it is their accountability that matters, not the existence or non-existence of NGO accountability.

Realizing win-win opportunities

In some cases trade liberalization can actually have direct positive effects on the environment. It is a common-sense recommendation by now, demanded by many others before (WTO 1997a; OECD 1998i; de Moor 1999), but it still needs to be realized and therefore repeated here yet once more: a future round of trade negotiations should focus on those trade liberalizations that are environmentally beneficial at the same time (so-called win-win opportunities). The following are examples of where these win-win opportunities lie:

- Reductions in agricultural subsidies, estimated by Myers and Kent (1998, pxvii) to be around US$325 billion worldwide. Subsidies lead to the overproduction of agricultural products with the ensuing overconsumption of environmental resources. Subsidies need not accrue in the form of direct and explicit payments to farmers, but can accrue indirectly in the form of tariffs which protect domestic agricultural production from cheaper imports. Direct subsidies can be especially harmful if they accrue in the form of the subsidization of fertilizer, the use of pesticides and irrigation.
- Reductions in fishery subsidies, estimated to be around US$22 billion worldwide (ibid). Subsidies lead to the overcapitalization of fishing fleets, to overharvesting and over-consumption (Porter 1999). Fishery subsidies have helped to bring many fish stocks to the verge of depletion (FAO 1999; ICTSD and IUCN 1999). Reductions in fishery subsidies have been supported in a common position paper by Australia, Iceland, New Zealand, the Philippines and the US (New Zealand 1999). The EU and Japan, big subsidizers of their fishing fleet, are less than enthusiastic though.
- Reductions in energy and road transport subsidies, estimated to be around US$205 billion and $225 billion respectively worldwide by Beers and van den Bergh (2001, p483).[11] These subsidies range from the direct subsidization of coal extraction in developed countries, especially Germany, to more indirect subsidies for fuel consumption, especially in the US. These subsi-

dies lead to too much energy consumption and to the consumption of an inefficient mix of energy, especially with respect to coal.

• The liberalization of trade in environmental services. Environmental services encompass air, water and noise-pollution abatement technologies, waste-water and solid-waste management, as well as environmental monitoring, analysis, assessment, research and development, construction and engineering (WTO 1995b). The liberalization of trade in these services will lower their costs and make them more widely available, especially in developing countries where there is a huge demand for these services. Liberalization in these sectors will also reward those countries that have set high environmental standards in the past and thus promoted the development of an industry that provides the necessary technology to comply with these standards. Vogel (2000, p268) reports that 'due to their strict emission standards for coal-burning power plants, both Germany and Japan dominate the world market in scrubbers which remove sulfur dioxide from power plant smokestacks'.

Of course, not all subsidies are the same. Some do not lead to environmental degradation, and some actually benefit the environment. Even a reduction of environmentally harmful subsidies might not help the environment much if it is not accompanied by appropriate environmental policies – for example, reductions in agricultural subsidies are likely to lead to more intensive forms of agricultural production in developing countries for export. If they are not accompanied by adequate environmental management, this could easily be detrimental to their environments. The worldwide environmental effects could then well be negative. Yet other subsidies, while possibly damaging the environment, have a good justification on other accounts. Agricultural subsidies in developing countries, for example, often are necessary to ensure some basic food security for the poorest people. Reductions of agricultural subsidies should therefore predominantly be undertaken in developed countries and must be carefully designed, compensating the poor and vulnerable so that their food security is not threatened. The existing WTO Agreement on Agriculture leads broadly in the right direction in demanding higher tariff reduction cuts from developed countries (an unweighted average of 36 per cent over six years) than from developing countries (24 per cent over ten years) with no commitments in the least developed countries (WTO 1997a, p7). However, much more needs to be done, and more differentiation between groups of countries and between various forms of subsidies should take place. The aim should be to phase out all price-distorting subsidies and to allow the continuation of subsidies only in the form of direct income subsidies or subsidies for efforts concerning the preservation of the environment and cultural heritage in rural communities (the so-called green box subsidies for the furtherance of the 'multi-functionality' of agriculture).

The reduction of agricultural subsidies, especially in the developed countries, is actually a good example of an opportunity that will not only increase trade and raise environmental quality, but will be supportive of development in poorer countries as well (sometimes referred to as win-win-win opportunities). Subsidized exports from developed countries into world markets lead to a lowering of prices that agricultural producers in developing countries can achieve and often threatens their very economic viability. A WWF (1999c) paper suggests that about 50 per cent of people in developing countries are employed in the agricultural sector and that 47 developing countries totally depend on agricultural exports for their development. For these countries, reduced agricultural subsidies in developed countries would amount to a drastic push for their development prospects.

Ensuring that environmental standards and schemes do not restrict market access for developing countries

Environmental product standards, packaging and recycling requirements and eco-labelling schemes form an important ingredient of a comprehensive environmental strategy. Used wisely, they can lead to a substantial reduction of environmental impacts from trade liberalization. However, often developing countries fear that the increasing use of these environmental instruments might restrict their market access as their enterprises, and especially their small and medium enterprises (SMEs), might lack the information, the know-how or the financial resources to comply with these standards, requirements and schemes (Jha, Markandya and Vossenaar 1999). Compliance can at times be quite expensive. Jha, Markandya and Vossenaar (ibid, p47) suggest that, for example, 'in the leather tanning sector in India, the costs of chemicals required to meet international standards were approximately three times higher than the costs of conventional chemicals'. The fear of developing countries is especially relevant as these mainly affect low value added products from sectors such as paper, textiles, leather, footwear, forestry and food products in which developing countries have a comparative advantage (WTO 1996a), where many SMEs operate and where price competition is fierce.[12]

The policy recommendation is that these fears can only be overcome if developed countries are willing to assist in capacity-building for, and the transfer of technical knowledge, especially with respect to environmentally sound technologies to, developing countries. Both the SPS Agreement and the TBT Agreement contain special provisions for assistance to developing countries, but as yet they need to be fully realized (see the dissatisfaction of developing countries with the special and differential treatment provisions in WTO agreements as discussed on p16).

8

GATT/WTO Dispute Settlement and the Environment

Chapter 7 described the importance of countries enacting strong environmental policies to mitigate and reduce the potential negative environmental effects of trade liberalization. The question is, then, whether countries have the autonomy to enact strong environmental policies. It is here that the second major critique of environmentalists sets in. The World Trade Organization (WTO) as the multilateral trading regime and its dispute settlement system is regarded as hindering countries from enacting such policies if they conflict with free trade. In the environmentalists' view at least, the WTO system is inherently biased against environmental protection, giving free trade priority over the environment. As Retallack (1997, p136) has put it: '[I]n every case brought before it to date, the WTO has ruled in favour of corporate interest, striking down national and sub-national legislation protecting the environment and public health at every turn.' Or in the words of Friends of the Earth International (FoE 1999c, p8): 'Governments are increasingly using (or threatening to use) the WTO to challenge legitimate existing and proposed domestic and international laws as "barriers to trade". They are able to do this because the WTO prioritises trade above all other societal values.' It is to an evaluation of such claims that we turn our attention in this chapter.

This chapter will look more closely at the most important disputes in which countries regarded trade measures in conformity with their WTO obligations or justified them with one of the environmental exceptions in Article XX of the General Agreement on Tariffs and Trade (GATT), whereas other GATT or WTO members regarded those measures as violating their trade rights and therefore brought them before a panel to decide. It is important to distinguish between measures that aim at product-related environmental effects, and measures that aim at non-product related environmental effects.[1] First, however, the rules of dispute settlement in the WTO (and the GATT before it) are presented in order to provide the reader with a better understanding of the dispute settlement process.

Dispute settlement in the WTO (and GATT)

In ratifying the WTO agreements, member countries have pledged to obey its obligations. If a WTO member chooses to violate its obligations explicitly, then the affected countries have the right to challenge this member before a WTO panel. More often, however, the WTO agreements leave room for interpretation so that it is truly disputed whether a member country has violated its obligations or not. Again, the affected countries have the right to ask a WTO panel to settle the dispute.

Dispute settlement among the GATT contracting parties existed already before the establishment of the WTO. However, the WTO dispute settlement, as regulated by one of the WTO agreements called the 'Understanding on Rules and Procedures Governing the Settlement of Disputes' or, in short, dispute settlement understanding (DSU), differs from the GATT dispute settlement in the following main aspects:[2]

- The WTO dispute settlement is a two-tier system in which a panel assesses the facts and comes to a legal conclusion. The panel consists of three (sometimes five) international trade lawyers or trade policy officials who are proposed by the WTO secretariat and usually agreed upon by the dispute partners consensually (Article 8), but may not come from one of the disputing parties as was possible under the GATT system.[3] All parties to a dispute can appeal against the panel's decision. The appellate body, which consists of three members for each case drawn at random from a pool of seven permanent members, will, however, not assess the facts anew or consider new facts. Rather, it is confined to an assessment of the panel's legal interpretations of the facts (Article 17). The GATT did not offer the possibility of appealing against a decision.
- Under the GATT system, all contracting parties had to approve a panel's decision to make it binding. As this meant that the losing party would need to give its approval as well, many GATT panel reports never became binding (including some environmentally relevant ones – see the next section). In a dramatic reversal, all WTO members need to disapprove of a panel's or (in the case of an appeal) an appellate body's report to prevent it from becoming legally binding. As this would mean that even the winning party would need to disapprove of the decision, these reports now almost automatically become approved by the so-called dispute settlement body (DSB).
- The dispute settlement system has been significantly streamlined under the WTO in setting a fixed timetable for panels and appellate bodies to follow. Disputes should not last longer than one year (three months longer if they are appealed against).

The proceedings of the panels and appellate bodies are not held in public. Against the explicit demand of developing countries (ICTSD 1998b), the appellate body in the shrimp/sea turtle case ruled that panels are allowed to take into account written statements from NGOs, so-called amicus curiae briefs that are not part of one party's solicited submission (WTO 1998b, paragraph 108) (see p144).[4]

After the adoption of the panel/appellate body report by the DSB, the losing party is given a 'reasonable period of time' to implement the report's recommendations (Article 21), which usually shall not exceed 15 months. While the DSU makes clear that full implementation is the preferred option, it allows the losing party to come to an agreement with the winning party and compensate it for any losses due to persistent non-implementation (and therefore violation of its WTO obligations). However, if the losing country fails to find an agreement on compensating the winning party and still refuses to implement the report's recommendations, the winning party can ask the DSB to allow suspension of its own WTO obligations towards the losing party for its part and to allow the imposition of retaliatory trade measures against the losing party, including so-called cross-retaliatory measures (that is, measures in other sectors or the suspension of WTO obligations in other WTO agreements than the ones that were relevant in the dispute). In the case of conflict, an arbitration panel will decide on a reasonable period of time for implementation and whether implementation has actually occurred. Critics from the developing world have argued that, de facto, retaliation is not an option for many developing countries as they cannot afford politically or economically to impose trade sanctions against a major developed country, which has prompted them to call for a reform of the understanding to allow for joint retaliatory action by all WTO members (South Centre 1999).

It is important to note that a country which has imposed a trade measure for environmental reasons in violation of its WTO obligations cannot be forced to remove this trade measure. On the contrary, it can maintain its measure if it is willing to compensate its trading partners which are negatively affected by the measure, or if it is willing to endure retaliatory trade sanctions. This point is not given enough attention in the relevant debates. While compensation and enduring trade sanctions are costly, a country that is strongly committed to the environmental cause it purports to advance can stick to its commitment if it wants to.

Measures aimed at product-related environmental or health effects

As concerns trade restrictions that aim at product-related environmental or health effects, there have been several major decisions so far. Most, but not all of them, ended with the dispute panel (or the appellate body respectively) ruling that the trade restriction was, partially at least, in non-comformity with GATT/WTO rules. However, even in these cases the dispute panel or appellate body has stressed that it had not decided against the protection of the environment, but merely against the intended or unintended effects of domestic regulation on imports from trading partners. In all these cases, the panel has shown ways on how to protect the environment without interfering with the trade rights of foreign countries. Let us have a closer look at these dispute settlement decisions.

United States – Prohibition of imports of tuna and tuna products from Canada

On 22 February 1982 a panel report was adopted that decided on the first dispute in which the environmental exceptions contained in Article XX of GATT played a major role (GATT 1983). Canada had seized 19 tuna fishing vessels and arrested their fishermen in waters it considered to be within its sole jurisdiction. The US disputed Canada's jurisdictional claims and imposed a ban on imports of tuna and tuna products from Canada in retaliation. This import ban was based on section 205 of the US Fishery Conservation and Management Act of 1976 which enabled the US to impose trade restrictions on countries that unilaterally claimed a 200-mile jurisdiction over tuna stocks and seized US tuna vessels within this area (ibid, paragraph 3.12). When Canada brought the import ban before a GATT panel, the US argued that the prohibition was in no way motivated by protectionism; rather it was undertaken 'in order to avoid and deter threats to the international management approach which the United States considered essential to conservation of the world's tuna stocks' (ibid, para 3.9) and therefore justified under Article XX(g).

In its decision, the panel noted that because similar import bans were imposed on other countries but Canada, the ban might not necessarily have been arbitrary or unjustifiable. Furthermore, since the ban was publicly announced and was clearly taken as a trade measure, it could not be considered a disguised restriction on international trade either. Consequently, the panel decided that the US import ban fell within the preamble of Article XX and therefore moved on to examine whether it was also covered by one of the specific exceptions, notably Article XX(g) (ibid, paragraph 4.8).[5]

In doing so, it noted that the US import prohibition was not 'made effective in conjunction with restrictions on domestic production or consumption' as required by Article XX(g). It also noted that the import restriction had evidently been imposed in retaliation for the arrest of US fishing vessels and therefore could not 'in itself constitute a measure of a type listed in Article XX' (ibid, paragraph 4.13). Consequently, the panel ruled that the US import prohibition was inconsistent with GATT.

The ruling was of no further factual consequence as the US had earlier already lifted the import ban in pursuance of an interim agreement between the US and Canada, which was followed by the conclusion of the Treaty on Pacific Coast Albacore Tuna Vessels and Port Privileges between the two countries (ibid, paragraph 4.2). However, the Canadian government insisted on a GATT panel ruling.

Assessment: The panel has made the right decision and has not unduly neglected environmental aspects. There quite simply was no real environmental justification for the US import restriction.

Canada – Measures affecting exports of unprocessed herring and salmon

In November 1987 a panel decided on Canada's export prohibitions of unprocessed salmon and herring (GATT 1987b), the report of which was adopted on 22 March 1988. Canada argued that export prohibitions were necessary to protect its fish stocks that it said were under threat of depletion. It argued further that it had also certain harvest limitations in place, so that the export prohibitions were covered by the exception in Article XX(g), as they were related to the conservation of an exhaustible natural resource and made effective in conjunction with the restrictions on domestic production or consumption. The US challenged these export prohibitions before GATT.

The panel, in looking at the wording of Article XX(g), struggled to interpret the formulation that measures covered under this exception must be 'related to' the conservation of exhaustible natural resources. It noted that this formulation is not as demanding as the formulations contained in other specific Article XX exceptions which require that a measure is 'necessary' or 'essential' to achieve a certain policy purpose. Nevertheless, it interpreted 'related to' quite restrictively as meaning 'primarily aimed at' the conservation of an exhaustible natural resource. In justification, the panel said that 'the purpose of including Article XX(g) in the General Agreement was not to widen the scope for measures serving trade policy purposes but merely to ensure that the commitments under the General Agreement do not hinder the pursuit of policies aimed at the conservation of exhaustible natural resources' (ibid, paragaph 4.6).

The panel proceeded to rule that Canada's export prohibitions could not be regarded as 'related to' the conservation of an exhaustible resource as it was not 'primarily aimed at' such conservation. This could be inferred from two facts. First, Canada did not prohibit the export of processed salmon and herring, thus not generally limiting the exploitation of its fish stocks. Second, Canada did not restrict access of its domestic producers to its unprocessed fish, thus effectively discriminating against foreign processors and privileging domestic ones (ibid, paragraph 4.7).

Assessment: In factual terms the GATT panel has made the right decision – an assessment that is supported by the fact that Canada accepted the adoption of the panel report. It is most doubtful that Canada's export prohibitions of unprocessed salmon and herring were motivated by genuine concern about the protection of these fish stocks. Because restrictions only applied to foreign producers, not to domestic ones, there is some reason for suspecting that the regulation served to disguise protectionist intentions. At the very least, one can say that Canada tried to protect its salmon and herring stocks entirely at the expense of foreign producers. The dispute panel objected to this, but it did not rule against a regulation which would protect the fish stocks more generally and would affect domestic and foreign producers alike. In other words, the panel did not question Canada's fundamental right to put policies in place that protect its fish stocks.

In interpretative terms, however, the GATT panel has been too restrictive, thereby confirming the environmentalists' suspicion that panels tend to favour free trade over environmental objectives. Article XX(g) demands that trade measures 'relate to' the conservation of exhaustible natural resources. To interpret this as 'primarily aimed at' clearly contradicts the everyday usage of the words and subjects environmental trade measures to an excessively restrictive test. This matters as Article 31 of the Vienna Convention on the Law of Treaties, often invoked by WTO panels, demands that a treaty 'shall be interpreted in good faith in accordance with the *ordinary* meaning to be given to the terms of the treaty in their context and in the light of its object and purpose' (added emphasis). It would have been better therefore had the panel ruled that the export prohibitions fell under the exception of Article XX(g), but violated the preamble of Article XX, which, *inter alia*, demands that measures 'are not applied in a manner which would constitute a means of arbitrary or unjustifiable discrimination between countries where the same conditions prevail'. As pointed out above, there is ample evidence that the restrictions constituted a means of arbitrary or unjustifiable discrimination.

The appellate body in a later case (United States – Standards for reformulated and conventional gasoline) distanced itself somewhat from the 'primarily aimed at' interpretation of the 'relate to' phrase. While not making a judgement on the interpretation itself, since none of the parties to the dispute requested the appellate body to do so, it did note that 'the phrase "primarily aimed at" is not itself treaty language and was not designed as a simple litmus test for inclusion or exclusion from Article XX(g)' (WTO 1996b, p18). However, since no appellate body has ever explicitly overruled the 'primarily aimed at' interpretation, it still remains a valid precedent in GATT/WTO case law.[6]

Thailand – Restrictions on importation of and internal taxes on cigarettes

In October 1990 a panel ruled against Thailand's restrictions on the importation of foreign cigarettes and its higher taxes on imported as opposed to domestically produced cigarettes (GATT 1990), the report of which became adopted on 7 November 1990. Thailand had justified its policies with health protection. The US had challenged the measures before GATT.

The panel ruled that because smoking constitutes a serious risk to human health 'measures designed to reduce the consumption of cigarettes fell within the scope of Article XX(b)' (ibid, paragraph 73). The panel stated 'that this provision clearly allowed contracting parties to give priority to human health over trade liberalization' (ibid). In order for a measure to be covered by Article XX(b) it has to be 'necessary' to protect human life or health, however. The panel interpreted 'necessary' in the sense that 'there were no alternative measures consistent with the General Agreement, or less inconsistent with it, which Thailand could reasonably be expected to employ to achieve its health policy objectives' (ibid, paragraph 75).

The panel suggested a whole range of possible restrictions on the sale and purchase of cigarettes that Thailand might have employed without violating the rights of foreign cigarette producers, including a ban on particularly unhealthy cigarette ingredients and on cigarette advertisements, as well as restrictions on the supply of cigarettes. In the end, it ruled against Thailand because its measure treated foreign cigarettes less favourably than domestic ones without this trade discrimination being necessary, in the sense above, to achieve its health objectives.

Assessment: As with 'Canada – Measures affecting exports of unprocessed herring and salmon', the GATT panel made the right decision on factual terms, which is also supported by the fact that Thailand accepted the adoption of the panel report. In putting restrictions and higher taxes only on imported, not on domestic cigarettes, Thailand clearly discriminated against foreign cigarettes without valid health reasons. Thailand's import prohibitions were seemingly dominated by economically protectionist considerations. At the very least, it can be said that Thailand tried to protect the health of its own population entirely at the expense of foreign cigarette producers. The dispute panel objected to this, but it did not rule against a regulation that would protect health in lowering the consumption of cigarettes.

However, in interpretative terms the panel ruling might have been too restrictive in its interpretation of the term 'necessary' in GATT Article XX(b). Whether this is the case or not is not entirely clear as the panel ruling itself is not entirely clear. Its interpretation of a measure to be considered as necessary 'only if there were no alternative measure consistent with the General Agreement, or less inconsistent with it', which a GATT contracting party can 'reasonably be expected to employ' to achieve its policy objectives is unclear about one important point: are other measures which are consistent or less inconsistent with GATT, considered as alternatives only if they are equally or similarly effective? Or are they already considered as alternatives if somehow they further the policy objective, even if they are much less effective than the disputed measures? From an environmental point of view the latter interpretation is to be rejected. A second measure cannot be considered an alternative if it is far inferior in its environmental (or health protection) effect. The GATT panel should have made clear that only equally or similarly effective measures can be considered as alternatives. This would not have changed the substance of its decision – the GATT consistent or less inconsistent measures it listed were equally or similarly, if not more, effective in reducing cigarette consumption, but it would have alleviated environmentalists' concern that GATT panels are biased towards free trade considerations at the expense of environmental objectives. Unfortunately, other GATT/WTO panels which have interpreted the term 'necessary' in Article XX(b) have similarly failed to be clear on this point (see WTO 1998d, pp13ff).

United States – Taxes on automobiles

In September 1994, a panel decided on several United States measures on cars: a luxury tax on cars sold for over US$30,000, a gas guzzler tax which applied to vehicles in general, and a minimum fuel economy regulation. This regulation required that the average fuel economy value calculated for each manufacturer's and importer's entire fleet of vehicles, the so-called corporate average fuel economy (CAFE), must not be short of a certain minimum (GATT 1994a). Importantly, part of the CAFE regulation required companies that both import cars and manufacture them domestically to calculate a separate average fuel economy for the domestically manufactured and the imported vehicles. The European Community challenged all three measures before GATT.

The panel found the two taxes to be consistent, but the CAFE regulation to be inconsistent with the national treatment obligation in GATT Article III:2. It went on to examine whether the CAFE regulation would be covered by Article XX(g), as claimed by the US. The panel ruled that the establishment of minimum fuel economy standards and the calculation of fleet average fuel economy values served the purpose of fuel conservation and could therefore be subsumed under this article. However, it noted that the particular part of the CAFE regulation that required separate fuel economy accounting for foreign imported fleets of vehicles could not be considered as being covered by Article XX(g) since 'the evidence submitted to the Panel suggested that separate foreign fleet accounting primarily served to inhibit imports of small cars' (ibid, paragraph 5.60).

Assessment: From an environmental perspective, there is nothing wrong with this panel report. The panel clearly regarded the conservation of fuel as a valid public policy objective and merely objected to one specific detail of the regulation which discriminated against foreign imported cars. Not surprisingly, therefore, then US Trade Representative Mikey Kantor – that is, the representative of the party whose trade measure was challenged – welcomed the panel's report in saying:

> *The panel has emphatically rejected the European claim that trade-neutral legislation intended to further energy conserva-*

> *tion goals and protect the environment could be attacked... The panel's finding also confirms that GATT's trade rules can be compatible with our laws that conserve natural resources and protect the environment. This decision is a recognition that our government – and those of other countries – have latitude to legislate and regulate in these crucial areas as long as they are not discriminating between domestic and imported products.* (cited in GATT 1994a, p1397).

The panel report was never adopted by GATT due to EU objections – that is, due to objections by the challenging party – which supports the assessment that the panel has not unduly neglected environmental aspects in coming to its decision.

United States – Standards for reformulated and conventional gasoline

In April 1996, an appellate body overruled an earlier panel report concerning US regulation of fuels and fuel additives (WTO 1996b). The regulation was quite complicated, but in essence required refiners to supply cleaner fuels and fuel additives relative to 1990 baseline standards. However, whereas US refiners were allowed to invoke their individual 1990 baselines, foreign refiners could not qualify for individual baselines and were faced with statutory baselines reflecting average 1990 US petrol quality instead (ibid, pp4–6). Brazil and Venezuela had challenged the regulation before GATT.

The appellate body reversed the panel's finding and came to the conclusion that the baseline establishment rules were 'primarily aimed at' exhaustible resource conservation. The panel had made the error of examining whether the 'less favourable treatment' of imported petrol was 'primarily aimed at' resource conservation, rather than the trade measure itself – that is, the baseline establishment rules as required by the wording of Article XX (ibid, pp13–19). The appellate body also found that the rules were 'made effective in conjunction with restrictions on domestic production or consumption', giving this requirement of Article XX(g) quite a non-restrictive interpretation in saying that it 'is appropriately read as a requirement that the measures concerned impose restrictions, not just in respect of imported gasoline but also with respect to domestic gasoline' (ibid, pp20). The baseline standards were thus covered under Article XX(g).

The appellate body continued to analyse whether the baseline standards were also covered by the preamble of Article XX. It ruled that the US regulation constituted 'unjustifiable discrimination' and a 'disguised restriction on international trade'. As justification it stated that the US could have either made individual baselines available also to foreign refiners or required statutory baselines for domestic refiners as well, thus in both cases avoiding discrimination against foreign refiners (ibid, p25). It was not convinced by the US objection that individual baselines for foreign refiners would have generated insurmountable administrative problems, saying that the US had failed to engage in serious efforts to achieve cooperative agreements with the home countries of foreign refiners to reduce these costs. On the US argument that to require statutory baselines for domestic refiners as well would have been too costly for them, the appellate body had the following to say:

> *Clearly, the United States did not feel it feasible to require its domestic refiners to incur the physical and financial costs and burdens entailed by immediate compliance with a statutory baseline... At the same time we are bound to note that, while the United States counted the costs for its domestic refiners of statutory baselines, there is nothing in the record to indicate that it did other than disregard that kind of consideration when it came to foreign refiners.*

Assessment: From an environmental perspective, there is nothing wrong with the appellate body's decision as it clearly did not rule against the right of the US to impose regulation in order to make cleaner fuels and fuel additives compulsory. It merely demanded that foreign and domestic suppliers of these fuels and fuel additives were treated on equal terms in either allowing individual 1990 baseline standards to all of them or requiring statutory baselines for all of them.

The reaction of the US government has consequently been rather modest, even though the appellate body, in substance, ruled against it. The then acting US trade representative Charlene Barshefsky said that the appellate body decision contained 'a number of positive messages about WTO rules and protection of the environment' (cited in Charnovitz 1996). The report became adopted on 20 May 1996. The United States Environmental Protection Agency has now agreed to evaluate foreign refiners on their individual baselines for minimum clean air standards as well, in order to remove the unequal treatment and to comply with the WTO ruling (ICTSD 1999d).

European Communities – Measures concerning meat and meat products (hormones)

In January 1998 an appellate body overruled an earlier panel report on European Communities (EC) measures concerning meat and meat products (hormones) (WTO 1998c). The US and Canada had challenged the EC import ban on beef from cattle raised with growth hormones. The appellate body in principle upheld the earlier panel ruling that the import ban violated provisions of Article 5 of the Agreement on the Application of Sanitary and Phytosanitary Measures (SPS Agreement), which forms part of the WTO system.

Contrary to the panel, however, the appellate body accepted

> *that the predominant motivation for both the prohibition of the*
> *domestic use of growth promotion hormones and the prohibi-*
> *tion of importation of treated meat, is the protection of the*
> *health and safety of its population. No suggestion has been*
> *made that the import prohibition of treated meat was the result*
> *of lobbying by EC domestic producers of beef* (ibid, paragraph
> 244).

The appellate body therefore overruled the panel which had found the import prohibition to result in 'discrimination or a disguised restriction on international trade' in the meaning of Article 5.5 of the SPS Agreement. However, according to the rules laid down in this agreement this is not enough to render SPS measures consistent with the agreement. In addition, the enacted measures must also be based on a risk assessment (see p29). On this point, the appellate body ruled, as the panel did before, that the scientific reports the EC had put forward as a risk assessment 'do not rationally support the EC import prohibition' (ibid, paragraph 197) and that for one specific growth hormone the EC had not put forward any risk assessment at all (ibid, paragraph 201). Consequently, it affirmed 'the ultimate conclusion of the Panel that the EC import prohibition is not based on a risk assessment within the meaning of Articles 5.1 and 5.2 of the SPS Agreement and is, therefore, inconsistent with the requirements of Article 5.1' (ibid, paragraph 208).

In three other important aspects it overruled the earlier panel decision in favour of a country imposing an SPS measure, however. First, it overruled the panel's finding that the prima facie burden of proof rests with the party imposing an SPS measure. Instead, it ruled that the party challenging the measure needs to provide prima facie evidence for the lack of a risk assessment. Only then is the burden of proof on the defending party to demonstrate that one way or the other the SPS measure is consistent with WTO rules (ibid, paragraphs 97–109). Second, the appellate body made clear that a risk assessment need not establish a minimum quantifiable magnitude of risk (ibid, paragraph 186) and that such an assessment need not be confined to quantifiable risks (ibid, paragraph 187). Third, the appellate body ruled that risk assessors may take into account the risks arising 'from potential abuse in the administration of controlled substances and from control problems', noting that the studies had found the application of the hormones to be safe merely for cases in which 'the hormones are administered in accordance with the requirements of good veterinary practice' (ibid, paragraph 206). The problem was that the European Communities had not provided an assessment of the risks involved in the use of growth hormones contrary to good veterinary practice.

As concerns the so-called precautionary principle, the appellate body's ruling confirmed the precarious standing of the principle within the WTO system.[7] The reader should recall that the precautionary principle is not explicitly integrated into the agreement, is only indirectly referred to and that it can only be invoked provisionally to suspend the requirement to provide a risk assessment. The appellate body, maybe not surprisingly, did nothing to strengthen the role of the principle. While refraining from making an explicit judgement on the status of the precautionary principle in international law, in tendency the appellate body seemed to side with those who dispute that the precautionary principle is internationally and widely accepted as a general or customary international law, noting 'that the precautionary principle, at least outside the field of international environmental law, still awaits authoritative formulation' (ibid, paragraph 123). Furthermore, it made clear that the precautionary principle cannot be invoked to absolve a country imposing an SPS measure from undertaking a risk assessment, in stating that 'the principle has not been written into the SPS Agreement as a ground for justifying SPS measures that are otherwise inconsistent with the obligations of Members set out in particular provisions of that Agreement' (ibid, paragraph 124).

In spite of the WTO having authorized the US to impose trade sanctions worth US$191.4 million against it, the European Union has refused to lift the ban. It now seeks to establish a comprehensive risk assessment with regards to hormone-treated beef. It has not given a deadline for when such an assessment is likely to become concluded. To avoid trade sanctions it has offered the US to compensate it for lost export revenues via increasing the US quota for exports of hormone-free beef into the EU (ICTSD 2000a). At the time of writing, this was still subject to ongoing negotiations. The EU is keen on avoiding trade sanctions as the US, controversially and possibly in violation of WTO rules, has threatened to impose cross-retaliatory sanctions in a carousel manner, periodically imposing sanctions on different groups of non-beef related products so as to maximize the likelihood of inflicting damage on EU export interests.

Assessment: The panel and appellate body have made a formally correct decision in the sense that their dismissal of the EU import ban on the grounds that the ban is not based on a risk assessment is in accordance with the SPS Agreement. However, the decision is nevertheless wrong from an environmental perspective, which means that the SPS Agreement itself is flawed. The reason for this flaw is that the agreement does not integrate the precautionary principle sufficiently. It is not even explicitly incorporated in the SPS Agreement, but merely indirectly referred to. Furthermore, WTO members may only provisionally suspend the requirement to provide a risk assessment on the grounds that there exists insufficient scientific information to judge the danger of allowing a certain good into its home market. In my view at least, the SPS Agreement as part of the WTO system therefore needs to be reformed so that the precautionary principle is fully incorporated. This policy recommendation is justified at the end of this chapter.

Australia – Measures affecting importation of salmon

In October 1998, an appellate body ruled on the import ban of fresh, chilled or frozen – that is, uncooked – salmon which had been imposed by Australia since 1975. The dispute was initiated by Canada, which has a formidable salmon export interest. Australia had justified the import ban by saying that it was trying to prevent the entry of fish diseases that were hitherto non-existent domestically into Australian salmon stocks. The appellate body overturned the panel, which had found the heat-treatment – that is, cooking – requirement rather than the import prohibition to be the sanitary or phytosanitary (SPS) measure in question. Nevertheless, it came to the same legal conclusion that Australia's so-called '1996 Final Report' could not be regarded a proper risk assessment within the meaning of Article 5.1 of the SPS Agreement as it did not properly evaluate 'the likelihood of entry, establishment or spread of a pest or disease ... and of the potential associated biological and economic consequences' as required by the definition of risk assessment contained in paragraph 4 of the Agreement's Annex A (WTO 1998f, paragraphs 131 and 135). In justification it relied on the Panel's factual findings

> that the 1996 Final Report ... lends more weight to the unknown and uncertain elements of the assessment than the 1995 Draft Report (on which the 1996 Final Report is based). This, on occasions, results in general and vague statements of mere possibility of adverse effects occurring; statements which constitute neither a quantitative nor a qualitative assessment of probability (ibid, paragraph 129).

In its evaluation of whether Australia's import ban had furthermore violated Article 5:5 of the SPS Agreement which states that '...each Member shall avoid arbitrary or unjustifiable distinctions in the levels it considers to be appropriate in different situations, if such distinctions result in discrimination or a disguised restriction on international trade', the appellate body upheld three important findings of the panel. First, it agreed with the panel that Australia had failed to impose the same comprehensive SPS measure on the import of herring used as bait and live ornamental finfish, even though evidence showed that the risk of importing foreign diseases was higher with respect to herring than with salmon. It regarded this differential treatment as 'arbitrary or unjustifiable' in the sense of Article 5.5 (ibid, paragraph 155). Second, it upheld the panel's finding that 'the substantial, but unexplained change in conclusion between the 1995 Draft Report [which recommended allowing the importation of ocean-caught Pacific salmon under certain conditions] and the 1996 Final Report [which recommended continuing the import prohibition]' (ibid, paragraph 170), together with 'the absence of controls on the internal movement of salmon products within Australia compared to the prohibition of the importation of ocean-caught Pacific salmon' (ibid, paragraph 174), provided not in itself and in isolation, but taken together, sufficient accumulative proof that the SPS measure also resulted in a 'disguised restriction on international trade' (ibid, paragraph 177).

The appellate body in this case made two important rulings in favour of a country imposing an SPS measure. First, it ruled that in examining whether an SPS measure should be regarded as 'more trade-restrictive than required' in the sense of Article 5.6 of the SPS Agreement, it was not for the panel to 'substitute its own reasoning about the implied level of protection for that expressed consistently by Australia' (ibid, paragraph 199) in finding the reference point for what is required. Expressed even more clearly: 'The determination of the appropriate level of protection ... is a *prerogative* of the Member concerned and not of a panel or of the Appellate Body' (ibid, emphasis in original). Second, and going one step further, it ruled that the country imposing an SPS measure can determine its own appropriate level of protection to be 'zero risk', if the 'risk' to be evaluated in a risk assessment is an ascertainable risk and not merely a theoretical uncertainty (ibid, paragraph 125).

Australia and Canada reached an agreement in May 2000 on how to implement the ruling of the appellate body. In exchange for Canada's consent not to seek WTO authorization for retaliatory trade sanctions against it, Australia has accepted removing its import ban of uncooked salmon. Instead, it wants to prevent the introduction of exogenous diseases into its salmon stocks via processing, packaging and certification standards that foreign salmon exporters have to obey (ICTSD 2000j). What complicates the situation is that the small Australian island state of Tasmania, which is particularly rich in salmon, has vowed to stick to the import ban of any uncooked foreign salmon. This has created tensions between the Tasmanian and the federal government. At the time of writing, talks were still ongoing without a conclusion in sight. It seems unlikely, however, that Canada would seek authorization for trade sanctions if the small state of Tasmania stuck to non-compliance of the WTO appellate body report's recommendations.

Assessment: The appellate body's finding that the import ban amounts to a 'disguised restriction on international trade' because of the change in conclusion between the 1995 Draft Report and the 1996 Final Report, together with the absence of similar controls within the Australian territory, is to be rejected. It would be foolish to presume that the generation of a risk assessment cannot evolve over time and that a government is bound to the conclusions that a mere draft report had found earlier on. To require time consistency in the process of policy formation would establish a non-justifiable intrusion of WTO rules into the sovereignty of member countries to formulate their policies. Similarly, it is inappropriate to require SPS measures within Australia to be as comprehensive as SPS measures aimed at imports into Australian territory, when many of the diseases the SPS measures are meant to prevent from entering Australia are not existent domestically so far.[8]

However, the appellate body was correct in ruling that the failure to impose the same comprehensive SPS measure on the import of herring as on the import of salmon is to be regarded as 'arbitrary or unjustifiable'.[9] Otherwise, a government could choose to impose comprehensive SPS measures only on those products in which international competition is fierce, even if the risk to be prevented is much lower than with respect to products in which international competition is less significant. As mentioned above, evidence showed that the risk of importing foreign diseases was higher with respect to herring, for which no similar trade ban existed, than salmon, which is a much more economically lucrative and competitive fish product.

European Communities – Measures affecting asbestos and products containing asbestos

On 9 October 1998, Canada requested the establishment of a dispute panel concerning the French ban on asbestos and products containing asbestos. Canada alleges that 'the prohibition by France of, inter alia, the manufacture, processing, import, placing on the domestic market, possession for sale, sale or transfer on any ground of asbestos and any product containing asbestos severely damages Canada's economic interests...' in violation of, inter alia, Article 2 of the TBT Agreement (WTO 1998h). Canada is the world's second largest producer and largest exporter of chrysotile asbestos (BNA 1999g).

In spite of the case still pending then, the European Union published the directive 1999/77/EC banning the use of chrysotile asbestos fibres and products containing them by January 2005. Chrysotile asbestos is the only form of asbestos still allowed within the EU, which argues that the ban is necessary because 'no threshold level of exposure has been identified below which chrysotile asbestos does not pose carcinogenic risks' (BNA 1999g). The EU's Scientific Committee on Toxicity, Ecotoxicity and the Environment will review the scientific evidence on this form of asbestos again and will decide on possible exceptions to the ban.

In September 2000, a panel decided in favour of the EU and upheld the French ban on imports as being justified under Article XX(b) of GATT (WTO 2000b). It ruled that asbestos fibres and non-asbestos fibres should be considered 'like products' in the meaning of GATT Article III and that the French ban on asbestos imports therefore violated this article (ibid, paragraph 8.150 and 8.158). It defended this ruling in stating that the different health impacts of asbestos and non-asbestos fibres must not influence a judgement on whether two products are considered like as it 'would largely nullify the effect of Article XX(b)' and 'would allow the Member concerned to avoid the obligations in Article XX, particularly the test of necessity for the measure under paragraph (b) and the control exerted by the introductory clause to Article XX concerning any abuse of Article XX(b) when applying the measure' (ibid, paragraph 8.130).

Once it decided that the import ban violated Article III of GATT, the panel had to move on to examine whether the violation could be justified with recourse to one of the exemptions contained in Article XX. The panel assessed whether the ban was 'necessary' in the meaning of Article XX(b), adopting the interpretation of the term from the panel report in the 'Thailand – Restrictions on importation of and internal taxes on cigarettes' case (see above). It concluded that there was no reasonably available alternative measure consistent with or less inconsistent with WTO obligations that France could have adopted, rejecting handling regulations (Canada's preferred option) as inadequate health protection measures (ibid, paragraph 8.222). Thus the import ban was covered by Article XX(b) of GATT and the panel had to progress to examining the chapeau of Article XX. It found that the import ban did not constitute 'arbitrary or unjustifiable discrimination between countries where the same conditions prevail' or a 'disguised restriction on international trade' and therefore satisfied the requirements of the chapeau (ibid, paragraph 8.241).

Canada appealed against the panel's ruling. In March 2001 the appellate body overruled the panel's decision (WTO, 2001). It rejected the panel's finding that the ban does not constitute a technical regulation within the meaning of the TBT Agreement. However, because it is not allowed to start a new process of fact finding, the appellate body saw itself unable to assess the ban with reference to the TBT Agreement (ibid, paragraph 83). Instead, it exclusively examined the compatibility of the ban with GATT rules. Noting that the 'carcinogenicity, or toxicity, constitutes ... a defining aspect of the physical properties of chysotile asbestos fibres' (ibid, paragraph 114), it rejected the panel's finding that asbestos fibres and non-asbestos fibres should be considered like products: 'We do not see how this highly significant physical difference *cannot* be a consideration in examining the physical properties of a product as part of a determination of "likeness" under Article III:4 of the GATT 1994' (ibid, emphasis in original). Thus the ban did not violate any WTO rules. In the alternative, it confirmed that the ban could be justified with recourse to Article XX(b) if it did violate Article III.

Assessment: Environmental NGOs heavily criticised the panel report for considering asbestos and non-asbestos fibres like products (Field et al, 2001). Since the appellate body has overruled the panel's decision, this critique does no longer apply. The appellate body has made the right decision.

Measures aimed at non-product related environmental effects

As concerns trade restrictions which aim at non-product related environmental effects, three major decisions have been made by trade panels and appellate bodies, respectively.

United States – Restrictions on imports of tuna (Tuna I)

In August 1991, a panel ruled on the by now famous case of US import restrictions of tuna caught with purse-seine nets which resulted in the incidental killing of dolphins in excess of the killing rate of US fishing vessels (GATT 1993). Substantial killing of dolphins can occur in the Eastern Tropical Pacific Ocean only, where schools of tuna and dolphin swim together and fishermen can intentionally encircle dolphin schools to catch tuna (Körber 2000). The restrictions were based on the US Marine Mammal Protection Act (MMPA). Mexico challenged the import prohibitions before GATT as its fishermen did employ purse-seine nets with a dolphin mortality rate in excess of the US fleet, and consequently Mexican fishermen were banned from exporting tuna to the US.

The fundamental question to be decided was whether the US had the right to invoke Article XX(b) of the GATT to impose trade measures because of the effects that non-product related process and production methods outside its own jurisdiction have on the environment – an issue that will be examined in more detail below. The panel declared the US import restrictions inconsistent with its GATT obligations and not covered by one of the general exceptions in Article XX. The panel report was circulated among GATT members on 3 September 1991, but Mexico, the complainant country, did not find it politically opportune to press for adoption at the time of the then still ongoing NAFTA negotiations (Hudec 1996, p167, footnote 107). Even if it had, the US would certainly have objected to the report's adoption.

Apart from the question of whether the US had the right to enact trade measures because of PPMs outside its own jurisdiction, the panel made two important observations in interpreting the requirement of necessity in Article XX(b). First, it seemed to imply that this requirement imposes the duty on the enacting country to demonstrate

> *that it had exhausted all options reasonably available to it to pursue its dolphin protection objectives through measures consistent with the General Agreement, in particular through the negotiation of international cooperative arrangements, which would seem to be desirable in view of the fact that dolphins roam the waters of many states and the high seas* (GATT 1993, paragraph 5.28).

Second, it seemed to superimpose the 'arbitrary or unjustifiable discrimination' test from the preamble to Article XX on the interpretation of the necessity requirement of Article XX(b):

> *The United States linked the maximum incidental dolphin taking rate which Mexico had to meet during a particular period in order to be able to export tuna to the United States to the taking rate actually recorded for United States fishermen*

during the same period. Consequently, the Mexican authorities could not know whether, at a given point of time, their policies conformed to the United States' dolphin protection standards. The Panel considered that a limitation on trade based on such unpredictable conditions could not be regarded as necessary to protect the health or life of dolphins (ibid).

Environmentalists critical of this ruling sometimes seem to overlook that the GATT dispute panel ruled in favour of the US on one important aspect. It upheld the Dolphin Protection Consumer Information Act which gave tuna processors access to a voluntary 'dolphin safe' label if they could demonstrate that the tuna was actually caught without harm to dolphins. In justification, the panel stated that because the labelling regulations applied to both domestic and foreign fishing boats, there was no discrimination (ibid, paragraph 5.43), given that 'any advantage which might possibly result from access to this label depends on the free choice of consumers to give preference to tuna carrying the "Dolphin Safe" label' (ibid, paragraph 5.42).

In April 2000 the US finally lifted the import ban on Mexican tuna after Mexico, due to political and economic pressure by the US, had decided to participate in the Agreement on the International Dolphin Conservation Programme (IDCP) and the US was satisfied with the Mexican implementation of it. Reports suggest that dolphin mortality in the Eastern Tropical Pacific Ocean has substantially decreased due to the IDCP. However, several environmental NGOs, led by the Earth Island Institute, have challenged the lifting of the embargo before the US Court of International Trade. While they have failed to achieve a temporary restraining order that would re-install the embargo until a final ruling of the Court, the case is still pending and no final decision has been taken. The same NGOs were more successful before a California District Court in a slightly different matter, however. In its ruling, this Court decided that the US government was not justified in changing its procedures for issuing 'dolphin-safe' labels. The US government, in accordance with the IDCP, had changed the labelling procedures from requiring that purse-seine nets should not be used in the process of tuna catching to allowing purse-seine nets if no dolphins were observed being killed or severely injured in the process of tuna catching. The US government has appealed against the ruling, but has decided to stick to the old procedures until a final ruling has been issued. This in turn has angered the Mexican government, which rightly fears that the lifting of the embargo will be rendered irrelevant as long as Mexican fishermen using purse-seine nets do not have access to 'dolphin-safe' labels, since tuna canneries and consumers are likely to insist on such labelling before buying tuna. It has threatened therefore to challenge what it regards as the non-implementation of the US side of the deal before the IDCP or the WTO, or even to withdraw completely from the IDCP (ICTSD 2000d). At the time of writing, no conclusion to this case was in sight.

United States – Restrictions on imports of tuna (Tuna II)

It is sometimes forgotten that there have actually been two panel rulings on 'United States – Restrictions on imports of tuna'. The second panel ruling came about because the US MMPA not only prohibited the direct importation of tuna caught with dolphin-unsafe technology, but also put an embargo on intermediate nations. In other words, it also prohibited the importation of, say, processed tuna from a third country if that country had itself imported tuna caught with dolphin-unsafe technology.

The European Economic Community and the Netherlands challenged this intermediate nations embargo before the GATT. The fundamental question to be decided was again whether the US had the right to invoke Article XX(b) of the GATT to regulate PPMs outside its own jurisdiction. As with the first panel, the second panel ruled that the US import restrictions were inconsistent with GATT and not covered under the general exceptions in Article XX (GATT 1994b). The panel report was circulated among GATT members on 16 June 1994, but was never adopted due to US objections. While the panels in the two tuna cases came to the same basic finding, there are also important interpretative differences with respect to the legality of extra-jurisdictional measures (see p139 for more detail).

United States – Import prohibition of certain shrimp and shrimp products

In possibly the most important ruling so far, an appellate body in October 1998 overruled an earlier panel report concerning the US import prohibition of certain shrimp and shrimp products (WTO 1998b). In essence, the US had prohibited the importation of these products from countries that were not certified by the US as employing harvesting methods that prevented the incidental killing of five species of sea turtles, the most common method being the use of so-called turtle excluder devices (TEDs). Without such methods, shrimp harvesting can lead to the substantial incidental killing of sea turtles, considered by the US to constitute 'the largest cause of human-induced sea turtle mortality' (WTO 1998a, paragraph 3.19). Puls (1999, p346) reports that before the US legislation, its domestic shrimp fishing led to the killing of 55,000 sea turtles annually. All seven currently recognized species of sea turtles are listed in Appendix 1 of the Convention on International Trade in Endangered Species of Wild Fauna and Flora (CITES), which means that they are considered as threatened with extinction and that their trade for commercial purposes is generally prohibited. India, Pakistan, Thailand and Malaysia suggested that they had undertaken measures to protect sea turtles other than TEDs, such as restrictions on egg harvesting and direct catch (WTO 1998a, paragraphs 3.4–3.16), and challenged the import prohibitions before the WTO. It is disputed whether sea turtles are highly migratory so that they cross national jurisdictions over waters beyond a regional scale (ibid, paragraphs 3.36–3.46).

The major issue at stake was yet again whether the US had the right unilaterally to impose trade measures because of non-product related PPMs outside its own jurisdiction. The appellate body ruled that the US import prohibitions were inconsistent with its WTO obligations and could not be covered under one of the general exceptions in GATT Article XX. The justification given for this ruling differs substantially from the two tuna panel rulings (see the next section below).

The appellate body was at pains to point out that it ruled against the way that the US imposed its own regulatory standards upon foreign countries, but that it did not rule against the need for protection for sea turtles. Indeed, the body reserved a full paragraph to emphasize this point:

> We have not *decided that the protection and preservation of the environment is of no significance to the Members of the WTO. Clearly, it is. We have* not *decided that the sovereign nations that are Members of the WTO cannot adopt effective measures to protect endangered species, such as sea turtles. Clearly, they can and should. And we have* not *decided that sovereign states should* not *act together bilaterally, plurilaterally or multilaterally, either within the WTO or in other international fora, to protect endangered species or to otherwise protect the environment. Clearly, they should and do* (WTO 1998b, paragraph 185, emphasis in original).

As an alternative to the unilateral imposition of import prohibitions, the appellate body strongly called for multilateral environmental agreements for the protection of endangered species (ibid, paragraph 166). In response to the appellate body report, the US has negotiated a non-binding Regional Agreement on the Conservation and Management of Marine Turtles and their Habitats in the Indian Ocean and South-East Asian Region with 22 countries, including the complainants. It also went from country-by-country certification to shipment-by-shipment certification, allowing shrimp imports if it can be proven that the shrimps on the ship have been caught without damage to sea turtles.[10] However, while not formally challenging this measure yet, it seems unlikely that the complainant countries will regard anything as compliant with the WTO ruling, short of removing the import ban on shrimp whatever the incidental sea turtle killing rate (ICTSD 2000c).[11] Indeed, Malaysia has already requested formal consultation with the US according to DSU rules on the matter (ICTSD 2000l).

The appellate body report was adopted on 6 November 1998. As the two tuna reports have never been adopted, the shrimp appellate body report in effect represents the only legally binding decision on the important question of whether countries can unilaterally impose trade restrictions because of the effects that foreign non-product related PPMs have on the environment, which is discussed in more detail below.

Chile – Port access restrictions

A further case involving trade measures aimed at non-product related environmental aspects was prevented at the last minute. It would have been the first time that a WTO panel would have had to decide on such a measure that was imposed by a developing country and challenged by developed countries. Indeed, it would have been the first time ever a developed party challenged the environmental regulations of a developing country more generally. (The GATT case 'Thailand – Restrictions on importation of and internal taxes on cigarettes' was about health regulations, not environmental regulations more narrowly defined.)

In 1991 Chile unilaterally banned imports of swordfish to protect dwindling South Pacific stocks. Chile also banned foreign ships from unloading swordfish catches in Chilean ports even if the catches were designated for third markets, not for Chile. Affected by this measure were, among others, EU vessels, especially Spanish ones. The EU argued that Chile is required to allow access to its ports according to Article V of GATT, which guarantees the free transit of goods through the territory of a WTO member. Chile claimed that its port restrictions are justified under GATT Article XX(g). It also argued that its measures were taken in pursuance of the United Nations Convention on the Law of the Sea (UNCLOS). Chile had invited the EU to let the dispute be decided by an arbitration tribunal according to UNCLOS rules. However, the EU seemed to prefer the WTO as a dispute venue, arguing that enforcement there is easier and the time limits on resolving the dispute tighter (ICTSD 2000b).

The EU had already submitted a request for the establishment of a panel and a number of countries with significant fisheries interests were accredited third-party status in the dispute. However, a settlement was reached on 25 January 2001 that allows limited access for EU vessels to Chilean ports and provides for bilateral and multilateral scientific and technical cooperation on the conservation of swordfish stocks (ICTSD 2001b).

Like products, PPMs and a country's jurisdictional reach

In the three relevant dispute settlements mentioned above, one question has been of overwhelming importance: if a country opposes non-product related PPMs by other countries outside its own jurisdiction, can it impose trade measures against those countries? This question actually breaks down into two separate questions. First, would these trade measures be in violation of the country's substantive WTO obligations? Second, if the answer to the first question is positive, could these measures still be justified with one of the exceptions of Article XX?

As concerns the first question, GATT and WTO panels have consistently ruled that trade measures against countries because of non-product related PPMs used by those countries violates the WTO obligations of the imposing country, in particular the national treatment obligation according to Article

III (and possibly also the most favoured nation treatment obligation according to Article I). This is because of the way the term 'like product' contained in these two articles has become interpreted. The clearest statement can be found in the Tuna I panel report. In this case, the US vigorously put forward its argument that its import prohibition of tuna caught with dolphin-unsafe technology was consistent with its national treatment obligations of Article III as it did not allow its own nationals to catch tuna without dolphin-safe nets and sell the tuna in the US market. The panel, however, found the US trade measures in violation of its national treatment obligations. Having noted that Article III only covered measures affecting products as such (GATT 1993, paragraph 5.11), it ruled that

> Article III:4 calls for a comparison of the treatment of imported tuna as a product with that of domestic tuna as a product. Regulations governing the taking of dolphins incidental to the taking of tuna could not possibly affect tuna as a product. Article III:4 therefore obliges the United States to accord treatment to Mexican tuna no less favourable than that accorded to United States tuna, whether or not the incidental taking of dolphins by Mexican vessels corresponds to that of United States vessels (ibid, paragraph 5.15, emphasis in original).

One can, of course, put the validity of the GATT panel's reasoning into doubt. If individuals care about whether the tuna they eat was caught in a dolphin-safe or unsafe way, then for them dolphin-safe tuna is obviously unlike dolphin-unsafe tuna. However, such counter-reasoning does not convince GATT/WTO panels. As Howse and Regan (2000, p2) note, the distinction between trade measures imposed because of the characteristics of a foreign product itself and trade measures imposed because of other countries' PPMs of their products has become 'conventional wisdom' and 'all process-based measures not directly related to physical characteristics of the product itself, are prima facie violations of GATT and therefore illegal unless they are justified under Article XX'. As the answer to the first question is therefore positive, we have to turn to the second question: Can trade measures imposed because of other countries' non-product related PPMs be justified under one of the general exceptions in Article XX? The answer is: yes in theory, no in practice. To understand why, the relevant issues need to be examined step by step.

Contrary to a common misunderstanding, it is not the extra-jurisdictional reach of PPM-related trade measures as such that renders them inconsistent with Article XX. On this important aspect, the GATT panel rulings in the two tuna cases clearly differed from each other. Whereas the panel in the Tuna I case came to the conclusion that the negotiation record 'indicates that the concerns of the drafters of Article XX(b) focused on the use of sanitary measures to safeguard life or health of humans, animals or plants within the jurisdiction of the importing country' (GATT 1993, paragraph 5.25ff), the panel in the Tuna II case rejected such a narrow interpretation. Instead, it observed that neither Article XX(b) nor Article XX(g) respectively limit the location of the 'human, animal or plant life or health' to be protected or the location of 'exhaustible natural resources' to be conserved. It therefore came to the conclusion that GATT rules do not proscribe 'in an absolute manner measures that related to things or actions outside the territorial jurisdiction of the party taking the measure' (GATT 1994b, paragraph 5.16). In coming to this conclusion, the panel specifically referred to Article XX(e), which excepts measures 'relating to the products of prison labour' from the substantive GATT obligations. Consequently, it 'could see no valid reason supporting the conclusion that the provisions of Article XX(g) apply only to policies related to the conservation of exhaustible natural resources located within the territory of the contracting party invoking the provision' (ibid, paragraph 5.20). According to the panel, this reasoning applies equally to Article XX(b) (ibid, paragraph 5.30).

It follows that it is not the extra-jurisdictional reach of trade measures as such that puts trade measures imposed because of other countries' nonproduct related PPMs outside the allowed exceptions contained in Article XX. Instead it is the fact that these trade measures are imposed *because* of other countries' PPMs. This is because, according to the Tuna II panel ruling, such trade measures could only achieve their conservation objectives if other countries were to change their PPMs. In other words, they could only achieve their objective if the trade measures had some coercive effect on other countries to change their conservation policies. According to the panel, such a coercive effect could not be justified under the Article XX exceptions, however. It ruled that if

> *Article XX were interpreted to permit contracting parties to take trade measures to implement policies, including conservation policies, within their own jurisdiction, the basic objective of the General Agreement would be maintained. If however Article XX were interpreted to permit contracting parties to take trade measures so as to force other contracting parties to change their policies within their jurisdiction, including their conservation policies, the balance of rights and obligations among contracting parties, in particular the right of access to markets, would be seriously impaired. Under such an interpretation the General Agreement could no longer serve as a multilateral framework for trade among contracting parties* (ibid, paragraph 5.26).

This ruling echoed a similar finding of the Tuna I panel. While the panel was at pains to assure that 'the provisions of the General Agreement impose few constraints on a contracting party's implementation of domestic environmental policies' (GATT 1993, paragraph 6.2), the panel was equally clear in ruling that trade measures with the intended coercive effect on other countries' policies are not covered by Article XX(b) as otherwise

> *each contracting party could unilaterally determine the life or health protection policies from which other contracting parties could not deviate without jeopardizing their rights under the General Agreement. The General Agreement would then no longer constitute a multilateral framework for trade among all contracting parties but would provide legal security only in respect of trade between a limited number of contracting parties with identical internal regulations* (ibid, paragraph 5.27).

However, the rulings in the two tuna cases are not legally binding interpretations of GATT rules with respect to trade measures against countries because of non-product related PPMs used by those countries. This is because none of the two panel reports became formally adopted by GATT, even though both panel rulings have received general support from 39 of the 40 GATT members taking a position (the fortieth being the US itself) (Hudec 1996, p117).[12]

The panel in the shrimp case had argued very similarly to the panel reports in the two tuna cases and even referred explicitly to the second tuna case in support of its reasoning, noting that while unadopted panel reports 'have no legal status in the GATT or WTO system ... a panel can nevertheless *find useful guidance in the reasoning of an unadopted panel report that it considers to be relevant*' (WTO 1998a, p287, footnote 652, emphasis in original). Not surprisingly, then, the panel found that the US regulation would 'undermine the WTO multilateral trading system' and could thus not be permitted under Article XX of the GATT (WTO 1998a, paragraph 7.44 and 7.62).

The appellate body, however, fully rejected this finding, noting that to maintain the multilateral trading system 'is not a right or an obligation, nor is it an interpretative rule which can be employed in the appraisal of a given measure under the chapeau of Article XX' (WTO 1998b, paragraph 116). Furthermore, without even mentioning either tuna case, it ruled in a noteworthy reversal of the two prior rulings that

> [I]t appears to us, however, that conditioning access to a Member's domestic market on whether exporting Members comply with, or adopt a policy or policies unilaterally prescribed by the importing Member may, to some degree, be a common aspect of measures falling within the scope of one or another of the exceptions (a) to (j) of Article XX. ... It is not necessary to assume that requiring from exporting countries compliance with, or adoption of, certain policies (although

> *covered in principle by one or another of the exceptions)*
> *prescribed by the importing country, render a measure a priori*
> *incapable of justification under Article XX. Such an interpreta-*
> *tion renders most, if not all, of the specific exceptions of Article*
> *XX inutile, a result abhorrent to the principles of interpretation*
> *we are bound to apply* (ibid, paragraph 121, italics in original).

After establishing that the imposition of trade measures because of PPMs outside a country's own jurisdiction can in principle be covered by Article XX, the appellate body went on to examine whether the US import ban violated the preamble of Article XX. It ruled that the ban amounted to an 'unjustifiable discrimination between countries where the same conditions prevail', stating that the 'most conspicuous flaw in this measure's application relates to its intended and actual coercive effect on the specific policy decisions made by foreign governments ... to adopt *essentially the same* policy (together with an approved enforcement program) as that applied to, and enforced on, United States domestic shrimp trawlers' (ibid, paragraph 161, emphasis in original). Further, it noted that the ban also affected '*shrimp caught using methods identical to those employed in the United States* ... solely because they have been caught in waters of *countries that have not been certified by the United States*' (ibid, paragraph 165, emphasis in original). The appellate body further pointed out that while the US had negotiated and concluded the Inter-American Convention as a regional international agreement for the protection of sea turtles, no serious efforts were undertaken to negotiate similar agreements with the complaining countries; this is in spite of the fact that Section 609(a) of the 1989 Sea Turtle Conservation Amendment to the US Endangered Species Act required the Secretary of State to initiate negotiations with all relevant foreign shrimp-harvesting nations.

Due to this and some other aspects of the regulation, the appellate body judged that the regulation

> *imposes a single, rigid and unbending requirement that*
> *countries applying for certification ... adopt a comprehensive*
> *regulatory programme that is essentially the same as the United*
> *States' program, without inquiring into the appropriateness of*
> *that program for the conditions prevailing in the exporting*
> *countries* (ibid, paragraph 177).

The appellate body also ruled that the US import ban amounted to 'arbitrary discrimination' as it found that the 'certification processes followed by the United States (...) appear to be singularly informal and casual' so that foreign countries could not be certain that they were 'applied in a fair and just manner' (ibid, paragraph 181).

So what is the end result of this rather lengthy inquiry into the relevant GATT and WTO case law? In principle, unilaterally imposed trade measures against countries because of their non-product related PPMs can be justified by one of the environmental exemptions in GATT Article XX. The extra-jurisdictional reach of such measures as such does not render them GATT-inconsistent. However, the requirements for unilateral non-product related trade measures to be GATT consistent are quite stringent and difficult to meet. According to the appellate body in the shrimp case, the US would have had to engage in bilateral or multilateral negotiations with shrimp-harvesting countries (ibid, paragraph 166). Only if these had proven to be unsuccessful could the US have introduced unilateral measures which would have needed to be designed so that differing conditions in different countries are taken into account (ibid, paragraphs 163–165), that all countries are granted the same 'phase-in' periods (ibid, paragraph 174), that the US undertakes the same effort in transferring sea-turtle-safe harvesting technology to all relevant parties (ibid, paragraph 175), and that the certification process is transparent and allows affected countries to be heard and to appeal against non-certification (ibid, paragraph 180). The appellate body in the shrimp case thus opened the theoretical possibility for the imposition of trade measures because of other countries' PPMs to be consistent with WTO rules. It seems fair to say, however, that at the same time it put up so many conditions that such measures would need to fulfil that in practice it would be quite difficult for them to pass scrutiny. But it remains true that these measures are not a priori GATT-inconsistent, which represents an important reversal of earlier rulings which render the relevant sections of the two tuna panel reports obsolete. In response, the government of Thailand, one of the successful challengers of the US legislation, aired the somewhat exaggerated concern that this finding could lead to 'an explosive growth in the number of environmental ... measures applied to PPMs and justified pursuant to Article XX' (cited in Richards and McCrory 2000, p335).

Assessment: The appellate body's intended clarification in the shrimp/sea turtle case on the issue of whether and, if so, how countries can impose unilateral trade measures because of PPMs of other WTO members has not been very helpful. In allowing these measures in theory, but putting up so many conditions that they would be hard to fulfil in practice, the appellate body has achieved more confusion than clarity. Instead of putting up clear rules, the appellate body has opened the possibility for extensive discussions on whether or not these conditions are fulfilled in future looming trade disputes. In my view, it would have been better to declare clearly such unilateral measures as violating WTO rules. I will argue for this position in more detail in the following section. However, I should state here that such a dismissal of the unilateral imposition of such trade measures should go hand in hand with a strengthening of the status of MEAs vis-à-vis WTO rules – a topic which will be taken up in the next chapter.

Policy recommendations

Making the dispute settlement process open and transparent

The DSU should be reformed in order to make the dispute settlement process more open and transparent.[13] Parties to the settlement process should be required to publish their submissions to a WTO panel or appellate body, hearings should be open to the public, all decisions should be published immediately and environmental and other stakeholder groups with a valid interest in the subject matter should be allowed to send so-called amicus curiae briefs to the panels for their consideration if they choose to do so. As mentioned above, the latter has already been made possible by a decision of the appellate body, but since developing countries have criticized that the appellate body had no right to interpret the existing DSU in this way, it would be appropriate to make this point explicit in a DSU reform.

The justification for the proposition to make the dispute settlement process more open and transparent is basically the same as the one given for the analogous proposition with respect to NAFTA's investor-to-state dispute settlement process in Chapter 5: if foreign countries challenge environmental policies enacted by, at least ideally, democratically elected and publicly accountable policy-makers, then the public should have the right to gain access to all relevant information at all stages. Doing so will also help the WTO to gain an increased acceptability as a more open and transparent dispute settlement process automatically defeats allegations of a hidden conspiracy against democratically enacted environmental policies.

The prospects for more openness and transparency in WTO dispute settlement are far from bright. On the specific and rather limited aspect of amicus curiae briefs practically all developing countries argue that they should be prohibited. They criticize the various dispute panels and appellate bodies for permitting them and call for a change of the DSU to explicitly prevent panels from considering them. Even among developed countries support for allowing amicus curiae briefs is at best lukewarm, with the notable exception of Canada and the United States (BNA 2000g).

The major argument of the opponents of such briefs is that even WTO members do not have the right to submit statements if they are not parties to the dispute. This argument is rather weak, however, as any WTO member with a substantial interest in the dispute matter can be registered as a third party, thus reserving its right to be heard by the panel and to submit written statements (Article 10 of DSU). Contrary to amicus curiae briefs, panels and appellate bodies do not have the right to ignore these third party statements. Furthermore, if such briefs became allowed, WTO members, even those that were not granted third party status, could of course submit them as well.

Ironically, while several panels and appellate bodies have expressed their general willingness to accept such briefs, in practice they have been extremely restrictive in actually accepting them. The appellate body in the case

'European Communities – Measures affecting asbestos and asbestos-containing products', for example, after inviting such briefs and laying down formal guidelines that they must comply with, summarily rejected all briefs submitted, stating that they had failed to comply with those guidelines (ICTSD 2000o). Not surprisingly, this decision was heavily criticized by the NGOs which had submitted briefs. As Aimee Gonzales, WWF International Senior Policy Advisor, has put it: 'What the WTO gave with one hand, it took with the other. We were encouraged by the WTO's invitation as a sign that it might have finally got the message about the importance of civil society participation. To then be summarily refused without reasons shows gross indifference to the interests of our constituencies and lack of due process' (quoted in ibid). A number of NGOs had therefore appealed unsuccessfully to the WTO appellate body to accept its brief (FIELD et al 2001).

Interpretative statement of GATT Article XX(b) and XX(g)

According to Article IX:2 of the Agreement Establishing the WTO, the Ministerial Conference and the General Council of the WTO 'have the exclusive authority to adopt interpretations of this Agreement and of the Multilateral Trade Agreements'.[14] A Ministerial or General Council Statement should provide an interpretation of GATT Article XX with respect to the following aspects.

- The term 'relate to' in Article XX(g) should be understood and interpreted by WTO panels and appellate bodies according to its everyday usage as 'have reference to' or 'be connected to' (*Oxford Concise Dictionary*), not as the more restrictive 'primarily aimed at', which found its way into GATT/WTO case law for the first time in the panel report on 'Canada – Measures affecting exports of unprocessed herring and salmon'. It is important to note that such a clarification would not open the floodgates for abusing protectionist measures under green disguise. This is because while such an interpretation will make it easier for disputed measures to be covered by Article XX(g) itself, they would still need to pass the test contained in the preamble to Article XX that measures must not constitute 'a means of arbitrary or unjustifiable discrimination ... or a disguised restriction on international trade'.

- Following the panel report on 'Thailand – Restrictions on importation of and internal taxes on cigarettes', the term 'necessary' in Article XX(b) has consistently been interpreted by panels and appellate bodies as requiring that 'no alternative measure consistent with the General Agreement, or less consistent with it' exist, which the challenged country could 'reasonably be expected to employ'. In principle, this interpretation seems to be justified. However, it should be made clear that measures consistent with GATT or less inconsistent with it can only qualify as alternatives if they achieve the environmental objective as effectively as the measure in dispute. Such an interpretation would be in line with, for example, similar provisions in the SPS Agreement. A footnote to its Article 5:6 clarifies that 'a measure is not more trade-restrictive than required unless there is another measure reasonably available, taking into account technical and economic feasibility, that achieves the appropriate level of sanitary or phytosanitary protection and is significantly less restrictive to trade'. As another example, consider NAFTA's exception clause for MEAs, where measures can only be considered alternatives if they are 'equally effective and reasonably available' (Article 104:1).

A plea against unilateral action with respect to foreign non-product related PPMs

Should countries be allowed unilaterally to impose trade measures on other countries because of their non-product related PPMs? We have seen earlier that the ruling of the appellate body's decision in the shrimp/turtle case suggests that while doing so might be consistent with WTO rules in theory, it set up so many conditions to fulfil that, in actual reality, hardly any measure would be deemed consistent. In this section I will go one step further and argue that it would have been best if the appellate body had clearly ruled out the legality of such unilateral action. I do realize, of course, that after this body's ruling it is unrealistic to expect that such explicit ruling out of unilateral action – for example, via a Ministerial Declaration – will become enshrined in WTO rules as at least the US, the world's foremost proponent of the merits of unilateral action, would never consent. Nevertheless, it is of great interest to assess the case in favour of and against unilateral action.

Types of environmental effects caused by PPMs

First, the type of non-product related PPM that is under consideration needs to be clarified. PPMs can have three different environmental effects: first, they can lead to environmental effects which are purely limited to the producing country; second, they can lead to environmental spill-over effects into specified third countries; third, they can lead to environmental spill-over effects on a global scale. Note that the spill-over effects need not be physical; they could be psychological as well. By this, it is meant that, for example, the cruel treatment of animals within the national boundaries of one country can have spill-over effects as individuals in other countries suffer from knowing about this cruel treatment. In the following it will be assumed that unilateral action is targeted towards PPMs that have environmental spill-over effects into third countries or on a global scale. This is because if the environmental effect is purely domestic, there is much less justification for unilateral action to start with. In other words, only the case that is most favourable to unilateral action is examined.

Arguments in favour of unilateral action

Paternalism grounded in superiority. This argument is the crudest and most difficult to defend in favour of unilateral action. It simply says that we (the domestic country, the developed world) know better than they (the foreign country, the developing world) do. Some of the extreme adversity of developing countries against allowing unilateral action, which would be mostly exercised by developed countries, might stem from their perception that such action is grounded in a paternalism that has its roots in Northern countries' domination of the world and alleged superiority from times of colonialism and imperialism. Developing countries' political leaders are simply fed up of being told by Northerners what they have to do and how they have to behave with respect to any issue, and hence with respect to the environment as well.

Paternalism grounded in altruism. A more sophisticated paternalistic argument in favour of unilateral action has been put forward by Maestad (1998). It says that if foreign governments disregard the environmental preferences of their own people, then our unilateral action will help these people to satisfy their preferences against the will of their political leaders. The problem with this argument is that it would be difficult to find many people in developing countries who would be grateful for such kind altruistic paternalism from developed countries. Martin Khor, for example, Director of Third World Network, is possibly the most prominent representative of a developing country NGO and an outspoken critic of the WTO, but an equally outspoken critic of unilateral action with respect to nonproduct related PPMs.

Domestic efficiency. This argument says that unilateral action is justified because it satisfies domestic environmental preferences. If Americans do not like the incidental killing of dolphins and sea turtles, and Europeans are aroused by the pain endured by leg-hold trapped fur animals outside their own jurisdiction, then imposing unilateral trade measures is a means to satisfy these preferences. As Chang (1995, p2184) has put it succinctly: 'Through these measures, we are merely trying to optimize our own production and consumption decisions: if the benefits to us (in terms of the public good of dolphins saved) exceed the costs we incur (flowing from higher tuna prices), then there has been an improvement in economic efficiency.' Note that this argument does not depend on individuals in any other country holding the same values as it disregards any but domestic preferences. The total disregard for non-domestic preferences becomes clear in the following quotation by Howse and Regan (2000, pp28ff):

> ... *the use of turtle-unfriendly methods by foreign fishermen creates the very same externality, and efficiency requires that that externality also be internalized, both (a) to avoid the ineffi-*

cient killing of turtles and (b) because if foreign fishermen are allowed to impose an externality which domestic fishermen are required to internalize, this will distort the allocation of production between foreign and domestic fishermen.

In this disregard also lies the greatest weakness of this argument in favour of unilateral action: while unilateral action might lead to efficiency improvements in the domestic country, it might also lead to a decrease in worldwide efficiency. What about the preferences of the tuna and shrimp fishers and the leg-hold trappers and their families? What about the preferences of people who do not think that the death and pain endured by dolphins, sea turtles and leg-hold trapped animals is in any sense worse than the death and pain endured by animals in slaughterhouses in developed (and other) countries? If the domestic preferences were shared widely internationally, then surely it should not be all that difficult to negotiate an MEA for the preservation and protection of these species. If the domestic preferences are particularly strong and much stronger than the international average, then the domestic country should be willing to assist financially those countries it wants to refrain from certain activities.

Sovereignty. The argument regarding sovereignty is that a country should have the sovereign right to decide which goods and services it wants to import and which ones it does not. Chang (1995, p2194) suggests that unilateral trade measures are 'an exercise of the traditional sovereign power any nation enjoys over its trade with other nations'. The counter-argument is that if all countries insisted on exercising their sovereign trade rights this would imply the death of the multilateral trade regime. This regime crucially depends on countries' willingness to surrender some of their sovereignty in exchange for gaining access to other countries' markets, made possible by the surrender of some of their sovereignty. It is a quid pro quo in furtherance of the participating countries' mutual interests. It is the defining prerequisite of a multilateral trade regime that countries must obey rules they have consented to beforehand and cannot simply insist on their sovereignty each time these rules run counter to their interests.

True environmentalism. This argument is that a true environmentalist does not care about national boundaries and is interested in protecting a species or the environment no matter where they happen to exist. Environmentalists want dolphins and sea turtles and other animals to be protected – period. If unilateral action is a means to achieve this protection, then they will support it. They are not impressed by the counter-argument that animals might equally or even more suffer in, say, slaughterhouses or animal testing as they are against inhumane conditions in slaughterhouses and against animal testing as well. They are special interest groups whose objective is the protection of animals and the environment. One cannot blame them therefore for not taking into account the preferences of those who do not care about animal and environmental protection.

Lack of an effective alternative. This is a very pragmatic argument to be used in conjunction with any of the other arguments made above. It says that unilateral action is the most effective, if not the only effective means to achieve environmental protection. Offering payments to countries that do not protect the environment in order to induce them to instigate protection might not find the necessary political support and might have perverse incentive effects by encouraging other countries to refrain from environmental protection in order to be paid to introduce protection. As Charnovitz (1994, p19) has put it succinctly: the problem with these side-payments is 'that the appetite for them can be insatiable'. MEAs, another option, are difficult to bring about, take time to negotiate and might well be insufficient from an environmental point of view. Unilateral action might then be regarded as the best means available. In this respect it is interesting to note that while there are many cases in which unilateral action has not been effective in the past, there are also many cases in which it has. Charnovitz (1994) reports that the mere threat of restrictions on the fish trade contained in the so-called Pelly Amendment to the US Fishermen Protective Act had an overall success rate of 56 per cent in the period 1974–1993. In other words, in 56 per cent of cases the threat induced the foreign country to alter the incriminated activity so that the Secretary of Commerce no longer had reason to determine that 'nationals of a foreign country, directly or indirectly, are conducting fishing operations in a manner or under circumstances which diminish the effectiveness of an international fishery conservation program' (Pelly Amendment as quoted in Charnovitz 1994, p9). As concerns the famous US–Mexican tuna–dolphin case, the import prohibition against Mexican dolphin-unsafe tuna eventually prompted Mexico to give in and participate in the International Dolphin Conservation Agreement.

Arguments against unilateral action

Power dominates. To allow unilateral action will mean that powerful countries will be authorized to enact this kind of action against equally powerful countries in some cases, but in most cases against less powerful countries. The reason is simply that there is then much less chance of retaliation, retaliation will be less severe if it occurs and the chances of unilateral action achieving its objective are also higher. Weaker countries are likely to end up exclusively at the receiving end of unilateral action.[15] Of course, Bangladesh and low-lying small island countries, for example, could enact in principle unilateral trade restrictions against the US, the world's foremost emitter of greenhouse gases, but in practice they could never do so. The attempt alone would be laughable. Allowing unilateral action will therefore mean that power dominates rules that were enacted to protect the weaker countries from the arbitrary exercise of power by the stronger countries. Multilateral regimes like the multilateral trade regime try to base international relations on rules rather than on power. Unilateral action is therefore like a foreign body in the multilateral trade regime that has the potential to destroy its host.

Coercion. A related argument is that power will be used to coerce weaker countries into doing as they are told. There can be no doubt that unilateral action in the case of dolphins and sea turtles, for example, was not enacted merely to save US citizens from the pain of unwillingly consuming dolphin-unsafe tuna and sea turtle-unsafe shrimp. If that had been the objective, an eco-labelling scheme would have done the job. Rather, these unilateral actions were driven by the coercive intent of pushing the targeted countries into obeying US regulations. In this sense, Bhagwati (1993, p170) is right in arguing that unilateral action is driven by 'the zeal to impose one's ethical preferences on other communities and nations' and 'to force others into accepting one's own idiosyncratic choice of ethical concerns'. Why dolphins? As they are not endangered, dolphins were certainly not targeted because of the risk of becoming extinct. Instead, dolphins were targeted because they appeal strongly to the moral sentiments of US citizens.[16]

The danger of protectionism in green disguise. The third argument against unilateral action is that it would open the floodgates for protectionists to capture the environmental agenda and further their own selfish material interest in green disguise. In this respect, it is interesting to note VanGrasstek's (1992) finding that linking trade with environmental issues fosters support for import restrictions in the US Congress. Similarly, DeSombre (1995) found that trade restrictions such as those in the 1978 wildlife expansion of the Pelly Amendment mentioned above, and in the African Elephant Conservation Act, which were merely supported by environmental groups and not by protectionist groups due to the lack of domestic industrial or farming interests, tended to be weaker, less likely to pass the US Congress or to be implemented than trade restrictions that were supported by protectionist groups. The coalition between trade unionists and some environmental groups in Seattle also falls in this category. Chang (1995, p2205), on the other hand, is not very worried about political and other support from protectionist interest groups for trade restrictions under the environmental flag. His argument is of such naivety that it is worthwhile quoting here: 'Finally, even if protectionist interest groups do lend political support to these trade sanctions, to the extent that they serve genuine and substantial environmental interests, this support may be a welcome development. In these cases, perhaps environmentalists can capture protectionism rather than being captured by protectionists.' Developing countries' representatives will not be very comforted by the prospects of environmentalists capturing protectionism rather than the other way around.

This is not to say that a protectionist motivation would always be present. Shrimp/sea turtle is presumably the case where it would be hardest to argue that US unilateral action was motivated by protectionist concerns. Instead it seems that it was predominantly, if not totally, driven by the wish to preserve sea turtles since the TEDs that US shrimp trawlers are required to use are relatively inexpensive – TED prices range from US$75–500 per shrimp trawl-net (WTO 1998a, paragraph 3.79).

Slippery slope. A related argument is that once the floodgates are opened for unilateral action for some aspect of animal or environmental protection, there will no longer be any holding on to the slippery slope towards the widespread use of unilateral action, not least because of the support of protectionist groups. Today it is dolphins and sea turtles that are favoured by unilateral action, tomorrow countries that allow animal testing, bird shooting, chicken farming, baby seal killing, fox hunting, leg-hold trapping, whale hunting, forest burning or the commercial use of nuclear energy could be targeted. If Hindu nations were able, maybe they would want to impose trade restrictions against all countries that slaughter cows. Or if countries that are likely to suffer from climate change were able, maybe they would want to impose trade restrictions against all the major developed country greenhouse gas emitters. Nor is unilateral action likely to be confined to environmental issues once it is permitted. It could be anything from child labour to human rights. The US state of Massachusetts and the city of Minneapolis have already passed resolutions that disadvantage companies that do business in Burma (Myanmar) with respect to winning public procurement tenders (Stumberg 1999; Alliance Project 2000). The next target could be companies that buy goods made in the sweatshops of India or by child labour in Brazil – there are no limits to the well-meaning idealist in search of targets upon which to impose unilateral sanctions.

Adverse effects on MEAs. Another argument against unilateral action is that it poisons the international diplomatic climate, especially between developed and developing countries. To allow unilateral action will run counter to the spirit of cooperation which the world is so direly in need of for the solving of international and global environmental problems. The unilateral imposition of trade measures is fiercely opposed, even by environmentalists from developing countries. Sunita Narain from the Delhi Centre for Science and Environment goes as far as denouncing it as 'environmental fascism' (personal communication), which in my view is way off the mark, but clearly shows the alienation to which unilateral action leads in the developing world. There can be no doubt that MEAs, if they are not an absolute prerequisite for the solution of these problems, then at least represent, in principle, the much more effective instrument. The point is that to allow unilateral action will have adverse effects on the likelihood of consensual agreement on MEAs and might thus actually harm the environmental interest it purports to promote.

Alternatives exist. The final argument against unilateral action is that alternatives exist. The detrimental effects of countries' PPMs on the global commons are best dealt with in MEAs, of which many already exist and work quite effectively (see Chapter 9). Truly global environmental problems call for truly global cooperation aimed at solving these problems, not for unilateral action. On this aspect, it is pertinent to note that the US, which so much likes to impose unilateral trade restrictions on other countries, has one of the worst records in terms of MEA membership. The US has not ratified the Basel Convention or the Convention on Biological Diversity. It has not even signed the United Nations Convention on the Law of the Sea or the Convention on the Conservation of Migratory Species of Wild Animals.

Another alternative is eco-labelling schemes. Fishermen who catch their tuna or shrimp with dolphin-safe and sea-turtle-safe devices can label their products accordingly and if consumers want to, they can ban products without such labels from their menu. These consumer choices can be a powerful means to persuade non-labelled producers to change their production methods or otherwise pay the price in the form of reduced export opportunities. The US import ban against Mexican tuna was completely futile as the voluntary labelling scheme for dolphin-safe tuna together with the major US canneries' decision to stop tuna imports from the Eastern Tropical Pacific Ocean had all but erased dolphin-unsafe tuna from US supermarkets (Esty 1994, p134; Körber 2000). The difference is that this form of persuasion and voluntary business decision is based on the free choice of consumers and processors, not on unilaterally imposed trade sanctions by one country against another one.

Conclusion

It is perfectly understandable that some environmentalists favour unilateral action, if only as a means of last resort (see, for example, von Moltke 1997; WWF 1999a). It provides its supporters with the feeling of having done the right thing and the media attention it arouses is not unwelcome. I have argued above that many of the arguments in favour of unilateral action are seriously flawed. The only really convincing arguments in its favour are that true environmentalism knows no jurisdictional boundaries and that unilateral action can be an effective, and sometimes possibly the only available means to achieve the environmental end. However, I have also argued that there are many good arguments against unilateral action. The most important ones from an environmental perspective are that alternatives to unilateral action exist and that unilateral action has adverse impacts on MEAs, one of these alternatives.

This is not to say that at times there cannot be a dilemma. On the one hand, unilateral action is undesirable for the reasons mentioned above. On the other hand, MEAs are difficult to bring about, often take time to conclude and might very well be insufficient from an environmental perspective. For example, the bilateral agreements reached with the three major leg-hold trapping countries – Canada, Russia and the US – were substantially less comprehensive than the initial unilateral import ban contemplated by the EU (European Communities 1997, 1998; Harrop 2000). Much to the distress of animal-welfare NGOs, these agreements set 'International Humane Trapping Standards', rather than banning leg-hold trapping completely (RSPCA 1999), whereas others argue that humane trapping standards ensure that animals do not suffer more than with many other common farming methods (North 2000). Eco-labelling schemes only have an indirect effect and, while they give consumers a choice, they can neither ensure that consumers will opt for the environmentally more friendly product nor ensure that foreign producers will switch to environmentally more benign PPMs.

As with all real dilemmas, there is no clear-cut solution. My own view is that as long as it has not been convincingly shown that attempts to solve these problems via MEAs are doomed to failure and that specific eco-labelling schemes are ineffective, WTO rules should not allow countries to resort to unilateral action aimed at non-product related PPMs in foreign countries. As this case clearly has not been made yet, unilateral action should not be allowed.

Integrating the precautionary principle into WTO rules

The incorporation of the precautionary principle within the WTO system is fundamentally unsatisfactory. No full account is taken of the widespread existence of uncertainty in modern life. This is for two reasons. First, and foremost, the precautionary principle is confined to one single agreement. This needs to be rectified: WTO members should have the right to base environmental measures upon the precautionary principle outside the limited confines of the SPS Agreement. The preferred option would be to include a relevant clause into the GATT. Second, the SPS Agreement allows only provisional measures to be justified with recourse to the precautionary principle and thereby ignores the persistence of scientific uncertainty.

Implicitly it seems to be guided by a view that considers only risks, but not uncertainties. Risk refers to a situation where the set of all possible states of the world, the probability distribution over the set of possible states, and the resulting consequences, can be objectively known with enough effort by scientists. Uncertainty, however, refers to a situation where the probability distribution over a set of possible states of the world and the resulting consequences cannot be known objectively (cf Neumayer 1999c, pp99–101). Because they cannot be known objectively, there cannot be definite scientific evidence. In these cases, scientists can merely provide their best guesses based on judgements – sophisticated and informed judgements, but guesses nevertheless. Scientists themselves will then differ, and sometimes quite dramatically so, with respect to the assessment of the dangers posed by uncertainties.

Unfortunately, uncertainties do not merely exist on the fringe. Instead, they are a central characteristic of modern life. Be it the potential danger that 'mad cow disease' (BSE) can be infectious for human beings as well, or the potential health dangers from beef stemming from hormone-treated cattle, or the dangers from genetically modified organisms – the central characteristic of these and other cases is the uncertainty of the danger posed. There is no scientific consensus on either the likelihood that the dangers will occur or the severity of the consequences should they occur. The SPS Agreement with its insistence on 'proving' the dangers with the help of a scientific risk assessment is misguided in its belief in the ability of science to provide definite and reliable evidence on novel and as yet insufficiently known dangers to human health.

For cases of uncertainty, the precautionary principle was designed. Its very essence is that preventive measures can be undertaken even if definite scientific evidence on the dangers imposed by something does not exist. In discussing the case 'European Communities – Measures concerning meat and meat products' above, we have seen that the SPS Agreement, while not ignoring the principle completely, does not fully integrate it. This should be rectified during the next round of trade negotiations. Article 5:7 of the SPS Agreement should be abolished in its current form, which reads as follows:

> *In cases where relevant scientific evidence is insufficient, a Member may* provisionally *adopt sanitary or phytosanitary measures on the basis of available pertinent information, including that from the relevant international organizations as well as from sanitary or phytosanitary measures applied by other Members. In such circumstances, Members shall seek to obtain the additional information necessary for a more objective assessment of risk and review the sanitary or phytosanitary measure accordingly within a reasonable period of time* (emphasis added).

Instead, a new Article 5:7 should be introduced, the wording of which could be as follows:

> *Scientific uncertainty due to insufficient relevant scientific information and knowledge regarding the likelihood and extent of dangers to human, animal or plant life or health within the territory of a Member, shall not prevent a Member from adopting preventive sanitary or phytosanitary measures in accordance with the precautionary principle and on the basis of available pertinent information. Preventive sanitary or phytosanitary measures in accordance with the precautionary principle shall not be applied in a manner which would constitute a means of arbitrary or unjustifiable discrimination between countries*

where the same conditions prevail, or a disguised restriction on international trade.

The first sentence of this new paragraph would give WTO members substantial leeway to justify preventive SPS measures with the precautionary principle. The second sentence, which provides the counterbalance to this right, would ensure that members cannot abuse the precautionary principle to discriminate arbitrarily or unjustifiably between countries or to restrict disguisedly international trade. Of course, such a formulation does not extinguish all ambiguities. Unfortunately, there does not exist an internationally agreed upon clear definition of the precautionary principle, which opens the space for a dispute over whether or not a specific action is covered by the precautionary principle or whether the principle is merely invoked to disguise the protectionist aims. In the end, it would still be for WTO panels and appellate bodies, then, to assess whether a country invoking an SPS measure based on the first sentence in this new Article 5:7 of the SPS Agreement obeyed also the requirements in the second sentence. But because, following this reform recommendation, the precautionary principle would be explicitly and fully integrated into the agreement, WTO panels and appellate bodies would be severely constrained in finding fault with measures based on the precautionary principle. WTO members would regain their sovereignty about deciding which dangers are acceptable to them and which are not. The following are two examples:

- The European Communities could continue to ban beef stemming from hormone-treated cattle. It imposed this ban on all countries that allow cattle to be treated with growth hormones, so there is no arbitrary or unjustifiable discrimination between countries where the same conditions apply. The appellate body in the pertinent case had no doubt 'that the predominant motivation for both the prohibition of the domestic use of growth promotion hormones and the prohibition of importation of treated meat, is the protection of the health and safety of its population' (WTO 1998c, paragraph 244). This, together with the fact that the European Communities naturally banned the application of growth hormones also within its own territory, means that the ban cannot be regarded as a disguised restriction on international trade.
- The potential for conflict between the Cartagena Protocol on Biosafety and WTO rules (see p172) would disappear. Hence countries could restrict the import of certain types of GMOs in accordance with the advance informed agreement procedure of the Protocol without fear of being challenged before a WTO dispute panel. But countries could go even beyond the rules of the Cartagena Protocol, which are sometimes restrictive due to pressure from the Miami Group during its negotiations – for example, in excluding many types of GMOs from the advance informed agreement procedure (see p168, and Cosbey and Burgiel 2000).

Countries that oppose GMOs, including GMOs that are used as food or feed such as genetically modified plants, could ban their import if they regarded their potential danger to human, animal or plant life or health as unacceptable. Again, they would need to apply this import ban without arbitrary or unjustifiable discrimination between countries where the same conditions prevail. They would also need to ban the production of these types of GMOs within their own territory.

Unfortunately, the prospects for such a reform to materialize are not very bright. When the European Commission submitted a so-called White Paper 'Communication from the Commission on the precautionary principle' (European Commission 2000b), which did not include a specific proposal for reform of the SPS Agreement though, for discussion in the WTO Committee on Sanitary and Phytosanitary Measures in March 2000, the US together with Argentina, Australia, Bolivia, Brazil, Canada, Chile, Hong Kong and Mexico immediately expressed their concern that the principle could be used as a protectionist measure (ICTSD 2000e). This is the more astonishing and disappointing as the Commission made it clear that one of the communication's aims was to 'avoid unwarranted recourse to the precautionary principle, as a disguised form of protectionism' (European Commission 2000b, p3). The communication is laudable in stating that 'what is an "acceptable" level of risk for society is an eminently *political* responsibility' (ibid, emphasis in original), thus making it clear that in the case of scientific uncertainty it is not for the scientists to decide on behalf of society to judge the acceptability of the risks (or rather the dangers). The communication is also laudable in its attempt to balance carefully the rights of those who invoke the principle with their obligations to obey certain rules. It demands that measures based on the precautionary principle should be, inter alia (ibid, p4):

• proportional to the chosen level of protection;
• non-discriminatory in their application;
• consistent with similar measures already taken;
• based on an examination of the potential benefits and costs of action or lack of action (including, where appropriate and feasible, an economic cost/benefit analysis);
• subject to review, in the light of new scientific data; and
• capable of assigning responsibility for producing the scientific evidence necessary for a more comprehensive risk assessment.

All these qualifications are unproblematic with the exception of the requirement that actions taken in pursuance of the precautionary principle should be 'based on an examination of the potential benefits and costs of action or lack of action (including, where appropriate and feasible, an economic cost/benefit analysis)'.[17] While nothing is to be said against an examination of the potential benefits and costs as such, the European Commission was ill-advised to include the concept of cost/benefit analysis here. The whole point about the precautionary principle is that it defies a cost/benefit analysis and that action can be undertaken to protect individuals against uncertainties independent of the cost/benefit relationship. The European Commission's White Paper does not go so far as requiring a cost/benefit analysis, but it is important to note here that to require such an analysis before applying the precautionary principle would defeat the very purpose of the exercise. In this respect, it is pertinent to note that the SPS Agreement does not include a cost/benefit analysis and that SPS measures can be undertaken, no matter whether or not they pass a cost/benefit test.

WTO Rules and Multilateral Environmental Agreements

This chapter looks at the potential conflicts between multilateral environmental agreements (MEAs) and WTO rules. Most of this potential originates in the use of trade measures by MEAs, which is why they are the major focus of this chapter. However, substantive provisions, not related to trade measures, in the Convention on Biological Diversity might also clash with the Trade Related Intellectual Property (TRIPs) Agreement, which forms one of the WTO agreements, and are therefore dealt with here as well.

Potential conflicts because of trade measures in MEAs

Theoretical considerations on the role of trade measures in MEAs

Trade measures in MEAs fulfil three functions. First, they can be used to deter internal and external free-riding; second, they can mitigate problems with so-called emission leakage; and finally, they can be used to further directly the objectives of an MEA in restricting trade in specified substances or species. These three functions will now be examined.

Economists have examined the strategic incentives that countries face with respect to internal and external free-riding in international environmental cooperation and have developed the concepts of self-enforcing and renegotiation-proof agreements.[1] What does this mean? Many environmental problems are truly international or global. They cannot be tackled by a single country alone, hence international cooperation is needed for a solution. But whereas environmental policy can use the enforcing power that sovereign nation states ideally have within their territory, in general international environmental policy cannot take recourse to a supranational authority with enforcing powers. The affected countries are confronted with a basic Prisoner's Dilemma, in the following sense: the countries have an interest in, say, reducing emissions or reducing the over-harvesting of an exhaustible natural resource and all the countries would be better off with international environmental cooperation, but each and every one of them also has an incentive to free-ride on the others' efforts and to enjoy the benefits of abatement or harvest limitations without incurring any costs of emissions or harvest reduction. (In the following I will speak of emissions only for expositional ease, but the argument applies to any form of environmental degradation.)

Therefore MEAs normally have to deter *external* free-riding – that is, they have to deter countries that would benefit from emissions reduction from not signing up to the agreement and staying outside. Equally, they have to deter *internal* free-riding – that is, they have to deter signatory countries from not complying with the requirements of the agreement. What is important is that the mechanism employed to achieve deterrence has to be self-enforcing in the sense that a recourse to an external enforcement agency is not feasible: no country can be forced to sign an agreement and signatories cannot be forced to comply with the agreement.

One of the mechanisms that could potentially achieve such deterrence is trade measures. Before coming to this point, let us first examine, however, what the problems are if trade measures (or a similar mechanism) were unavailable. Then the only variable left to a country is the amount of pollution it emits. Hence, the only mechanism left is to threaten not to undertake any emissions reduction in order to deter external free-riding or to decrease emissions by less than that required by the agreement in order to punish non-compliant countries and to deter internal free-riding. This threat has to be credible in the sense that it is in the interest of the threatening country (or countries) actually to execute the threat whenever other countries try to free-ride. In other words, a threat cannot be credible if a country is worse off after executing the threat than it would be without execution. Non-credible threats cannot deter because potential free-riders will anticipate that they could get away with free-riding without being punished. Moreover, an agreement that establishes such a mechanism to deter free-riding has to be renegotiation-proof. This means that the threat has to be credible also in the sense that the threatening country (or countries) must be better off actually executing the threat than refraining from execution and renegotiating a new agreement with the free-riding country (or countries). Agreements that are not renegotiation-proof cannot deter because potential free-riders will anticipate that they could strike another deal after free-riding and could therefore get away without being punished.

What are the consequences of the requirements of self-enforcement and renegotiation-proofness on international environmental cooperation? If trade measures (or a similar mechanism) are unavailable, then one basic result holds: a self-enforcing and renegotiation-proof agreement will either consist of only a small subset of affected countries or, if many countries are parties to the agreement, the gains from cooperation relative to the non-cooperative equilibrium are very small. In other words, large-scale cooperation will either not take place as only a few countries will sign the agreement or if it does take place it is virtually irrelevant as the agreed cooperation improves only marginally on what would have been achieved by unilateral action in the absence of the agreement.[2] Cooperation is either narrow (instead of wide) or shallow (instead of deep).

This result leads to pessimistic expectations about the solution to an environmental problem for which international cooperation is most needed. For example, in cases where the benefits to be gained from emissions abatement are high and the costs are low (for example, ozone-depleting substances), the end result that cooperation will either be narrow or, if it is wide, it will not be deep, matters little as countries have big incentives to solve the problem unilaterally. The same might even be true if the benefits of emissions abatement are relatively low, as long as the costs are low as well. Similarly, in cases where the benefits of abatement are low and the costs are high, the end result of the economic theory of international environmental cooperation is insignificant as even the full cooperative outcome would achieve little because of the high costs involved. The cases for which the end result is really relevant are those where the benefits of emissions abatement are high, but so are the costs (for example, greenhouse gas emissions). These are exactly the cases for which finding the solution to environmental problem will demand the widest and deepest cooperation (Barrett 1991, pp14ff).

What is the intuitive reason for this rather pessimistic result? In order to deter free-riding, an agreement must specify that the non-free-riding countries are permitted to increase their emissions relative to an agreement without free-riding in order to punish other free-riders for not decreasing their emissions at all (external free-riding), or by not as much as requested by the agreement (internal free-riding). In order to deter free-riding, the damage to the potential free-rider caused by the increase in emissions must be greater than the potential benefit from free-riding. The wider and deeper the cooperation is, the higher the benefit is from free-riding, so that the damage to the potential free-rider must also increase in order to deter free-riding. The problem is, however, that the bigger the damage is to the potential free-rider, the bigger the damage is to the punishing countries themselves as well. This self-inflicted damage due to the emissions increase limits the punishment that is available for free-rider deterrence. It must not hurt the punishing countries more than the damage caused by the free-riding, otherwise it will not be credible as the potential free-rider knows that it is not in the best interest of the punishing countries to execute the punishment.

What is more, there must be no incentive for the punishing countries and the free-riders to renegotiate the agreement and strike another deal. For this condition to hold, the punishment must not be too great or the damage to the free-riding country will be great, as will be its incentive to renegotiate another agreement. For these two reasons the credible punishment that is available cannot be very substantial, which means that it cannot deter much free-riding. Because external free-riding can be deterred only to a small extent, free-riding is ubiquitous and the number of countries participating in an agreement is small. Alternatively, because internal free-riding can be deterred only to a small extent, an agreement can improve little relative to the non-cooperative equilibrium in order to keep the incentives for non-compliance small, if the number of signatories is large.

Trade measures are a way of overcoming the negative effects of the requirements of self-enforcement and renegotiation-proofness in the field of international environmental cooperation. Barrett (1997b) shows how linking an international environmental agreement with trade can promote cooperation. Trade measures are a more credible threat to deter free-riding than an increase in emissions because, according to Barrett, trade measures mainly harm the free-rider, whereas an emissions increase considerably harms the punisher as well.[3] Hence, with trade measures free-riding can be deterred more effectively as a more substantial punishment becomes credible, so wider and deeper cooperation can be achieved as a self-enforcing and renegotiation-proof equilibrium.[4]

Another problem that can be addressed by restrictive trade measures is so-called leakage, which describes the phenomenon that a decrease in emissions by the participants to an agreement is counteracted by an increase of emissions by non-members. Such an increase can be a deliberate decision by the free-riding countries. Because the decrease in emissions by the participants lowers the marginal social damage of emissions by the non-participants, their 'non-cooperative' self-interest response is to let their emissions rise. These non-members will therefore usually find it in their own best interest to increase emissions deliberately. However, this is just part of the story. The other reasons why emissions of non-participants might rise are more subtle and can hardly be traced back to a deliberate policy by these countries to exploit the emissions reductions of others. To understand this point, take the example of carbon dioxide emissions. If a subset of all countries – for example, only developed countries and transition countries as with the Kyoto Protocol – agrees on limiting their carbon dioxide emissions, then production of carbon-intensive goods and services becomes relatively more expensive in these countries. The comparative advantage in these goods and services shifts to the non-participating countries that increase their production of carbon-intensive goods and services. Similarly, some especially carbon-intensive industries might migrate from signatory to non-signatory countries. Also, the reduction in demand for fossil fuels due to the limitation of carbon dioxide emissions by the participants to the agreement will lower world fossil fuel prices, which increases demand for fossil fuels in non-member countries. All of these feedback mechanisms lead to an increase of emissions by non-participants quite involuntarily – that is, without the participating countries being able to blame the non-members for deliberately exploiting their emissions reduction. How significant leakage would be depends on the underlying assumptions about the number of countries that form an agreement, the size of reduction in emissions and the instruments that are used to achieve a reduction of emissions. Econometric estimates show that leakage could be anywhere between around 5 per cent and 30 per cent.[5] In any case, leakage potentially can be an important obstacle for MEAs and trade measures imposed on non-members can help to mitigate the problem.

The deterrence of internal and external free-riding, as well as the mitigation of leakage, are not the only purposes for which trade measures are used, however. In some MEAs, as will be discussed in the next section, restrictions on trade in specified substances or species is the very objective of the MEA, rather than an instrument to deter free-riding. This will always be the case when trade itself is considered to be endangering the preservation of species (CITES) and biodiversity (Convention on Biological Diversity) (CBD)), or endangering human life and health (Basel Convention, Rotterdam Convention and the Agreement on Persistent Organic Pollutants (POPs)). Let us therefore turn now to how trade measures and the threat of trade measures have been used in actual MEAs.

Trade measures in practice

Maybe surprisingly, these theoretical considerations notwithstanding, the vast majority of MEAs do not contain any trade measures. A 1994 survey revealed that while many of the then 180 international treaties and other agreements on environmental matters contained trade-related aspects, only 18 actually employed trade measures (WTO 1994). However, in seven of the most important MEAs, discussed below, trade measures play a prominent role and those measures are bound to play a major role in future amendments to the Kyoto Protocol for the reduction of greenhouse gas emissions.

The Montreal Protocol

The aim of the Montreal Protocol on Substances that Deplete the Ozone Layer is to phase out ozone-depleting substances (ODSs) – that is, substances responsible for the thinning of the ozone layer in the stratosphere which filters out ultraviolet radiation. The major ODSs covered by the Protocol – the so-called controlled substances – are chlorofluorocarbons (CFCs) and halons. At the time of writing, 175 countries have ratified the Montreal Protocol, which gives it almost universal support. Only five countries were WTO members but not parties to the Protocol.

The Protocol's major trade provisions are contained in its Article 4. It bans imports (Article 4.1) and exports (Article 4.2) of controlled substances between parties and non-parties of the Protocol, unless the non-parties can demonstrate that in spite of not being formally a party to the Protocol, nevertheless they comply with its obligations (Article 4.8). Article 4.3 also bans the import of products containing controlled substances from non-parties. In principle, Article 4.4 of the Protocol even provides the possibility to ban or restrict the import from non-parties of products made with, but not containing, controlled substances. However, such restrictions were soon deemed infeasible by the parties to the Protocol. These provisions were therefore never made operational and it must be regarded as highly unlikely that they would ever become operationalized.[6]

One problem that countries are faced with is the illegal trade in ODSs. To contain this problem, the Montreal Amendment to the Montreal Protocol, which at the time of writing has been ratified by 37 nations and brought into force in November 1999, introduces a mandatory licensing system for the import and export of ODSs from 2000 onwards with developing countries enjoying the possibility of delaying the introduction of such a licensing system for methyl bromide and hydrochlorofluorocarbons (HCFCs) until 2002 and 2005 respectively.

Have all these trade provisions been effective in bringing about multilateral environmental cooperation? As an answer to this question depends on counter-factual evidence, there cannot be an unambiguous answer as we cannot know what would have happened if the trade provisions had not existed. Furthermore, it is next to impossible to separate the effects of the threat of trade measures (sticks) from the effects that the promise of financial assistance for developing countries (carrots) contained in Article 10 of the Protocol had on encouraging the participation of the developing world. Many experts agree, however, that the threat of trade restrictions against non-parties has been important in bringing about almost universal participation (see, for example, French 1994, p62; Brack 1996, p55; Barrett 1997b, p346; OECD 1997c).

The Convention on International Trade in Endangered Species of Wild Fauna and Flora (CITES)

CITES is not an MEA with trade among many other provisions. Rather, its very aim is to restrict the international trade in endangered species. At the time of writing, the Convention has been ratified by 138 countries, of which only 10 were WTO members but not parties to the Convention.

CITES' major trade provisions are as follows. Appendix I names species (around 600 animals and 300 plant species) that are threatened with extinction and whose trade for commercial purposes is generally prohibited with few exceptions (Article III). Appendix II names a further 4000 animals and 25,000 plants species that might become threatened with extinction if their trade is not regulated. Their export is only allowed if the exporter has acquired an export permit from the state of export, testifying that the export will not be detrimental to the survival of that species, that the specimen have not been obtained in contravention of the protection laws of the exporting state, and that any living specimen will be so prepared for transport that the risk of injury, damage to health or cruel treatment is minimized (Article IV). Similar to the Montreal Protocol, trade in the species listed in Appendix II and, in rare circumstances, even in Appendix I is possible with non-parties if these countries can demonstrate that they comply fully with the Convention (Article X). If a party fails to comply with the Convention's obligations, it can lose its right to be treated as a party and can be treated essentially as a non-party.

Experts' assessment of the effectiveness of CITES and therefore on the trade provisions contained therein are mixed (OECD 1999d, p22). Crocodilians and elephants are the cases where CITES might have significantly helped to improve their conservation. It has been less effective with respect to, for example, rhino and tiger species, and has been indifferent with respect to the conservation status of some other species (ibid). Martin (2000, p30) comes to the rather sobering conclusion that 'if the convention is benefiting species then, even after careful study, it has not been demonstrated'. Unlike the Montreal Protocol, CITES does not contain substantial financial assistance to help developing countries comply with the Convention, which has been regarded as one of the major reasons for the poor implementation of species trade-control systems in these countries and consequently substantial illegal poaching and trafficking (OECD 1999d, p26). Another shortcoming is that CITES is unbalanced in regarding the international trade in wildlife all too often as a threat to preservation rather than as a means to raise the preservation value of endangered species if it is properly regulated (Martin 2000; 't Sas-Rolfes 2000). Complete trade bans often merely raise the value of illegal trafficking and render stringent controls more difficult.[7]

The Basel Convention

Similar to CITES, restrictions on trade are at the heart of the Basel Convention on the Control of Transboundary Movements of Hazardous Wastes and Their Disposal. It aims to 'ensure that the management of hazardous wastes and other wastes including their transboundary movement and disposal is consistent with the protection of human health and the environment whatever the place of disposal' (preamble). At the time of writing, the Convention has been ratified by 136 countries, but not by the United States, which has signed but not ratified the Convention. Some 28 countries were WTO members but not parties to the Convention.

The major trade provisions of the Basel Convention are as follows. Trade in hazardous waste is subjected to a comprehensive control system which is based on the principle of prior informed consent (PIC). This means that a country can only export these materials to another country if it has gained the prior written consent from the importing country and all transit countries (Article 6). Trade in these materials with non-parties is prohibited (Article 4:5) unless agreements with these non-parties have been concluded which 'do not derogate from the environmentally sound management of hazardous wastes and other wastes as required by this Convention' (Article 11:1). A party has the right to ban the entry or disposal of foreign hazardous waste in its territory (Article 4:1). Furthermore, an amendment to the Convention generally bans trade in these materials between so-called Annex VII (OECD countries) and non-Annex VII countries. However, at the time of writing, this amendment had been ratified by only 20 countries and it is unclear whether it will reach the necessary ratifications to enter into force (cf Krueger 1999, pp106–108).

Similar to CITES, the Basel Convention does not contain any substantial provisions for financial assistance to developing countries to assist them in implementing their obligations. This has been regarded as one of the major reasons for the poor implementation of hazardous waste trade-control systems in these countries and the consequent substantial illegal trading, which will become exacerbated once the amendment to the Convention banning trade between OECD and non-OECD countries comes into force (ibid, pp27ff).

In terms of effectiveness, Krueger (1999, p62) suggests that 'in as far as the goal was to eliminate the worst forms of hazardous waste dumping on developing countries, the trade restrictions of the Convention can generally be deemed a success'. However, it is unclear to what extent the trade measures were necessary to achieve this effect, for, as Krueger (ibid) suggests:

> *By publicizing and condemning the practice of exporting hazardous wastes for final disposal to poor countries, the Basel Convention arguably put a great deal of political pressure on exporting countries to stop this practice. In this way, the creation of a Convention that changed the norms of international practice was perhaps as effective as the actual trade measures themselves.*

Furthermore, it is unclear what the effect of the Basel Convention has been on the overall amount of transboundary hazardous waste movements as reliable data are practically non-existent (OECD 1999d, p24). It could well be that the Convention has also deterred some transboundary movements which would have actually been in the environmental interest – for example, movements to environmentally preferable recycling or waste-disposal facilities in other countries (ibid). The notification requirements could lead to a more environmentally sound management of transboundary movements of hazardous waste, but much depends on how effectively it will be administered.

The Rotterdam Convention

The Convention on the Prior Informed Consent Procedure for Certain Hazardous Chemicals and Pesticides in International Trade (Rotterdam Convention) was adopted and opened for signature in Rotterdam in September 1998. It is an MEA in pursuance of Chapter 19 of Agenda 21 on

'Environmentally sound management of toxic chemicals, including prevention of illegal international traffic in toxic and dangerous products'.[8] Its objective is 'to promote shared responsibility and cooperative efforts among Parties in the international trade of certain hazardous chemicals in order to protect human health and the environment from potential harm and to contribute to their environmentally sound use' (Article 1). It needs to be ratified by 50 countries and is not in force yet.

Annex III of the Convention specifies the chemicals that are subject to the Prior Informed Consent (PIC) procedure (initially, Annex III encompasses 30 chemicals). This means that a country may only export one of these chemicals to another country if it has sought and received the PIC of the importing country. Furthermore, the exporting country has the duty to provide for 'labelling requirements that ensure adequate availability of information with regard to risks and/or hazards to human health or the environment, taking into account relevant international standards' (Article 13:2). This applies to all chemicals listed in Annex III, all chemicals banned or severely restricted in the exporting country's territory (Article 13:2) as well as to all chemicals subject to environmental or health labelling requirements (Article 13:3). Exports of chemicals, the use of which are banned or severely restricted in the exporting country's territory, are subject to laborious information requirements for export notification as laid down in Annex V of the Convention.

Countries need not give their consent to import Annex III chemicals. According to Article 10 of the Convention, each party has the right not to consent to import or merely consent to import, subject to specified conditions, any of the chemicals contained in Annex III. However, if a country decides to ban imports or consent to import only under specified conditions, then according to Article 10:9 it has to 'simultaneously prohibit or make subject to the same conditions' the import of the chemical from any other country and the domestic production of the chemical for domestic use. In other words, a country cannot ban or severely restrict imports of a chemical from one country, but not another, or to ban or severely restrict imports of a chemical, but not domestic production.

The Agreement on Persistent Organic Pollutants

In December 2000, in Johannesburg, 122 countries concluded negotiations on a multilateral Agreement on Persistent Organic Pollutants (POPs Agreement). It is supposed to be signed formally at a meeting in Stockholm in May 2001 and will enter into force once it has been ratified by at least 50 countries. The objective of the agreement is the eventual elimination of eight POPs: aldrin; chlordane; dieldrin; endrin; heptachlor; hexachlorobenzene; mirex; and toxaphene. The use of another four POPs becomes severely restricted: dichlorodiphenyltrichloroethane (DDT) for use against malaria; dioxins; furans; and polychlorinated biphenyls (PCBs).

POPs are considered of special danger to human health and the environment as they are persistent and can accumulate in the environment, and therefore can be passed on from one generation to the next. Article D of the agreement allows the importation of the relevant POPs only for the purpose of environmentally-sound disposal or for a specified use permitted explicitly by the agreement. Exportation is only allowed for the same purposes and only to either parties to the agreement or to non-parties that can document that they comply with the provisions of the agreement.

The Convention on Biological Diversity

The Convention on Biological Diversity, which was one of the few tangible results of the United Nations Conference on Environment and Development in Rio de Janeiro in 1992, has as its objectives 'the conservation of biological diversity, the sustainable use of its components and the fair and equitable sharing of the benefits arising out of the utilization of genetic resources' (Article 1). At the time of writing, it had 177 parties – that is, practically universal membership, with the notable exception of the US which has signed but not ratified the Convention. Only three countries are WTO members but not parties to the Convention.

The CBD does not provide explicitly for trade measures, but it can have important trade implications in restricting access to genetic resources: 'Recognizing the sovereign rights of States over their natural resources, the authority to determine access to genetic resources rests with the national governments and is subject to national legislation' (Article 15:1). However, parties 'shall endeavour to create conditions to facilitate access to genetic resources for environmentally sound uses by other Contracting Parties and not to impose restrictions that run counter to the objectives of this Convention' (Article 15:2). Access should be 'on mutually agreed terms' (Article 15:4) and 'subject to prior informed consent of the Contracting Party providing such resources' (Article 15:5).

The Cartagena Protocol on Biosafety

Living modified organisms, better known as genetically modified organisms (GMOs), represent a special threat to biodiversity as they represent an exogenously introduced disturbance of the existing ecosystems and, in some cases at least, can mutate, migrate and procreate. Furthermore, GMOs, which are directly used as food or feed, can pose a potential danger to human or animal health. The use of GMOs therefore needs to be controlled, which is the objective of the Cartagena Protocol on Biosafety. It was finalized in Montreal in January 2000, was signed by 81 countries at the time of writing and needs the ratification of 50 countries to become effective.

The Cartagena Protocol comes under the Convention on Biological Diversity (CBD), Article 19:3 of the CBD calls upon parties to consider 'the need for and modalities of a protocol setting out appropriate procedures, including, in particular, advance informed agreement, in the field of the safe transfer, handling and use of any living modified organism resulting from biotechnology that may have adverse effect on the conservation and sustainable use of biological diversity'. The Cartegena Protocol does just that. It would be beyond the scope of this book to provide a comprehensive analysis of the Protocol, which can be found in Cosbey and Burgiel (2000), Swenarchuk (2000) and Falkner (2000). Suffice it to say here that the single most important element of the Protocol is an advance informed agreement procedure similar to the prior informed consent mechanism of the Rotterdam Convention. The country of potential import can put conditions on the import or even ban the import. However, many types of GMOs are not subject to this procedure:

- Pharmaceuticals addressed by other relevant international agreements or organizations (Article 5).
- GMOs in transit to another country (Article 6:1).
- GMOs destined for contained use (Article 6:2).
- GMOs intended for direct use as food or feed, or for processing (Article 7:2).
- GMOs that have been declared 'not likely to have adverse effects on the conservation and sustainable use of biological diversity, taking also into account risks to human health' by a decision of the Conference of the Parties (Article 7:4).

Critics of GMOs invoke a whole range of reasons for their opposition, including environmental, ethical, spiritual and religious reasons (see, for example, Institute of Science in Society 1999a,b; Lappé and Bailey 1999). Their supporters, on the other hand, do not fail to mention that GMOs might also help to overcome hunger in the developing world. African scientists, for example, are therefore divided over whether or not to support modern biotechnology (ICTSD 2000i). Critics counter that hunger is not a problem of insufficient food supply, but of the inequitable access to food resources. Again, it would be vastly beyond the scope of this book to provide an assessment of these arguments. Instead, we will concentrate in this chapter on the potential for conflict between the Protocol and the WTO system.

The Kyoto Protocol and potential follow-up conventions

In its current form the Kyoto Protocol, which sets up obligations for so-called Annex 1 countries (OECD countries and the economies in transition in Eastern Europe, including the Russian Federation) to reduce emissions of greenhouse gases, does not contain substantial trade provisions. In the words of Brack, Grubb and Windram (2000, p127): 'It is almost an exaggeration to say that the non-compliance provisions of the climate change regime are in their infancy – they are not really yet developed that far.' Article 17 of the

Protocol employs so-called emissions trading provisions as part of the flexibility mechanisms contained in the Protocol, which means that countries and potentially private entities as well can trade emissions reduction obligations with each other. Once the specifics of the emissions trading system have been decided upon, pertinent questions will be asked regarding whether the emissions trading system will fall under WTO rules and the disciplines contained therein – for a good discussion of these aspects see Brack, Grubb and Windram (ibid, pp117–123).

At the time of writing, the Protocol has not come into force yet, with unlikely prospects of this ever happening (see Barrett 1998). The problem is that US ratification is far from assured (see p70). As non-ratification by the US would potentially deter other countries from ratifying the Protocol as well, this, together with the fact that 55 countries comprising at least 55 per cent of emissions must ratify, could well mean that the Protocol will never formally come into force. This need not render it irrelevant, however, as often countries obey international obligations they have signed up to even though these obligations never became formally binding via ratification. Only the future will tell.

Trade measures in MEAs and WTO rules: Do they conflict?

No World Trade Organization (WTO) member has ever challenged any trade measure that another WTO member had purportedly undertaken in compliance with an MEA. Hence, no relevant WTO case law and no binding interpretation exists – as yet. Nevertheless, one can examine whether trade provisions in MEAs appear to clash with WTO rules. The answer is, as will be discussed below, that they might do, as the potential for conflict clearly exists.

Most MEAs with explicitly mandated or permitted trade provisions restrict trade between parties and non-parties, or even trade between parties. These restrictions might violate the general most favoured nation treatment obligation in the General Agreement on Tariffs and Trade (GATT) Article I. If these restrictions take the form of import or export bans, export certificates or access restrictions rather than duties, taxes or other charges, they might violate the general elimination of quantitative restrictions obligation in GATT Article XI. If countries in alleged pursuance of or compliance with MEAs applied regulations or taxes differently to imported than to domestically produced goods and services, they might also violate their national treatment obligation contained in GATT Article III. If they applied product standards or sanitary or phytosanitary measures that affected domestic and foreign producers differently, they might violate their TBT Agreement or SPS Agreement obligations. However, the trade provisions contained in MEAs that appear to violate one or the other GATT obligations, can still be considered WTO consistent if they are covered by the general exceptions of GATT Article XX or similar provisions in one of the other WTO agreements. In the following, we will look first only at the Montreal Protocol, CITES, the Basel

Convention and the CBD, the most relevant MEAs in force. After that, we will take a closer look at the Cartagena Protocol, which plays a special role due to its far-reaching embracement of the precautionary principle.

The Montreal Protocol, CITES, the Basel Convention and the CBD

The ozone layer, as well as endangered species and biodiversity (genetic resources), constitute an exhaustible natural resource in the meaning of Article XX(g). The article further demands that trade measures 'are made effective in conjunction with restrictions on domestic production or consumption', which is true for the Montreal Protocol, the CBD and the Basel Convention. However, problems could arise with respect to CITES as its provisions for the regulation of domestic wildlife use contrary to its provisions for the regulation of international wildlife trade are rather rudimentary. Trade measures must also 'relate to' the conservation of an exhaustible natural resource, which has been interpreted by the GATT/WTO dispute settlement as 'primarily aimed at' such conservation (see p122). All three MEAs should pass this test as their very aim is the conservation of an exhaustible natural resource. However, a problem could arise if a WTO panel narrowly interprets the objective of trade measures, especially in the Montreal Protocol and the CBD, as merely broadening the participation of countries in deterring free-riding, rather than directly protecting an exhaustible resource. Could these trade measures, then, still be considered 'primarily aimed at' conservation?

All four MEAs furthermore purport to protect either human, animal or plant life or health in the meaning of Article XX(b). The article requires further that trade measures are 'necessary' for such protection, which has been interpreted by the GATT/WTO dispute settlement as requiring that 'no alternative measures either consistent or less inconsistent' with WTO rules exist (see p124). This requirement could potentially pose an insurmountable hurdle for all four MEAs. Could taxes or transferable emission permits have phased out ODS as effectively and rapidly as the trade restrictions contained in the Montreal Protocol? Could direct harvest and wildlife-management regulations prevent the extinction of endangered species similarly to the trade restrictions contained in CITES? Are trade restrictions really necessary to prevent environmental and health damage from transborder shipments of hazardous waste? Even accepting the validity of 'limited capabilities of the developing countries to manage hazardous wastes and other wastes' (preamble of the Basel Convention), is a complete ban on the trade in hazardous waste between OECD and non-OECD countries really necessary? Are there really no less GATT-inconsistent measures for the preservation of biodiversity than restrictions on access to genetic resources? Would less GATT-inconsistent measures need to be as effective as the trade restrictions to be considered alternatives? It would be beyond the scope of this book to attempt to answer these questions. Suffice it to say here that it is open to debate at least whether the trade measures contained in the four MEAs could pass the 'necessity' test of Article XX(b).

If trade measures in MEAs are covered by one of the exceptions in Article XX(b) or XX(g), they must still pass the requirements set by the preamble of the article. This seems to be rather easy with respect to the requirement that these measures are not applied in a manner that would constitute 'a disguised restriction on international trade', as the four MEAs are explicit and rather transparent in their provision for trade restrictions (least so the CBD, however). It is more doubtful, but still arguable, that they are 'not applied in a manner which would constitute a means of arbitrary or unjustifiable discrimination between countries where the same conditions prevail'. This clause is usually interpreted by GATT/WTO panels as the requirement to balance carefully the environmental objectives of the trade measures with the trade rights of negatively affected WTO members. As all four MEAs have very widespread multilateral support, it can be argued that the international community of nation states has given its blessing to the objectives contained in the MEAs and to the trade measures they employ. Furthermore, the Montreal Protocol, CITES and the Basel Convention do not discriminate against non-parties as such, as these can still enjoy all the trade benefits of parties if, in spite of the remaining non-parties, they comply with the substantial obligations of the agreement. The CBD does not have such a provision for non-parties. However, its almost universal membership means that the number of non-parties is very small indeed. >From this perspective, one could argue that the trade measures in all four MEAs would have a good chance to pass the preambular test of Article XX.

So far we have focused on trade measures between parties, and either non-parties or non-complying parties as specifically mandated or explicitly allowed by the MEAs. It has been shown that while the potential for WTO inconsistency clearly exists, it is far from clear that these measures actually are WTO inconsistent. Things are different with respect to the measures an MEA party might undertake without a specific mandate or permission contained in an MEA. Such a country could still argue that while these measures are not specifically mandated or allowed for by an MEA, they are undertaken nevertheless in pursuance of and compliance with mandated MEA obligations. Whether these would pass scrutiny for WTO consistency is much less clear and cannot be answered in general as the answer very much depends on the concrete measures undertaken and the manner in which they were applied.[9]

That countries like to invoke MEAs at times in justification for clearly protectionist measures can be seen by two of the cases we looked at in Chapter 8: 'United States – Prohibition of imports of tuna and tuna products from Canada', justified, inter alia, as furthering the objectives of the Inter-American Tropical Tuna Commission and the International Convention for the Conservation of Atlantic Tunas (GATT 1983, paragraph 3.10); and 'Canada – Measures affecting exports of unprocessed herring and salmon', whereby Canada in its submissions referred to international agreements on fisheries and the United Nations Convention on the Law of the Sea (GATT 1987b, paragraph 3.39).

The Cartagena Protocol on Biosafety

The major potential for conflict between the Cartagena Protocol on Biosafety and the WTO system does not lie in its trade measures as such, but in the Protocol's explicit and repeated embracing of the so-called precautionary principle in the body of the Protocol. Article 1 of the Protocol proclaims that the objective of the Protocol is 'in accordance with the precautionary approach contained in Principle 15 of the Rio Declaration on Environment and Development'. Article 10:6 gives considerable significance to the principle:[10]

> *Lack of scientific certainty due to insufficient relevant scientific information and knowledge regarding the extent of the potential adverse effects of a living modified organism on the conservation and sustainable use of biological diversity in the Party of import, taking also into account risks to human health, shall not prevent that Party from taking a decision, as appropriate, with regard to the import of the living modified organism in question ...*

The reader should recall that the precautionary principle is not explicitly but only indirectly referred to in the SPS Agreement. Also, it can only be invoked in provisional suspension of the requirement to perform a risk assessment (see p30). With regard to these two important aspects, the Cartagena Protocol considerably differs from the SPS Agreement. Herein also lies the potential for conflict as the following hypothetical scenario shows: a country which is a member of the WTO and a party to the Cartagena Protocol bans the import of GMOs without sufficient scientific information for a risk assessment, but invoking the precautionary principle. The exporting country, which is a WTO member, but not a party to the Protocol, regards these trade measures as violating the other country's obligations under the SPS Agreement as no risk assessment is provided and challenges the measures before a WTO panel.

Given this potential for conflict, parties have fought hard over how the relationship between the Protocol and the WTO system would be spelled out in the Protocol. Those who are major exporters of GMOs and regard the precautionary principle with suspicion as they fear that it will be used to restrict imports of GMOs, were gathered in the so-called Miami Group (Argentina, Australia, Canada, Chile, the United States and Uruguay). The Miami Group wanted to include an article in the main body of the Agreement, stating that nothing in the Protocol would affect the parties' rights and obligations under other existing international agreements, which basically meant the WTO Agreements. Such a clause is actually included in the CBD's Article 22:1 which states that 'the provisions of this Convention shall not affect the rights and obligations of any Contracting Party deriving from any existing international agreement, except where the exercise of those rights and obligations would cause a serious damage or threat to biological diversity'.

Most other countries and environmentalists rejected this approach as they regarded it as a subordination of the Protocol under a trade agreement.[11] In the end stood a compromise that merely restates the conflicting views on the issue and that followed the precedent set by the Rotterdam Convention on the Prior Informed Consent Procedure for Certain Hazardous Chemicals and Pesticides in International Trade. The Miami Group had to accept that a relevant text was merely included in the less binding preamble, but pushed through the formulation that 'this Protocol shall not be interpreted as implying a change in the rights and obligations of a Party under any existing international agreement'. However, the very next paragraph confirms the view of all other countries and environmentalists that 'the above recital is not intended to subordinate this Protocol to other international agreements'. Thus, a potential for conflict clearly exists and, given the massive export interests of GMO-producing countries from the Miami Group, it seems only a question of time until a dispute before the WTO is initiated.

How can this conflict be resolved? The heart of the problem lies in the SPS Agreement's unsatisfactory dealing with insufficient scientific evidence. I have argued in detail on pages 153 why the SPS Agreement needs to be reformed, to the effect that the precautionary principle becomes fully and directly incorporated and is invokable not only provisionally. Doing so would remove the major potential for conflict between the Cartagena Protocol and the WTO Agreements so that both could co-exist in mutual support.

Reconciling trade measures in MEAs and WTO rules

Given that the potential for conflict between the trade provisions in MEAs and WTO rules exists, it is pertinent to examine different options for dealing with this potential.

Wait and see

The easiest way to deal with the potential for conflict is to do nothing for the time being and to embark on policy reform only if it was found to be necessary in the future.

Assessment: No trade provision contained in MEAs has ever been challenged before GATT/WTO. Even if it was, a panel or the appellate body might still uphold the provisions, as argued above. The most likely potential future dispute will not be about mandated or specifically allowed trade provisions, however, but about measures, not demanded or specifically allowed, but undertaken by a country in alleged pursuance of and compliance with an

MEA. But even in this case it might be best to wait and see how a WTO panel and the appellate body would rule. If it turned out that in either case these came to a conclusion that is unsatisfactory from an environmental perspective, one could still have recourse to one of the other options analysed below. This wait-and-see approach is therefore very much influenced by the idea that something that is not obviously broken does not need fixing.

Wait and see is the preferred option of the vast majority of developing countries (WTO 1996c), but is regarded as inadequate by most developed countries (for example, Canada 1999b; European Communities 1999; Norway 1999), with the possible exception of the US (BNA 2000d). Always suspicious towards the developed countries' inclination to protect themselves against cheaper imports from poorer countries, they see the more far-reaching options discussed below as potentially biased against their trading rights in their de facto effects, if not in their design. On the other hand, many observers have spoken out against the wait-and-see approach. WWF (1996, p10), for example, suggests that the wait-and-see approach 'calls for political reinforcement of the current uncertainties and trade biases of the WTO and thus of their potential "chill" effect on the use of environmentally effective trade measures in MEAs'.

I would concede that the wait-and-see approach does not solve the conflict. On the other hand, the conflict so far exists merely potentially and wait and see is the best way to find out whether the conflict will actually materialize. In as far as a dispute between parties and non-parties to an MEA is more likely to arise before the WTO than a dispute between the parties to an MEA (where countries can use the consultation and, if existent, the dispute-settlement facilities of the MEA), the likelihood of a WTO challenge is very small indeed. As noted above, with the exception of the Basel Convention there is only a handful of countries that are not parties to these arguably most important MEAs, but members of the WTO. Furthermore, for many countries non-ratification has other reasons than opposition to the MEA and might still come about as time passes by. Maybe more importantly still, the vast majority of countries that are WTO members but not parties to one of the four MEAs are small and very poor developing countries that have not so far initiated any dispute before the WTO and are highly unlikely to do so regarding trade provisions contained in one of the MEAs.[12]

Furthermore, it might be the only option realistically available. As will be discussed below, all other options need the approval of most, if not all developing countries WTO members, and they strongly favour the current status quo. I will also argue in favour of amending the GATT to provide an MEA exception clause along the blueprint given by NAFTA. This could be achieved in the next round of trade negotiations if developed countries can convince the developing countries of the benefits of such an approach (or bribe them with concessions in other areas to concord). Until then, the best and indeed the only option is to wait and see.

Require environmental experts on panels and appellate bodies

A second option slightly beyond the wait-and-see approach is to change the composition of WTO panels and appellate bodies so that in any potential future dispute involving the trade provisions of MEAs, one or more of the panellists must have explicit expertise in environmental matters in addition to expertise in international trade law. This proposal addresses, at least with respect to MEAs, a common concern shared by many: that trade lawyers with no particular expertise in environmental matters decide on environmentally related disputes. The hope would be that with the infusion of environmental expertise, the panel might come to decisions that take environmental aspects better into account.

Assessment: To require environmental experts on panel and appellate bodies is neither necessary nor sufficient for solving conflicts between trade provisions in MEAs and WTO rules. Already panels have the right to seek information from outside expert groups (Dispute Settlement Understanding Article 13) and they actually do so. The panel in the shrimp/sea turtle case, for example, has confronted five environmental experts with an exhaustive list of investigating questions (WTO 1998). This, together with the possibility of environmental NGOs to submit position papers, so-called amicus curiae briefs, as explicitly allowed for by the appellate body in the shrimp/sea turtle case, should guarantee the sufficient provision of environmental expertise. Furthermore, in past dispute settlements it does not appear that decisions which were regarded by some as environmentally unfriendly were taken because of a lack of environmental expertise, but rather because of a specific legal interpretation of the WTO rules.

Certification by MEA secretariat

MEAs could be designed so that their secretariats have the option to certify trade measures undertaken by countries in alleged pursuance of or compliance with an MEA (Marceau 1999, p150). The idea is that such certification could serve as further evidence in a potential future dispute that the trade measure is genuinely undertaken for the alleged objective.

Assessment: This seems to be a good idea that can lead to some further clarification should a future dispute arise. However, this option stops a long way short of reconciling the conflict itself.

Restricting access to the WTO dispute settlement

The Understanding on Rules and Procedures Governing the Settlement of Disputes (Dispute Settlement Understanding (DSU)) could be amended to the effect that countries which are members both of an MEA and of the WTO are either required to settle their dispute via the dispute settlement mechanism of the MEA, and would therefore be prohibited from entering the WTO dispute settlement process, or would be required to try to exhaust the possibilities of an MEA dispute settlement first before they have recourse to the WTO dispute settlement. The EU seems to be in favour of such an approach (European Communities 2000b). Amendment of the DSU can only be undertaken by consensus, however (Article X:8 of the Agreement Establishing the WTO).

Assessment: This option is not very helpful for two reasons. First, the dispute settlement in MEAs is usually institutionally weak with no streamlined timetable and no enforcement mechanism via retaliatory and cross-retaliatory trade sanctions as existent in the WTO system. Some MEAs do not even have provisions for a dispute settlement. WTO members might therefore be more than hesitant to forgo their right to challenge trade measures before the WTO either completely or until the dispute settlement mechanisms of the relevant MEA are exhausted. Second, and more importantly, this option can only apply to cases where both countries are members of both the WTO and the relevant MEA. A future dispute can also arise between two countries where only one country is a member of the MEA and imposes trade measures on the other country as a non-party to the MEA. As non-parties cannot challenge a trade measure before the MEA, they would automatically have to challenge the measure before the WTO.

Temporary waiver

Article IX:3 of the Agreement Establishing the WTO provides for the temporal waiving of WTO obligations, which could be used to waive certain obligations with respect to trade provisions in MEAs. Waiving decisions should normally be taken by consensus, otherwise by a three-fourths majority. A waiver must be temporary with a fixed date of termination and is allowed in exceptional circumstances only (Article IX:4).

Assessment: A temporary waiver is a non-option as it would not really solve any conflict. It does not provide any security or permanence. It is ad hoc and unpredictable (Schoenbaum 1997, p283; Rutgeerts 1999, p84).

Interpretative statement

According to Article IX:2 of the Agreement Establishing the WTO, the Ministerial Conference and the General Council of the WTO 'have the exclusive authority to adopt interpretations of this Agreement and of the Multilateral Trade Agreements'. An interpretation becomes adopted if it gains the support of three-fourths of WTO members. For example, in 1996 the EU had put forward a proposal for an interpretation of Article XX(b) so that, under certain conditions, a trade measure undertaken by a country in pursuance of an MEA would automatically be regarded as 'necessary' in the meaning of the article and would therefore merely have to pass the test of the preamble to Article XX (WTO 1996c, p5).[13] The conditions were that the 'MEA was open to participation by all parties concerned with the environmental objectives of the MEA, and reflected, through adequate participation, their interests, including significant trade and economic interests' (ibid).

Switzerland in a later submission went one step further in suggesting that such trade measures should be exempted from the scrutiny of Article XX entirely, including the chapeau (Switzerland 2000). This submission was probably influenced by the importance that WTO panels and appellate bodies had put on the chapeau of Article XX in the meantime (see the relevant analysis in Chapter 8).

Assessment: An interpretative statement to GATT articles has the important advantage over the amendment of GATT articles discussed below that it does not need ratification. However, it is somewhat unclear how far-reaching an interpretative statement can be. This is because Article IX:2 of the Agreement Establishing the WTO states that the paragraph allowing interpretative statements 'shall not be used in a manner that would undermine the amendment provisions in Article X'. Even the EU proposal might be contested by many as calling for an amendment to GATT Article XX rather than an interpretation. To be on the safe side, it seems therefore much more appropriate to go the way via amending GATT articles if substantive change is required.

Amendment to GATT

The most far-reaching option is to amend the GATT. A proposal for amendment needs a two-thirds majority and has effect only for those members who have accepted the amendment (Article X:3 of the Agreement Establishing the WTO).[14] The amendment would need ratification by the accepting countries (Wold 1996, p916). GATT could be amended in a number of ways – for example:

- Brack (1996, p82), without embracing the suggestion, considers the introduction of a 'sustainability clause', which would set out 'agreed principles of environmental policy – such as the polluter pays principle and the precautionary principle – against which trade measures can be judged'.
- Several countries have proposed the establishment of a number of pre-specified ex ante requirements for an MEA to be granted exception from WTO obligations (see WWF 1996 and WTO 1996c). These requirements were supposed to be more or less binding and were regarded with suspicion by environmental NGOs such as the WWF as they would introduce 'new criteria, guidelines, or legal tests that are grounded in trade, not environment, policy considerations' (WTO 1996c, p10). WWF, for

its part, has called for a general exception for MEAs without providing any detailed proposal, however (ibid, pp29ff).

- Hudec (1996, pp120–142) has proposed a new exception to Article XX, which would introduce a two-tier approach modelled on the existing Article XX(h), which excepts international commodity agreements. According to this proposal, in its first part such a new exception would lay down pre-specified criteria as to the substance, structure and negotiating procedure that an MEA would need to fulfil to qualify for the exception. In its second part, the new exception would allow the submission of any MEA to WTO members for approval and the granting of the exceptional status, which would be possible whether or not the criteria in the exception's first part were met or not. Similarly, Housman and Zaelke (1995, pp324–327) suggest a number of criteria for an MEA to be protected from challenge before the WTO.

- A similar suggestion, but one going one step beyond the GATT amendment, is to conclude a special agreement on trade-related environmental measures (TREMs) (suggested, for example, by Cosbey 2000). In its chapter on MEAs, the TREMs Agreement would have to specify 'what constitutes an MEA under the agreement, how different types of trade measures should be treated, and what types of complementary measures must be applied under what circumstances' (ibid, p5). Brack (2000, pp294–296) has put forward a similar idea for a WTO Agreement on MEAs which would need to specify a definition of an MEA and of trade measures, and would need to put down rules for a dispute settlement.

- A final possibility to amend GATT is to introduce an MEA exception clause in following the blueprint set by the North American Free Trade Agreement's (NAFTA's) Article 104 which governs the relationship to environmental and conservation agreements. Its first paragraph states that 'in the event of any inconsistency between this Agreement and the specific trade obligations set out in' CITES, the Montreal Protocol, the Basel Convention and two further bilateral agreements between NAFTA partners 'such obligations shall prevail to the extent of the inconsistency, provided that where a Party has a choice among equally effective and reasonably available means of complying with such obligations, the Party chooses the alternative that is the least inconsistent with the other provisions of this Agreement'. Its second paragraph opens the possibility for the inclusion of further future MEAs in stating that 'parties may agree in writing to modify Annex 104.1 to include any amendment to an agreement referred to in paragraph 1, and any other environmental or conservation agreement'.

Assessment: The 'sustainability clause' will mitigate, but will not solve the conflict. The Agreement Establishing the WTO already contains a commitment to sustainable development in its preamble. Article 31:3(c) of the Vienna Protocol on the Law of Treaties requires to take into account other 'rules of international law applicable to the partners' and it is standard practice of panels and appellate bodies to take international environmental principles, such as the polluter pays principle, into account.

To establish pre-specified criteria that MEAs must comply with in order to qualify for the exception of GATT obligations is, in my view at least, inferior to an MEA exception clause following the blueprint given by NAFTA. The exact wording of these criteria will be highly contested and open to interpretation. The criteria necessarily need to be kept non-specific. For example, it would not make much sense to specify the exact number of parties or the range of interests to be represented as this would have to differ from MEA to MEA. Equally contested will be who has the right to decide on whether the criteria are fulfilled.

The much clearer and cleaner approach is to state explicitly which MEAs are exempted. This could take the form of either an environmental side agreement (a special agreement or an MEA code in WTO language) or the form of a simple MEA exception clause in a renegotiated GATT.[15] During the next round of trade negotiations the CBD, CITES, the Basel Convention and the Montreal Protocol, including their amendments, could be exempted explicitly. The same holds true for other MEAs with similar widespread international participation. What about future MEAs? To require consensus for inclusion of a future MEA might be appropriate for an agreement like NAFTA with only three partners. It would be too demanding for the WTO, however. I would suggest that other MEAs also become exempted if three-fourths of WTO members are in favour. Such a decision rule would ensure that no MEA is exempted if the majority of developing countries, the major proponents of the wait-and-see approach, is not in favour. On a case-by-case basis countries could decide whether they regard the MEA in question to be satisfactory on such criteria as the number of parties, the range of interests represented or the existence of a fair compromise between trade measures (sticks), and financial and technological assistance (carrots) to grant them exemption from WTO obligations.

Against such a proposal, Caldwell (1994, p192) raises the fear that an MEA exception clause might reinforce 'the perception, particularly frustrating to the environmental community, that the GATT and the goals of liberalized trade it represents have priority over all other concerns'. This misses the point, however, as an MEA exception clause actually gives precedence to MEAs over the GATT. It is therefore the environmental objective of the exempted MEAs that has priority over GATT's goals of liberalized trade, not vice versa.

It should be noted that for those MEAs that do not become explicitly exempted by WTO members, no presumption is implied that measures taken in their pursuance could be challenged successfully before the WTO. Those trade measures could still be justified under GATT Article XX or other provisions in one of the WTO Agreements, and the normal rules of dispute resolution would apply. Also, should a WTO panel or an appellate body ever find a trade measure taken in pursuance of an MEA in violation of WTO rules, there would be enormous pressure on countries to exempt the MEA in retrospect. Non-exemption of a MEA at some point of time therefore does not leave the MEA without any protection from being challenged before the WTO.

Conclusion

If, as suggested above, the potential for a clash between trade measures employed in MEAs and WTO rules exists, then it will be just a matter of time until a country will challenge such a measure. When this will be is difficult to say. It could well be within the next two years or so, but it could also be that nothing happens for at least another decade. Even if a measure became challenged, it is far from clear that a WTO dispute panel or appellate body would find the measure in conflict with WTO rules. Obviously, much depends on the concrete measure and its design, but as suggested above there are good arguments to presume that such a panel or body might find the measure to be covered by one of the environmental exceptions contained in GATT Article XX. It is reasoning such as this that makes the wait-and-see approach so attractive. Most, especially developing, countries therefore support this approach.

In spite of its attractiveness, the wait-and-see approach does not provide a solution, however. It is an unimaginative and short-sighted approach. Instead I would submit that we need to be more anticipative and seek a more long-term solution. Such a solution is the MEA exception clause proposed above. It is simple and clear, leaving very little room for ambiguity. As it would need the consent of the vast majority of developing countries, it cannot be denounced as biased against their interest. Combined with the possibility for specific trade measures undertaken by countries to become certified by MEA secretariats, it offers the best policy option to reconcile trade measures in existing and future MEAs with WTO rules.

Potential conflicts between substantive CBD provisions and the TRIPs Agreement

It is contested whether some of the substantive provisions of the CBD, discussed above, might clash with Article 27:3(b) of the TRIPs Agreement. The reader should recall that this article allows the patentability of 'non-biological and microbiological processes' and calls upon WTO members to 'provide for the protection of plant varieties[16] either by patents or by an effective *sui generis*[17] system or by any combination thereof'.

Most developed countries and their business groups argue that there is absolutely no reason to presume that the TRIPs Agreement clashes with the objectives of the CBD, which are 'the conservation of biological diversity, the sustainable use of its components and the fair and equitable sharing of the benefits arising out of the utilization of genetic resources' (CBD Article 1) (ITCSD 1998a). A position paper of the International Chamber of Commerce (ICC) makes this point very succinctly: 'It is ICC's position that both the CBD and TRIPs are important international conventions, equally binding on their numerous signatories. They deal with different topics. They are fully consistent with each other and must both be fully implemented by their signatories.' Those who hold this position argue that the availability of patents provides the right incentives for companies to invest into research for making pharmaceutical or agricultural use of biological diversity. The ensuing rise in the value of biodiversity would render the preservation and sustainable use of biodiversity more worthwhile relative to activities that would lead to its destruction. Furthermore, developed countries' companies would be more willing to share the use of relevant technologies with developing countries if their intellectual property rights are protected.

Critics, among them most developing countries and many environmentalists, argue that the TRIPs Agreement is in conflict with the spirit, if not the letter, of the CBD. Their major separate, but interrelated, arguments are as follows:

- The TRIPs Agreement is practically silent on the 'fair and equitable sharing of the benefits arising out of the utilization of genetic resources' as enshrined in Article 1 and, with special reference to making use of the knowledge, innovations and practices of indigenous and local communities, in Article 8(j) of the CBD (IISD and UNEP 2000, p55). The fear is that developed countries' companies will appropriate the lion's share of the benefits from genetic resource use if they are granted patents on modifications that are sufficient to be considered a new and inventive step, and are capable of industrial application as required by Article 27:1 of the TRIPs Agreement – a phenomenon that critics regard as 'biopiracy' (CUTS 1997). Cosbey (1999) asserts that 'there has been a steady and substantial transfer of resources from South to North as the valuable products of informal innovation have been appropriated cost-free'.
- It is feared that, in the agricultural field, the patentability of non-biological and microbiological processes would lead to restrictions on the transfer of technology to developing countries, which would run counter to the provisions for access to and the transfer of technology for developing countries in Article 16 of the CBD.[18]
- It is feared that the patentability of non-biological and microbiological processes would lead to a concentration of market power in the hands of a few companies from the developed world and to the domination of monocultures in the crops supplied by these companies, as farmers rush away from their traditional varieties to use standardized high-yielding crops. This could threaten the biodiversity of cultivated species (IISD and UNEP 2000, p56).

- It is also feared that the TRIPs Agreement is biased against the traditional innovations of farmers. As Cosbey (1999) points out: '... by most interpretations there will be no protection for the varieties produced by informal innovation – by farmers selecting for desired characteristics generation after generation'. This is often referred to as the neglect by the TRIPs Agreement of so-called farmers' rights as opposed to breeders' rights.

- Lastly, if patents are granted in very broad terms, this might counteract its supposed effect of encouraging research and development. As IISD and UNEP (2000, p57) note: 'Patents have been granted, for example, for such broad categories as sunflower seeds with high oleic acid content. To the extent that such a patent stifles innovative research into improved ways of producing high oleic acid sunflowers, strong intellectual property rights protection defeats one of its main avowed goals.' The granting of very broad patents might also lead to highly problematic consequences on equity. Cosbey (1999) quotes the Director-General of the International Plant Genetic Resources Institute as stating the following concern: 'The granting of patents covering all genetically engineered varieties of a species, irrespective of genes concerned or how they were transformed, puts in the hands of a single inventor the possibility to control what we grow on our farms and in our gardens.'

A review of Article 27:3(b) of the TRIPs Agreement is currently under way under the auspices of the WTO as part of the so-called built-in negotiating agenda from the Uruguay Round Agreements and as explicitly called for in the article. Developed countries argue that this obligatory review should be confined to assess whether countries, especially developing countries, have provided the patents or effective *sui generis* systems for the protection of plant varieties. Many developing countries have not yet provided either patents or *sui generis* systems, however. As a minimum demand, they have called for an extension of the deadline, which for developing countries was 1 January 2000 (2006 for the 29 so-called least developed WTO members). Given the fact that the Seattle meeting has not led to any conclusion on this contested matter, WTO members have found a so-called gentlemen's agreement, which says that non-implementation will not be challenged before the WTO until further negotiations find a way out of the deadlock (ICTSD 2000f).[19] However, the US has made it clear that it will only see itself bound to this agreement with respect to developing countries who encounter real problems in implementation and not with respect to developing countries who want an extension of the deadline because ultimately they do not want the implementation of the provisions at all (ibid).

But non-implementation seems to be the ultimate goal of developing countries who want the substance of the article itself to be addressed in its review and ultimately want to get rid of its provisions (ICTSD 1998a). Kenya (on behalf of the African Group, but representative for the vast majority of developing countries) has demanded that the review process 'should clarify that plants and animals as well as microorganisms and all other living organisms and their parts cannot be patented, and that natural processes that produce plants, animals and other living organisms should also not be patentable' (Kenya 1999b, p4). It also seeks explicit clarification of the article so that it does not contravene the CBD (ibid, p5). More specifically, it wants the insertion of a footnote to Article 27:3(b) allowing countries to pass laws that provide for:

1   the protection of the innovations of indigenous and local farming communities in developing countries, consistent with the Convention on Biological Diversity ...;
2   the continuation of the traditional farming practices, including the right to save, exchange and save seeds, and sell their harvest;
3   the prevention of anti-competitive rights or practices which will threaten the food sovereignty of people in developing countries ...

The case of the CBD is somewhat unique in that it is the only one so far in which it is one of the WTO Agreements which is in potential conflict with an MEA, rather than the other way around. The reader should note that, similar to the case of GMOs, many critics reject the patentability of any form of life for much more general reasons than a potential clash with CBD obligations, including environmental, ethical, spiritual and religious reasons (see, for example, Institute of Science in Society 1999b and Indigenous Peoples' Statement 1999). It would be vastly beyond the scope of this book to assess these arguments. Here, I will therefore not make a judgement on the appropriateness or otherwise of allowing the patentability of any form of life. Instead I will confine myself to assessing if this particular article of the TRIPs Agreement is in conflict with the CBD.

I would argue that this is not the case. That the TRIPs Agreement is silent on an equitable sharing of the benefits of biodiversity use does not mean that the patent or *sui generis* systems to be enacted could not include rules that lead to such an equitable sharing. Even the ICC (1999) admits that if equitable sharing of the benefits from inventions that make use of indigenous knowledge does not take place, this could reasonably be called 'biopiracy'. Similarly, just because the TRIPs Agreement does not contain an explicit reference to the preservation of biodiversity does not mean that the patent or *sui generis* systems to be enacted could not be designed in a way that promotes biodiversity preservation. It is true that Article 16:3 of the CBD subjects patents and other intellectual property rights 'to national legislation and international law in order to ensure that such rights are supportive of and do not run counter to its objectives'. However, those who see a clash with the TRIPs Agreement often seem to forget that this agreement also allows members to

> *exclude from patentability inventions, the prevention within their territory of the commercial exploitation of which is necessary to protect ordre public or morality, including to protect human, animal or plant life or health or to avoid serious prejudice to the environment, provided that such exclusion is not made merely because the exploitation is prohibited by their law* (Article 27:2).[20]

Furthermore, the fact that Article 27:3(b) of the TRIPs Agreement allows developing countries to provide an 'effective *sui generis* system' as an alternative to patents should give these and other countries some leeway to design these systems to their benefit and to the benefit of biodiversity preservation. They are not required to accede to the International Convention for the Protection of New Varieties of Plants (UPOV Convention), an existing *sui generis* system, which critics argue is biased towards developed countries' interests (for more detail on this Convention, see Cosbey 1999 and Dutfield 2000). In conclusion, therefore, as mentioned above, one might reject the provisions in Article 27:3(b) of the TRIPs Agreement for many other reasons, but there is no a priori reason to presume that this article is to be revoked because it clashes with the CBD.[21]

Conclusion and Summary of Policy Recommendations

This book has fulfilled two objectives. First, it has identified the problematic aspects of the relevant issue areas within the multilateral investment and trade regimes which, from an environmental perspective, need to be addressed via policy reform. Second, it has developed policy recommendations to solve these problems in a way that the economic development aspirations of developing countries are not negatively affected. Table 10.1 provides a summary of the results arrived at from the book's analysis of investment, trade and the environment – a summary that is structured into issue area, alleged problematic aspects, evidence and the policy recommendation offered as a solution. This table, together with the analysis behind it contained in the main chapters of this book, can be read as a blueprint for those who want to 'green' the multilateral investment and trade regimes in a way that is beneficial to developing countries as well.

In my perspective, the most important of these recommendations are as follows:

- Assistance to institutional capacity-building and local empowerment to help developing countries in setting efficient environmental standards and enforcing these standards.
- The establishment of a special environmental negotiation group in the next round of trade negotiations addressing the negative environmental consequences of trade liberalization.
- The realization of trade liberalization measures that are both economically beneficial and environmentally benign (win-win options) as a primary objective in the next round of trade negotiations.
- An interpretative statement concerning the General Agreement on Tariffs and Trade (GATT) Articles XX(b) and XX(g).
- Full integration of the precautionary principle into WTO rules.
- The introduction of a Multilateral Environment Agreement (MEA) exception clause.

Table 10.1 Summary of policy recommendations

Issue area	Alleged problematic aspects	Evidence	Recommended solution
Pollution haven	Inefficiently low or non-enforced environmental standards in developing countries	Some anecdotal evidence, very limited systematic statistical evidence	Assistance to institutional capacity-building and local empowerment for developing countries
Regulatory chill	Failure to raise environmental standards in developed countries	Some anecdotal evidence; systematic statistical evidence almost impossible to get	Upward harmonization of environmental standards Increased efforts to conclude MEAs
Roll-back	Knocking down of environmental standards via investor-to-state dispute settlement	No evidence so far	Make investor-to-state dispute settlement an open and transparent process No change in substantive investment protection provisions required
Environmental consequences of trade liberalization	Trade liberalization harms the environment in certain locations or even worldwide	Limited, some anecdotal, some systematic	Systematically assess the environmental consequences of trade liberalizations Establish a special environmental negotiation group Seek NGO participation Realize win-win options Ensure that environmental standards and schemes do not restrict market access for developing countries

Issue area	Alleged problematic aspects	Evidence	Recommended solution
WTO dispute settlement	WTO panels and appellate body rulings are biased in favour of free trade and against environmental interests	Some problematic aspects of GATT/WTO case law notwithstanding, there is no evidence for a systematic bias against environmental interests	Make dispute settlement open and transparent Provide interpretative statement of GATT Articles XX(b) and XX(g) Integrate precautionary principle into WTO rules
	WTO rulings severely restrict unilateral action with respect to foreign non-product related PPMs	Claim is justified	Clarify rules that unilateral action with respect to foreign non-product related PPMs is inconsistent with WTO rules
MEAs and WTO rules	Trade measures and other provisions in MEAs might clash with WTO rules	Potential for clash clearly exists even though no country has ever challenged an MEA-related measure and therefore no WTO case law exists yet Cartagena Protocol on Biosafety might clash with SPS Agreement. Convention on Biological Diversity does not necessarily clash with TRIPs Agreement	Introduce an MEA exception clause into GATT, which lists excepted MEAs and allows for the inclusion of further MEAs by a three-fourths majority vote Incorporate precautionary principle into WTO rules No need for policy reform

It can be seen from this summary of the most important policy recommendations, as well as from the more detailed list contained in Table 10.1, that no radical reform of the multilateral investment and trade regimes is advocated in this book. Instead, all these recommendations aim at a rather piecemeal reform. No fundamentally different structure of governance – for example, in the form of a new World Environment Organization (WEO) with far-reaching competences or a complete renegotiation of World Trade Organization (WTO) Agreements, is suggested.[1] This is for two reasons. First, it is this author's firm belief that the recommended policies would be both sufficient and appropriate to achieve the objective of reforming the multilateral investment and trade regimes so that adequate environmental protection can be provided without jeopardizing the economic development aspirations of developing countries. Second, any reform proposals that go substantially beyond the ones advocated in this book would be unlikely to be politically realizable. This is an important point as the best proposals are rendered pointless if they have no realistic chance of becoming realized.

Even realizing the policies recommended in this book will not be easy. Some of the recommendations stand to encounter resistance from developed countries, others from developing countries. For example, assistance for institutional capacity-building and local empowerment costs money and is likely to find lip-service support from developed countries, but opposition when it comes to paying the bill.[2] And introducing an MEA exception clause into GATT following the North American Free Trade Agreement (NAFTA) blueprint is likely to meet resistance from developing countries. It will prove to be a demanding task for those who care about the environment and believe that the multilateral investment and trade regime should favour developing countries at the same time to gather enough political support for a realization of these policies.

What can be said is that the feasibility of all recommended policies would increase if they could be realized as a package. To stick to the two examples given above: developed countries might be willing to step up assistance to institutional capacity-building and local empowerment in developing countries if they could achieve a more secure status for MEAs with respect to WTO rules in return. Conversely, developing countries might be more willing to accept an MEA exception clause within GATT if they could be sure that they will receive additional assistance. A more secure status for MEAs might in turn induce some countries that tend to opt for unilateral action (especially the US) to seek multilateral action with respect to species preservation and environmental protection instead. Thus, all issue areas are linked together, either directly and explicitly so or because politically negotiators are likely to link one issue with another. The best way to deal with this interlinkedness of issues would be to form a special negotiation group in the next round of investment and trade negotiations, which has the competence to formulate proposals that cut across traditional issue areas. As mentioned in Chapter 7, p112, it would be important to include representatives from ministries other than the environment into this negotiating group. A group that was confined to representatives from environmental ministries would most likely have low political status, a confined negotiation mandate and limited support from the more influential factions within participating countries' governments.

All in all, I am not too optimistic that it will be possible to realize the policy recommendations contained in this book or similar ones that have the same effect. On the one hand, the WTO itself seems to have become much more environmentally sensitive, taking the environmentalists' critique against it more seriously, as can be seen by a special study commissioned by the WTO just before the Ministerial Meeting in Seattle (Nordström and Vaughan 1999). On the other hand, this increased sensitivity has yet to translate into successful outcomes of negotiations under the auspices of the WTO. These negotiations can often be incredibly frustrating and not lead anywhere near a conclusion of rather obvious problems. Actually, this is one of the reasons why unilateral action is held in great esteem by some countries. In the end, however, there will be no alternative to multilateral action and hence there is no alternative to the greening of the multilateral investment and trade regimes. Similarly, there will be no alternative to ensuring that this greening takes place in a way that is supportive of the economic development aspirations of developing countries, because their political weight in these matters will increase continually and they can block all reform proposals if they want. We must all work together to make it happen – the sooner the better. Hopefully this book will contribute to a clarification and better understanding of the relevant issues and thus ultimately to the achievement of these goals.

Appendix

Environmental Provisions in Regional and Bilateral Trade and Investment Agreements

Greening Trade and Investment deals only with the multilateral investment and trade regimes. This appendix provides a short overview of environmental provisions contained in regional bilateral trade and investment agreements – see Table A.1. In addition, for comparison the WTO is included as well. Note that completeness is not claimed here since not all existing agreements could be included. Rather, the table focuses on the most important ones, especially with respect to bilateral agreements. The Asia-Pacific Economic Cooperation (APEC) and the proposed Free Trade Area of the Americas (FTAA) have not been included as they do not yet represent trade or investment agreements. The agreement between Canada and Chile – while representing possibly the most environmentally advanced bilateral agreement so far – has not been included due to its strong similarity with provisions contained in the North American Free Trade Agreement (NAFTA) as a consequence of Chile's desire to enter the NAFTA in the near future.

Table A.1 is divided into basic and more advanced environmentally friendly provisions. It can be seen that even rather basic provisions such as environmentally friendly preambular language, provisions for environmental cooperation among the trading partners, an environmental exceptions clause, regular meetings of government officials on environmental issues and a separate environmental chapter or protocol cannot be found in every agreement.

As concerns more advanced environmental provisions, the situation is bleaker still. Provisions for the encouragement of upward harmonization of environmental standards, a clause demanding enforcement of environmental regulations, a clause dissuading countries from lowering environmental standards for the purpose of attracting foreign investment are equally missing in most agreements as is the incorporation of the precautionary principle and a sustainability assessment. Indeed, the NAFTA and the

European Union (EU) are the only regimes that include practically all provisions. Interestingly, while the US seems to be committed to an inclusion of environmental provisions in new agreements as can be seen by the recently concluded bilateral agreement with Jordan, the EU has concluded several recent bilateral association agreements with Southern Mediterranean countries with very weak provisions. This puts into some doubt the EU's commitment to greening investment and trade agreements. As those bilateral agreements are supposed to become transformed into a regional agreement by 2010 (the Mediterranean Free Trade Zone), it remains to be seen whether the EU will strive for including advanced environmental provisions on a multilateral regional level (see Neumayer 2001f).

One possible interpretation of the overview given in Table A.1 is that agreements tend to have only weak environmental provisions if no developed country is party to the agreement. From another perspective, however, one could point out that only highly integrated and comprehensive agreements tend to have more advanced environmental provisions. In other words, while it is true that regional agreements among developing countries tend to have weak environmental provisions, this might be because the agreement itself tends to be rather weak in its trade and other integration provisions as well.

Mercosur might represent a case in point here. While to some extent still in its early phase of development, it has been characterized as 'the most ambitious scheme of regional integration since the creation of the European Community in 1957' (Tussie 2000, p. 189). Interestingly, as Mercosur strives to become a regional agreement that is more integrated and comprehensive than others among developing countries, it also tends to include more environmental provisions, as can be seen from the Table.

More comparative research is needed with respect to what lessons, if any, can be learned from the experience with certain agreements for others. The question is whether provisions in one agreement can meaningfully be transposed into another. For example, the Common Market for Eastern and Southern Africa (COMESA) includes the precautionary principle via simply taking over the relevant formulation from the Treaty establishing the European Union. Does such copying make sense or do environmentally friendly provisions need to be tailored towards the specific problems facing members to a regional agreement?

Finally, a note of caution with respect to the interpretation of Table A.1. It merely states whether the relevant provisions are existent in principle, occasionally subjected to a qualification. It does not, however, question their actual relevance and the extent of their realization in practice. Environmental cooperation, for example, may not take place to any significant extent even if provided for in the agreement. And if it does happen, it may or may not have significant environmental effects. A comparative analysis of these more far reaching questions represents a priority for future research.

Table A.1 Overview of environmental provisions in regional and bilateral agreements

Basic provisions	WTO	EU[1]	NAFTA[2]	Mercosur[3]	Andean Community[4]	CARICOM[5]	ASEAN/AFTA[6]	SADC[7]	COMESA[8]	EU-Med.[9]	US-Jordan[10]
Basic provisions											
Environmentally friendly preambular language	✓	✓	✓	✓[11]	✗	✓[11]	✗	✗	✗	✗	✓
Separate environment chapter/protocol	✗	✓	✓	✓	✗	✗	✗	✗	✓	✗	✓[12]
Environmental exceptions clause	✓	✓	✓	✗	✗	✗	✗	✗	✗	✓	✓
Environmental cooperation	✗	✓	✓	✓	✓	✓	✓	✓	✓	✓	✗
Regular meetings of government officials on environmental issues	✗	✓	✓	✓	✗	✓	✓	✓[11]	✗	✗	✗
Advanced provisions											
Encouragement of upward harmonization of environmental standards	✗	✓	✓[13]	✓	✗	✗	✗	✗	✗	✗	✓[14]
Enforcement clause	✗	✓[15]	✓	✗	✗	✗	✗	✗	✗	✗	✓
Not-lowering clause	✗	✗	✓	✗	✗	✗	✗	✗	✗	✗	✓
Precautionary principle integrated	✓[16]	✓	✓[17]	✗	✗	✗	✗	✗	✓	✗	✗
Sustainability assessment	✓[18]	✓[11]	✓	✗	✗	✗	✗	✗	✗	✗	✓

Key: ✓ provision exists; ✗ provision does not exist

1 European Union, comprising Austria, Belgium, Denmark, Finland, France, Germany, Greece, Ireland, Italy, Luxembourg, the Netherlands, Portugal, Spain, Sweden and the United Kingdom.

2 North American Free Trade Agreement, comprising Canada, Mexico and the United States.

3 Mercado Común del Sur, comprising Argentina, Brazil, Paraguay and Uruguay.

4 Comprising Bolivia, Colombia, Ecuador, Peru and Venezuela.

5 Caribbean Community, comprising Antigua and Barbuda, Bahamas, Barbados, Belize, Dominica, Grenada, Guyana, Jamaica, Montserrat, Saint Lucia, St. Kitts and Nevis, St. Vincent and the Grenadines, Suriname, and Trinidad and Tobago.

6 Association of Southeast Asian Nations (ASEAN)/ASEAN Free Trade Area, comprising Brunei Darussalam, Cambodia, Indonesia, Laos, Malaysia, Myanmar, Philippines, Singapore, and Thailand.

7 Southern African Development Community, comprising Botswana, Lesotho, Malawi, Mauritius, Mozambique, Namibia, South Africa, Swaziland, Tanzania and Zimbabwe. Three further members (Angola, Democratic Republic of Congo and the Seychelles) have not yet joined the Southern African free trade agreement.

8 Common Market for Eastern and Southern Africa, comprising Angola, Burundi, Comoros, Democratic Republic of Congo, Djibouti, Egypt, Eritrea, Kenya, Madagascar, Malawi, Mauritius, Namibia, Rwanda, Seychelles, Sudan, Swaziland, Tanzania, Uganda, Zambia and Zimbabwe.

9 Bilateral association agreements between the EU and Southern Mediterranean countries. At the time of writing, modern agreements have been negotiated with Egypt, Israel, Jordan, Morocco, Tunisia, and the Palestinian Authority.

10 Bilateral free trade agreement between the US and Jordan.

11 Limited.

12 Separate environment article.

13 Indirect encouragement only: Parties are encouraged to harmonize their standards and no country is allowed to lower its standards.

14 No provision for upward harmonization, but provision encouraging raising of environmental standards.

15 The Treaty establishing the European Union only contains enforcement provisions for environmental regulation based on directives or secondary environmental legislation at the Community level, not for environmental regulations enacted in the absence of Community harmonization.

16 Only included in one WTO agreement, the Agreement on the application of Sanitary and Phytosanitary Measures, and only rudimentarily: Art. 5.7 of this agreement allows members only provisionally to adopt a precautionary approach in the face of scientific uncertainty.

17 Only rudimentary integration in the chapters on sanitary and phytosanitary and standards-related measures. Similar to the WTO case, a precautionary approach in the face of scientific uncertainty is allowed provisionally only.

18 Not undertaken by WTO itself, but by some of its members (for example, Canada and EU).

Notes

Preface

1   See Neumayer (1999a, 1999b, 2000a, 2000b, 2001c, 2001d, 2001e).

Introduction

1   More precisely, regimes should be understood here as 'implicit or explicit principles, norms, rules, and decision-making procedures around which actors' expectations converge in a given area of international relations' (Krasner 1983, p2).
2   Foreign investment can be broken down into FDI and portfolio equity flows. Whereas FDI involves a long-term management interest in the acquired or newly set-up enterprise, portfolio equity investment does not lead to lasting management control.
3   For an introductory overview of some of these regional free trade agreements from an environmental perspective see, for example, Charnovitz (1995), Tussie and Vasquez (1997), Esty and Geradin (1997), Neumayer (2001a, 2001f).
4   That more emphasis is put on NAFTA rules is because they are most relevant to investment issues, such as investor-to-state dispute settlement. This does not mean that the author would regard the NAFTA regime to deal with environmental issues more successfully than the EU.

Chapter 1

1   The difference between GNP and GDP is that GDP includes output produced by foreigners within a country and excludes output produced by nationals abroad. The difference for most countries is usually quite small and does not matter here.
2   Analysis undertaken by UNCTAD shows that foreign portfolio equity investment flows are indeed generally more volatile than FDI flows to developing countries (see UNCTAD 1998a, p14ff). The reader should recall that the former does not entail a lasting management interest in the acquired enterprise, whereas the latter does.
3   To a certain extent, incentives might increase the amount of available investment as, *ceteris paribus*, they raise the return on investment and thereby the opportunity costs of consumption. Also, incentives, especially subsidies, can be justified on efficiency grounds if foreign investment generates positive externalities to the wider host economy.
4   At that time, EFTA contracting parties comprised Austria, Finland, Iceland, Norway, Sweden and Switzerland.

5   Similar side agreements were concluded for other issues as well, most notably the North American Agreement on Labour Cooperation.
6   OECD countries comprise the developed countries plus (since 1994–1996) the Czech Republic, Hungary, Mexico, Poland and South Korea.
7   For a joint NGO statement on the MAI, see Anonymous (1997). The assertion by one NGO activist that '*we* put the MAI in the "deep freeze" in the OECD' (Strand-Rangnes 1999, added emphasis) is certainly exaggerated, but not completely without foundation. For a comprehensive list of links to NGO web pages see the 'Annotated List of MAI Websites' at
http://www.corpwatch.org/trac/globalization/treaties/mailinks.html
8   This perception is shared by many observers. See, for example, Witherell (1998, p1), Lalumière and Landau (1998, p3), Hillyard (1998, p37), Henderson (1999, p48).
9   The WTO has had a working group on investment since 1996. Hence the question is whether to turn this working group into a negotiating group.
10 See also the statement of Third World Intellectuals (1999) against any linkage of trade with the environment or labour issues.
11 On another occasion I have argued that the strategy to insist on a mere renegotiation of existing agreements is not politically viable (Neumayer 1999b). Developing countries will find it in their best interest to support a new and comprehensive round of trade negotiations as it will be the only way to achieve the quid pro quos that are necessary to achieve a rectification of some of the results of the Uruguay Round. It is somewhat naive to believe that the developed countries will simply renegotiate old agreements without any prospect of gaining something in exchange.

Chapter 2

1   Chapeau and preamble mean the same here.
2   The precautionary principle says that preventive measures to avoid environmental harm should (or at least can) be undertaken before there is definite scientific evidence proving that certain activities cause environmental harm. It has been enshrined as Principle 15 into the Rio Declaration on Environment and Development at the UN conference in 1992, but under the name of precautionary approach: 'In order to protect the environment, the precautionary approach shall be widely applied by States according to their capabilities. Where there are threats of serious or irreversible damage, lack of full scientific certainty shall not be used as a reason for postponing cost-effective measures to prevent environmental degradation.'
3   That is, a system specifically designed for a specific type of intellectual property.
4   Investment in services is covered by GATS, the General Agreement on Trade in Services, and is not explicitly addressed here – see Sauvé (1994, pp9–13) for an overview.

Chapter 3

1   This chapter is mainly written from an economic perspective. For good summaries and analyses of the relevant debate in the legal literature, see Swire (1996), Revesz (1998), and Esty and Geradin (2000).
2   Equivalently, one can define efficiency as the level at which the marginal social damage of pollution is equal to the marginal abatement cost of pollution. If standards are not set at their efficiency level, then a country's welfare can be

increased via either reducing or increasing pollution. A simple thought experiment can clarify this point: if, say, the marginal social damage of pollution is higher than the marginal abatement cost, then there is excessive pollution and a country's welfare would increase by abating one further unit of pollution (the marginal unit of pollution). This is because of our assumption that the marginal social damage is higher than the marginal abatement cost and holds true up until the two marginal costs are just equal to each other. Conversely, if the marginal abatement cost of pollution is higher than the marginal social cost of pollution, then there is excessive pollution abatement (that is, pollution is reduced by 'too much'). A country's welfare would increase by allowing one further unit of pollution (the marginal unit of pollution). This is because of our assumption that the marginal abatement cost is higher than the marginal social damage and holds true up until the two marginal costs are just equal to each other, which represents the efficient environmental standard.

3   Eskeland and Harrison (1997) provide statistical evidence from US data that energy use is highly correlated with different measures of emissions.

4   Spearman's r is –.506, significant at the .05 level and –.689, significant at the .01 level, respectively.

5   See also Neumayer (2001a).

6   The borders between Eastern and Western European countries and the US-Mexican border are some of the few cases where this kind of transboundary pollution can be a potentially significant problem. Spill-overs from the developing world into the developed world are much more common, however, if we look at psychological spill-overs rather than physical pollution. Mexico's incidental killing of dolphins in its tuna fishing or India's, Pakistan's, Thailand's and Malaysia's incidental killing of sea turtles in their shrimp harvesting are prominent examples of hurting people's environmental sentiments in developed countries, especially the US (see p136).

7   The World Bank does not control for differentials in export–import ratios in overall goods and services, which, strictly speaking, it should do. As this ratio is .9 for low-income and 1.03 for high-income countries in 1995 (data taken from World Bank (1997)), the World Bank's (1998a, p113) conclusions remain valid, however: even after taking into account differences in the overall export–import ratio, low-income countries import many more goods from dirty industries than they export.

8   This conclusion is based on an analysis of the sources provided in the technical notes to OECD (1998g).

9   These cover the chemical industry, petroleum refining without extraction, the production of synthetics and rubber wares, iron and metal mining, as well as founding, paper and pulp production and processing.

10 As these figures include public environmental expenditures as well, which do not directly represent costs to the private sector, they tend to overestimate the true cost of compliance with environmental standards for the private sector.

11 They are not intended to be hierarchical.

12 The amendment would only be binding on the parties accepting it.

13 The baptists–bootleggers metaphor is due to the prohibition on the sale of alcohol in the US during 1920–1933 which was strongly supported by two groups: by baptists for non-materialist religious reasons and by bootleggers as they profited from illegal trading.

Chapter 4

1   The GCC counts 39 US corporations and industry associations among its members (BNA 2000a). The companies mainly come from the steel, oil, agriculture, electricity, rail and chemical industries. The associations include such important ones as the

American Petroleum Institute, the US Chamber of Commerce, the Chemical Manufacturers Association and the National Mining Association. GCC lost several prominent members, including Royal Dutch Shell, BP Amoco, DaimlerChrysler, Ford and Texaco. Shell and BP changed their position and support the Kyoto Protocol by now, and Chrysler had to change its position after being taken over by Daimler. Ford and Texaco, on the other hand, left the coalition merely for image reasons as it considered its continued membership to be detrimental towards its reputation. However, both companies have pledged to continue opposing the Kyoto Protocol as well as any other mandatory greenhouse gas emission cuts (BNA 1999c, BNA 2000a).

2   As a substitute, EU countries are now considering the imposition of minimum excise duties to a wide range of energy products. However, even this rather minimalist solution is currently blocked by opposition from environmental 'laggers' such as Ireland and Spain (ENS 1999).

3   This is the case, for example, with the German ecological tax reform, where energy-intensive manufacturing firms can get a rebate on their tax. The draft European Council Directive in its Article 10 promised this rebate for all energy-intensive firms. Similar exemptions apply with respect to the Danish and Swedish carbon/energy taxes (Brack, Grubb and Windram 2000).

4   For a detailed explanation of the quite complicated legal issues involved see Brack, Grubb and Windram (2000, pp81–90); Schoenbaum (1997, pp308–312); Düerkop (1994, pp820–823); Demaret and Stewardson (1994). However, a final judgement on this question cannot be made as no WTO panel has ever decided on it.

Chapter 5

1   As a consequence, Ethyl's challenge of Bill C–29 in the domestic Canadian legal system never went to trial.

2   Under NAFTA rules, investors cannot challenge subnational governments directly, but the federal governments are held responsible for actions of its states or provinces.

3   These are position papers which aim to provide tribunals with information that otherwise might remain unnoticed.

Chapter 6

1   At that time, Bob White was President of the Canadian Labour Congress and President of the Trade Union Advisory Committee to the OECD.

2   It is unclear whether these propositions would have actually been included had an MAI been concluded. OECD (1998c) suggests that 'a large majority (of the negotiating group) expressed support for the overall approach and believed that it could be a basis for further work'.

3   And there can be no doubt that this strong political message would have exerted considerable pressure on developing countries to accede.

Chapter 7

1   Comparative advantage is not to be confused with absolute advantage. A country can have an absolute advantage in producing all goods and services if it can produce these more productively than its competitors. It can never have a comparative advantage in all goods and services, however, as comparative advantage refers

to the opportunity costs of production: with limited amounts of labour, capital and resources, production of one good always means that other goods cannot be produced.

2   Note the emphasis on different factor endowments. The fact that about two-thirds of trade takes place between similarly endowed developed countries (Baldwin and Martin 1999, p12) demonstrates that other factors such as economies of scale, product differentiation and monopolistic competition have a major influence on international trade patterns, but it does not contradict the principle of comparative advantage.

3   However, Copeland and Taylor (1999) also show that under certain conditions trade liberalization can lead to a lock-in of an inefficient spatial pattern of specialization in the sense that the country with the most vulnerable environment specializes in dirty production, whereas its trading partner produces the clean goods.

4   The phenomenon is sometimes also known as the California effect, a term also coined by Vogel, as other US states followed California's lead in setting more stringent air emission standards for cars.

5   For a more elaborate critique of the actual significance of the 'trading up' phenomenon, see Swire (1996).

6   The reader should note that this result represents a possibility, but is not robust to changes in the specification of the model. More comprehensive models are ambiguous with respect to whether trade liberalization increases global pollution (see Copeland and Taylor 1997).

7   The EKC is a bell-shaped curve in a diagram with environmental pollution on the ordinate and (per capita) income levels on the abscissa. It is named after the economist Simon Kuznets who hypothesized a similar relationship with economic growth, but for income distribution on the ordinate.

8   For the case of sulphur dioxide concentrations only, Antweiler, Copeland and Taylor (1998) come to a different conclusion. In their study, the scale and technique lead to a net reduction in these emissions, which, in the words of the authors, 'yields a somewhat surprising conclusion: freer trade appears to be good for the environment'.

9   The proposals put forward in this section should be considered additional to the recommendations given in Chapter 8 regarding the openness and transparency of the dispute settlement process, which have some relevance for NGOs.

10   In this respect it is interesting to note that the International Trade Organization (ITO), which, as Chapter 1 has shown, can be regarded a predecessor to the WTO in many respects, had far-reaching provisions for the inclusion of NGOs (Charnovitz and Wickham 1995).

11   Myers and Kent (1998, pxvii) provide the higher estimate of US$703 billion for the two sectors together.

12   Jha, Markandya and Vossenaar (1999, p39) report from an UNCTAD study that these sectors comprise about one-third of the value of total exports and half of the value of manufactured exports of developing countries.

Chapter 8

1   Non-product related means that the environmental effect does not form part of the product produced. The environmental effect is fully related to the PPM with which the product was produced.

2   Wofford (2000) argues in some detail that these changes have helped the WTO dispute settlement system to adopt a more judicial and professional approach in accordance with standard international legal practice.

3   If a developing country is involved in the dispute it can demand that one of the panellists is from the developing world (Article 8.10).

4   This clarification of the rules contained in the DSU has been confirmed by another ruling of the appellate body in a non-environment related case (WTO 2000a, paragraph 42). Interestingly, in that case it was a business group that submitted the brief, which demonstrates that the rights of submission will be exerted by non-state groups other than NGOs in the usual sense as well. The renewed acceptance of amicus curiae briefs in these and other cases as well has angered many countries that think that such acceptance should only be granted, if at all, after a change of the DSU by WTO members (BNA 2000i).

5   Note that, as pointed out on p124, following the appellate body report in 'United States – Standards for reformulated and conventional gasoline' panels are required to examine first whether a trade measure falls within one of the specific exceptions of Article XX and then proceed to examine further whether it conflicts with the preamble. Before that decision, panels very often proceeded in the reverse order as was the case here.

6   According to Wofford (2000, p590), the concept of precedent, even if formally non-existent, does exist de facto in the WTO dispute system.

7   The precautionary principle says that preventive measures to avoid environmental harm should (or at least can) be undertaken before there is definite scientific evidence proving that certain activities cause environmental harm.

8   For a similar view, see Charnovitz (2000, p181).

9   For a contrary view, see Charnovitz (ibid, pp189ff).

10   United States environmental NGOs are unsatisfied with this response, however, and have already successfully challenged the shipment-by-shipment device before the US Court of International Trade (ICTSD 1999d; ICTSD 2000l). However, the Court decided not to require the government to change its guidelines, saying that 'given the facts and circumstances of this case, which obviously transcend purely domestic concerns, this court is unable to conclude that the government's position is not substantially justified' (quoted in ICTSD 2000l).

11   This does not apply to Pakistan which successfully managed to become certified by the US in July 2000 (US Department of State 2000).

12   According to Hudec (1996, p167, footnote 108) '[t]o old GATT hands, the degree of support shown for these two panel rulings amounts to virtual unanimity, because the rest of the 110-odd GATT member countries either do not attend Council meetings or almost never speak anyway'.

13   Note that such reform can only be undertaken by consensus (Article X:8 of the Agreement Establishing the WTO).

14   To become adopted, such an interpretation needs the support of three-fourths of WTO members.

15   A notable exception is the Chilean restrictions on port access, which amount to a ban on transshipments of swordfish (see p138).

16   Things are somewhat different with respect to sea turtles, which indeed are endangered and therefore listed in Appendix 1 of CITES.

17   Principle 15 of the Rio Declaration on Environment and Development from 1992 seems to embrace a similar reasoning in stating that 'lack of full scientific certainty shall not be used as a reason for postponing *cost-effective* measures to prevent environmental degradation' (added emphasis).

Chapter 9

1   The major contributions are Barrett (1990, 1991, 1994a, 1994c, 1997a, 1997b);

Carraro and Siniscalco (1993); Endres and Finus (1998); Finus and Rundshagen (1998a, 1998b).

2   Cooperation can be wider and deeper if the emissions abatement is characterized by fixed costs, so that the average costs fall over a certain range of abatement, or if the emissions abatement creates positive technological externalities, so that abatement by one country reduces the abatement costs of other countries – see Heal (1994).

3   A necessary condition is, however, that the trade measures are executed by a minimum number of countries and not just by one country alone (Barrett 1997b, p347). Indeed, cooperating countries that fail to execute trade sanctions against free-riders might themselves face trade measures.

4   Trade measures are cheaper than transfer payments as they do not impose any costs as long as the deterrence of free-riding is successful.

5   For an overview, see Smith (1998).

6   In addition to these explicit trade measures addressed at non-parties, parties to the Montreal Protocol might enact a number of measures in compliance with the Protocol, which can have relevant effects on the trade with other parties. These include, for example, quantitative restrictions on the imports of, and excise taxes on ODSs, and restrictions on the import of ODS technologies.

7   Furthermore, CITES is biased towards mammals and especially to the ones that humans find 'attractive' at the expense of the relative neglect of endangered non-mammals (Webb 2000). Interestingly, Metrick and Weitzman (1996) have found the same bias for the US Endangered Species Protection Act.

8   Agenda 21 was concluded at the United Nations Conference on Environment and Development (UNCED) in Rio de Janeiro in 1992.

9   One test case could have been the Chilean ban on the trans-shipments of swordfish, briefly described on p138, but it never went before a panel.

10   Similarly, Article 11:8 for the special case of living modified organisms intended for direct use as food or feed, or for processing.

11   For a general critique of this approach, see Saladin (1999).

12   The most conspicuous exception being, of course, the United States, a non-party to both the CBD and the Basel Convention.

13   Because the proposal was never formally submitted to the Committee on Trade and Environment (CTE), it is called a 'non-paper' in WTO nomenclature.

14   Amendments to GATT Articles I and II need consensus (Article X:2).

15   Note that such a clause would need to be outside GATT Article XX and would therefore not be subject to its chapeau requirements.

16   Plant varieties are improved versions of plants through breeding techniques with the purpose of making them stable and uniform (South Centre 1997, p28).

17   That is, a system specifically designed for a specific type of intellectual property. One such *sui generis* system is the International Convention for the Protection of New Varieties of Plants (UPOV Convention).

18   Note, however, that even the CBD demands that 'such access and transfer shall be provided on terms which recognize and are consistent with the adequate and effective protection of intellectual property rights' (Article 16:2).

19   Note that many provisions other than Article 27 have also not been implemented yet by developing countries and that the gentlemen's agreement covers all non-implementation issues, not just those with respect to Article 27. On 1 May 2000 the US announced that it would initiate two disputes against developing countries which are non-related to Article 27 of the TRIPs Agreement (ICTSD 2000h).

20   In the absence of relevant WTO case law on Article 27 of the TRIPs Agreement, it is unclear whether a panel would apply the same restrictive interpretation to the term 'necessary' as meaning 'least trade restrictive' as panels have interpreted the similar formulation of GATT Article XX(b).

21 One last remark: Critics of the patentability provisions contained in Art. 27:3(b) sometimes seem to forget that this article actually provides countries with the discretion to explicitly exclude certain life forms from patentability. This is true for all plants and animals as well as all essentially biological processes for the production of plants or animals. It is also true for all non-genetically modified micro-organisms found in nature.

Chapter 10

1 A WEO has been suggested by, for example, academics (Newell and Whalley 1999) as well as Renato Ruggiero (1999), then WTO Director-General, by French President Jacques Chirac (BNA 2000h) and recently by Laura Tyson, the defeated US presidential candidate Al Gore's economic adviser (ICTSD 2000m). Unfortunately, apart from Newell and Whalley (1999), these individuals do not seem to have a clear idea of what exactly the WEO is supposed to do, which is one of the reasons the EU has established an informal working group to study the pros and cons of such a new institution (BNA 2000h).

2 Menyasz (2000) quotes David Runnalls, President of the Winnipeg-based International Institute for Sustainable Development, as saying: 'The agreement at the 1992 Earth Summit in Rio de Janeiro to trade developing countries' support for the "Northern" agenda of biodiversity, deforestation, and climate change for a commitment from the developed countries to trade concessions, foreign aid, and technology transfers has produced little in the way of concrete results. The developed country side of that bargain never materialised.'

References

Abimanyu, A (1996) 'Impact of free trade on industrial pollution: do pollution havens exist?', *ASEAN Economic Bulletin*, vol 13, pp39–51

Ad Hoc Working Group on the MAI (1998) *MAI: Democracy for Sale?*, New York: Apex Press

AEA (1999) *Position of the American Electronics Association (AEA) on the European Commission's Draft Directive on Waste from Electrical and Electronic Equipment (WEEE)*, Washington, DC: American Electronics Association

AFL–CIO (1998) *Statement on the Multilateral Agreement on Investment*, 14 October, Washington, DC: AFL–CIO Executive Council

Agreement on Internal Trade Panel (1998) *Report of the article 1704 panel concerning a dispute between Alberta and Canada regarding the Manganese-based Fuel Additives Act*, Winnipeg: Agreement on Internal Trade

Ahlander, A-M Satre (1994) *Environmental problems in the shortage economy – the legacy of Soviet environmental policy*, Cheltenham: Edward Elgar

Albrecht, J (1998) 'Environmental policy and the inward investment position of US "dirty" industries', *Intereconomics*, July/August, pp186–194

Alliance for Sustainable Jobs and the Environment (1999) *Houston Principles of the Alliance for Sustainable Jobs and the Environment*, Eureka: Alliance for Sustainable Jobs and the Environment

Alliance Project (2000) 'Minneapolis City Council Passes "Free Burma" Resolution', press release, 19 May 2000, Saint Paul: Alliance Project

Anderson, K (1992) 'The Standard Welfare Economics of Policies Affecting Trade and the Environment' in Kym Anderson and Richard Blackhurst (eds) *The Greening of World Trade Issues*, Michigan: University of Michigan Press

Anonymous (1997) *Joint NGO statement on the multilateral agreement on investment (MAI)*, online available at http://corpwatch.org/trac/feature/planet/mai_ngo.html

Anonymous (1999) 'Ottawa's flip-flop on PCBs cost $85M, with suit pending – $20M in damages sought: Ohio firm seeking compensation for government policy', *Financial Post*, 25 November

Antweiler, W, B R Copeland and M S Taylor (1998) *Is free trade good for the environment?*, Working Paper 6707, Washington, DC: National Bureau of Economic Affairs

API (2000) *What is the US oil and natural gas industry's position on the Kyoto Protocol?* Washington, DC: American Petroleum Industry

Appleton (1998) *Statement of claim under the arbitration rules of the United Nations Commission on International Trade Law and the North American Free Trade Agreement between SD Myers Inc and the Government of Canada*, Ontario: Appleton & Associates International Lawyers

Appleton (1999) *Statement of claim under the arbitration rules of the United Nations Commission on International Trade Law and the North Amerian Free Trade Agreement between Pope & Talbot Inc and the Government of Canada*, Ontario: Appleton & Associates International Lawyers

Appleton, A E (1997) *Environmental Labelling Programmes: International Trade Law Implications*, London: Kluwer Law International

Arbitral Tribunal (2000a) *Interim award in the matter of an arbitration under chapter eleven of the North American Free Trade Agreement between Pope & Talbot Inc and The Government of Canada*, 26 June 2000

Arbitral Tribunal (2000b) *Partial award in a NAFTA arbitration under the UNCITRAL arbitration rules in the matter S.D. Myers Inc versus Government of Canada*, 13 November 2000

Arbitral Tribunal (2000c) *Award in the matter of an arbitration between Metalclad Corporation versus United Mexican States*, Case Arb (AF)/97/1, Washington, DC: International Centre for the Settlement of Investment Disputes (Additional Facility)

Arbitral Tribunal (2001) *Decisions of the tribunal on petitions from third persons to intervene as 'amici curiae' in the matter Methanex Corporation versus United States of America*, 15 January 2001

Arden-Clarke, C (1993) 'An Action Agenda for Trade Policy Reform to Support Sustainable Development: A United Nations Conference on Environment and Development Follow-Up' in Durwood Zaelke, Paul Orbuch and Robert F Housman (eds) *Trade and the Environment: Law, Economics, and Policy*, Washington, DC: Island Press

Australian Parliament Joint Standing Committee on Treaties (1999) *Multilateral Agreement on Investment: Final Report*, March 1999, Canberra: Joint Standing Committee on Treaties

Bairoch, P and R Kozul-Wright (1996) *Globalization Myths: Some Historical Reflections on Integration, Industrialization and Growth in the World Economy*, Discussion Paper 113, Geneva: United Nations Conference on Trade and Development

Balasubramanyam, VN (1998) *The Multilateral Agreement on Investment (MAI) and Foreign Direct Investment in Developing Countries*, International Business Research Group Discussion Paper EC 10/98, Lancaster: Lancaster University, Department of Economics

Balasubramanyam, V N, M Salisu and D Sapsford (1996) 'Foreign Direct Investment and Growth in EP and IS Countries', *Economic Journal*, vol 106, no 434, pp92–105

Baldwin, R E and P Martin (1999) *Two Waves of Globalisation: Superficial Similarities, Fundamental Differences*, Working Paper 6904, Cambridge, Mass: National Bureau of Economic Research

Barrett, S (1990) 'The problem of global environmental protection', *Oxford Review of Economic Policy*, vol 6, no 1, pp68–79

Barrett, S (1991) 'Economic analysis of international environmental agreements: lessons for a global warming treaty' in OECD (ed) *Responding to Climate Change: Selected Economic Issues*, Paris: OECD

Barrett, S (1994a) 'Self-enforcing international environmental agreements', *Oxford Economic Papers*, vol 46, no 5, pp878–894

Barrett, S (1994b) 'Strategic Environmental Policy and International Trade', *Journal of Public Economics*, vol 54, no 3, pp325–338

Barrett, S (1994c) 'The Biodiversity Supergame', *Environmental and Resource Economics*, vol 4, no 1, pp111–122

Barrett, S (1997a) 'Heterogeneous International Environmental Agreements' in Carlo Carraro (ed) *International Environmental Negotiations – Strategic Policy Issues*, Cheltenham: Edward Elgar

Barrett, S (1997b) 'The strategy of trade sanctions in international environmental agreements', *Resource and Energy Economics*, vol 19, no 4, pp345–361

Barrett, S (1998) 'Political economy of the Kyoto Protocol', *Oxford Review of Economic Policy*, vol 14, no 4, pp20–39

Bartik, T J (1988) 'The effects of environmental regulation on business location in the United States', *Growth and Change*, vol 19, pp22–44

BDI (1998a) 'Die Spitzenverbände der Wirtschaft warnen: "Ökosteuern sind ein Irrweg..."', press release, 28 August 1998, Köln: Bundesverband der Deutschen Industrie

BDI (1998b) 'BDI anläßlich der Ökosteuerpläne der rot-grünen Koalition: "Die gewerbliche Wirtschaft darf nicht mit zusätzlichen Ökosteuern belastet werden!"', press release, 5 November 1998, Köln: Bundesverband der Deutschen Industrie

Beers, C van and J C J M van den Bergh (1997) 'An empirical multi-country analysis of the impact of environmental regulations on foreign trade flows', *Kyklos*, vol 50, pp29–46

Beers, C van and J C J M van den Bergh (2001) 'Perseverance of perverse subsidies and their impact on trade and environment', *Ecological Economics*, vol 36, no 3, pp475–486

Beghin, J and M Potier (1997) 'Effects of trade liberalisation on the environment in the manufacturing sector', *World Economy*, vol 20, no 4, pp435–456

Ben-David, D, H Nordström and L A Winters (2000) *Trade, Income Disparity and Poverty*, Special Studies 5, Geneva: World Trade Organization

Bhagwati, J (1993) 'Trade and the environment: The false conflict?' in Durwood Zaelke, Paul Orbuch and Robert F Housman (eds) *Trade and the Environment: Law, Economics, and Policy*, Washington, DC: Island Press

Bhagwati, J (1998) 'The capital myth: The difference between trade in widgets and dollars', *Foreign Affairs*, vol 77, no 3, pp7–12

Birdsall, N and D Wheeler (1993) 'Trade policy and industrial pollution in Latin America: Where are the pollution havens?', *Journal of Environment & Development*, vol 2, pp137–149

BMU (2000) *Die Ökologische Steuerreform – der Einstieg und ihre Fortführung*, Berlin: Bundesumweltministerium

BNA (1997) 'Losses of 3 million jobs predicted from Kyoto Agreement by industry group', *Environment Reporter*, vol 28, no 32, 12 December 1997, Washington, DC: Bureau of National Affairs

BNA (1998a) 'Reaction mixed on US signing of treaty; opponents urge quick vote on ratification', *Environment Reporter*, vol 29, no 28, 13 November 1998, Washington, DC: Bureau of National Affairs

BNA (1998b) 'US firm seeks arbitration under NAFTA investor-state provisions', *International Trade Reporter*, vol 15, no 29, 29 July 1998, Washington, DC: Bureau of National Affairs

BNA (1998c) 'Canadian, US officials to present solution of water export issue to IJC', *International Trade Reporter*, vol 15, no 49, 16 December 1998, Washington, DC: Bureau of National Affairs

BNA (1999a) 'Mexico prevails in first decision issued under NAFTA Chapter Eleven', *International Trade Reporter*, vol 16, no 46, 24 November, Washington, DC: Bureau of National Affairs

BNA (1999b) 'Mexican environment official airs issues raised in Chapter 11 dispute', *International Trade Reporter*, vol 16, no 50, 23 December, Washington, DC: Bureau of National Affairs

BNA (1999c) 'Ford leaves Global Climate Coalition, cites distraction from environment moves', *Environment Reporter*, vol 30, no 31, 10 December 1999, Washington, DC: Bureau of National Affairs

BNA (1999d) 'US investor seeks $50 million from Mexico in case involving excise tax', *International Trade Reporter*, vol 16, no 24, 16 June 1999, Washington, DC: Bureau of National Affairs

BNA (1999e) 'Panel expected to be constituted soon in Canadian firm's $725 million NAFTA claim', *International Trade Reporter*, vol 16, no 3, 20 January 1999, Washington, DC: Bureau of National Affairs

BNA (1999f) 'Chicago Council calls on Congress, EPA to eliminate MTBE in reformulated gasoline', *Environment Reporter*, vol 30, no 33, 24 December 1999, Washington, DC: Bureau of National Affairs

BNA (1999g) 'Commission issues directive banning use of chysotile asbestos, fibers as of 2005', *International Trade Reporter*, vol 16, no 32, 11 August 1999, Washington, DC: Bureau of National Affairs

BNA (2000a) 'Industry lobbying group to continue opposition to emission reduction mandates', *Environment Reporter*, vol 31, no 10, 10 March 2000, Washington, DC: Bureau of National Affairs

BNA (2000b) 'CEC dismisses complaints against US based on NAFTA Chapter 11 challenge', *International Environment Reporter*, vol 23, no 15, 19 July, Washington, DC: Bureau of National Affairs

BNA (2000c) 'NAFTA claimant makes effort to open arbitration hearings to public', *International Trade Reporter*, vol 17, no 12, 23 March, Washington, DC: Bureau of National Affairs

BNA (2000d) 'WTO rules allow parties to forgo rights in multilateral environment pacts', *Environment Reporter*, vol 31, no 11, 17 March 2000, Washington, DC: Bureau of National Affairs

BNA (2000e) 'UPS files NAFTA Chapters 11, 15 claim against Canada Post Corp for $156 million', *International Trade Reporter*, vol 17, no 7, 27 April 2000, Washington, DC: Bureau of National Affairs

BNA (2000f) 'Asian nations claim European proposal on electronic waste unfair barrier to trade', *International Environment Reporter*, vol 23, no 16, 2 August 2000, Washington, DC: Bureau of National Affairs

BNA (2000g) 'WTO members make unfriendly noises on friends of the court dispute briefs', *International Trade Reporter*, vol 17, no 33, 17 August 2000, Washington, DC: Bureau of National Affairs

BNA (2000h) 'EU working group formed to examine creation of World Environment Organization', *International Environment Reporter*, vol 23, no 15, 19 July 2000, Washington, DC: Bureau of National Affairs

BNA (2000i) 'WTO members make unfriendly noises on friends of the court dispute briefs', *International Trade Reporter*, vol 17, no 33, 17 August 2000, Washington, DC: Bureau of National Affairs

Borensztein, E, J De Gregorio and J-W Lee (1998) 'How does Foreign Direct Investment Affect Economic Growth?', *Journal of International Economics*, vol 45, no 1, pp115–135

Brack, D (1996) *International Trade and the Montreal Protocol*, London: Earthscan and Royal Institute of International Affairs

Brack, D (2000) 'Environmental treaties and trade: Multilateral environmental agreements and the multilateral trading system' in Gary Sampson and W Bradnee Chambers (eds) *Trade, Environment, and the Millennium*, Tokyo: United Nations University Press

Brack, D, M Grubb and C Windram (2000) *International Trade and Climate Change Policies*, London: Earthscan and Royal Institute of International Affairs

Brander, J A and M S Taylor (1998) 'Open access renewable resources: Trade and trade policy in a two-country model', *Journal of International Economics* 44, pp181–209

Brown, W A Jr (1950) *The United States and the restoration of world trade*, Washington, DC: The Brookings Institution

Bundesbank (1994, 1997, 1999) *Kapitalverflechtung mit dem Ausland*, Deutsche Bundesbank, Frankfurt

Caldwell, D Jake (1994) 'International environmental agreements and the GATT: An analysis of the potential conflict and the role of a GATT "waiver" resolution', *MD Journal of International Law & Trade*, vol 18, pp173–198

Canada (1999a) *WTO and Transparency – Communication from Canada*, WT/GC/W/350, Geneva: World Trade Organization

Canada (1999b) *Canadian Approach to Trade and Environment in the New WTO Round – Communication from Canada*, WT/GC/W/358, Geneva: World Trade Organization

Canada (1999c) *Strategic Environmental Assessment of the New Round of Multilateral Trade Negotiations at the WTO*, Ottawa: Department of Foreign Affairs and International Trade

Canada (2001) *Framework for conducting environmental assessments of trade negotiations*, Ottawa: Department of Foreign Affairs and International Trade

Canadian Parliament Sub-Committee on International Trade, Trade Disputes and Investment (1997) *Canada and the Multilateral Agreement on Investment*, Report, Ottawa: Parliament of Canada, Standing Committee on Foreign Affairs and International Trade

Carraro, C and Siniscalco, D (1993) 'Strategies for the International Protection of the Environment', *Journal of Public Economics*, vol 52, no 3, pp309–328

CEC (1996) *Potential NAFTA Effects: Claims and Arguments 1991–1994*, Ottawa: Commission for Environmental Co-operation

CEC (1999) *Assessing environmental effects of the North American Free Trade Agreement (NAFTA) – an analytical framework (phase II) and issue studies*, Ottawa: Commission for Environmental Co-operation

CEC (1999) 'Canada, Mexico and the United States join forces to reduce toxic substances, protect birds and save a major river basin as CEC Council meeting concludes in Banff', press release, 28 June 1999, Montreal: Commission for Environmental Cooperation

Chang, H F (1995) 'An economic analysis of trade measures to protect the global environment', *Georgetown Law Journal*, vol 83, pp2131–2213

Chao, C-C and E S H Yu (1997) 'International capital competition and environmental standards', *Southern Economic Journal*, vol 64, pp531–541

Charnovitz, S (1994) 'Encouraging environmental cooperation through the Pelly Amendment', *Journal of Environment & Development*, vol 3, no 1, pp3–28

Charnovitz, S (1995) 'Regional trade agreements', *Environment*, vol 37, no 6, pp16–20 and 40–45

Charnovitz, S (1996) 'New WTO adjudication and its implications for the environment', *International Environment Reporter*, vol 19, no 19, 18 September, Washington, DC: Bureau of National Affairs

Charnovitz, S (2000) 'Improving the Agreement on Sanitary and Phytosanitary Standards', in G Sampson and W B Chambers (eds) *Trade, Environment, and the Millennium*, Tokyo: United Nations University Press

Charnovitz, S and J Wickham (1995) 'Non-governmental organizations and the original international trade regime', *Journal of World Trade*, vol 29, no 5, pp111–122

Cheang, Seung Wha (1997) 'GATTing a green trade barrier – eco-labelling and the WTO Agreement on Technical Barriers to Trade', *Journal of World Trade*, vol 31, no 1, pp137–159

Chichilnisky, Graciela (1994) 'North-South Trade and the Global Environment', *American Economic Review*, vol 84, no 4, pp851–874

Citizens Trade Campaign (1999) '$1 billion NAFTA lawsuit threatens California environmental safeguard', news release, 16 June 1999, Washington, DC: Citizens Trade Campaign

Clarke, T (1998) *Towards a Citizens' MAI: An Alternative Approach to Developing a Global Investment Treaty Based on Citizens' Rights and Democratic Control*, Ottawa: Polaris Institute

Colby, M E (1991) 'Environmental management in development: The evolution of paradigms', *Ecological Economics*, vol 3, no 3, pp193–213

Cole, M A, A J Rayner and J M Bates (1998) 'Trade liberalisation and the environment: The case of the Uruguay Round', *World Economy*, vol 21, no 3, pp337–347

Copeland, B R and M S Taylor (1994) 'North-South Trade and the Environment', *Quarterly Journal of Economics*, vol 109, pp755–787

Copeland, B R and M S Taylor (1997) *A Simple Model of Trade, Capital Mobility, and the Environment*, Working Paper 5898, Cambridge, Mass: National Bureau of Economic Research

Copeland, B R and M S Taylor (1999) 'Trade, spatial separation, and the environment', *Journal of International Economics*, vol 47, pp137–168

Cortney, P (1949) *The Economic Munich*, London: Pitman & Sons

Cosbey, A (1999) *The Sustainable Development Effects of the WTO TRIPs Agreement: A Focus on Developing Countries*, Winnipeg: International Institute for Sustainable Development, online available at http://www.ictsd.org

Cosbey, A (2000) *Institutional Challenges and Opportunities in Environmentally Sound Trade Expansion: A Review of the Global State of Affairs*, North-South Agenda Papers 41, Miami: North-South Center, University of Miami

Cosbey, A and S Burgiel (2000) *The Cartagena Protocol on Biosafety: An Analysis of Results – an IISD briefing note*, Winnipeg: International Institute for Sustainable Development

CUTS (1997) *TRIPs, Biotechnology and Global Competition*, Jaipur: CUTS Centre for International Trade, Economics and Environment

CUTS (1999) *Southern Agenda for WTO: A Civil Society Perspective*, Jaipur: CUTS Centre for International Trade, Economics and Environment

Daly, H (1993) 'The perils of free trade', *Scientific American*, November, pp24–29

Dasgupta, S, A Mody, S Roy and D Wheeler (1995) *Environmental Regulation and Development: A Cross-country Empirical Analysis*, Policy Research Working Paper 1448, Washington, DC: World Bank

Dasgupta, S, B Laplante and N Mamingi (1997) *Capital Market Responses to Environmental Performance in Developing Countries*, Policy Research Working Paper 1909, World Bank, Washington, DC

Dasgupta, S, H Hettige and D Wheeler (1997) *What improves environmental performance? Evidence from Mexican industry*, Development Research Group Working Paper 1877, World Bank, Washington, DC

De Mello, L R Jr (1997) 'Foreign direct investment in developing countries and growth: A selective survey', *Journal of Development Studies*, vol 34, no 1, pp1–34

De Mello, L R Jr (1999) 'Foreign direct investment-led growth: Evidence from time series and panel data', *Oxford Economic Paper*, vol 51, no 1, pp133–151

de Moor, A (1998) *Perverse Incentives – Subsidies and Sustainable Development: Key Issues and Reform Strategies*, San José: Earth Council

Demaret, P and R Stewardson (1994) 'Border tax adjustments under GATT and EC law and general implications for environmental taxes', *Journal of World Trade*, vol 28, pp5–65

DeSombre, E R (1995) 'Baptists and bootleggers for the environment: The origins of United States unilateral sanctions', *Journal of Environment & Development*, vol 4, pp53–75

Dowell, G, S Hart and B Yeung (2000) 'Do corporate global environmental standards create or destroy market value?', *Management Science*, vol 46, no 8, pp1059–1074

Düerkop, M (1994) 'Trade and environment: International trade law aspects of the proposed EC directive introducing a tax on carbon dioxide emissions and energy', *Common Market Law Review*, vol 31, pp807–844

Dunkley, G (1997) *The Free Trade Adventure: The Uruguay Round and Globalisation – A Critique*, Melbourne: Melbourne University Press

Dutfield, G (2000) *Intellectual Property Rights, Trade and Biodiversity: Seeds and Plant Varieties*, London: Earthscan

Eastman, Z (1999) 'NAFTA's Chapter 11 – for whose benefit?', *Journal of International Arbitration*, vol 16, no 3, pp105–118

Endres, A and M Finus (1998) 'Renegotiation-Proof Equilibria in a Bargaining Game over Global Emission Reductions – Does the Instrumental Framework Matter?' in N Hanley and H Folmer (eds) *Game Theory and the Environment*, Cheltenham: Edward Elgar

ENS (1999) 'European tax deal deferred to 2000', *Environment News Service*, 15 November 1999

Environment Canada (1999) 'Government to act on Agreement on Internal Trade (AIT) panel report on MMT', news release, 20 July 1998, Ottawa: Environment Canada

Erlandson, D (1994) 'The BTU tax experience: What happened and why it happened', *Pace Environmental Law Review*, vol 12, no 1, pp173–184

Eskeland, G S and A E Harrison (1997) *Moving to Greener Pastures? Multinationals and the Pollution Haven Hypothesis*, Working Paper 1744, Washington, DC: World Bank

Esty, D C (1994) *Greening the GATT*, Washington, DC: Institute for International Economics

Esty, D C (1998) *Why the World Trade Organization Needs Environmental NGOs*, Geneva: International Centre for Trade and Sustainable Development

Esty, D C (2000) 'Environmental governance at the WTO: Outreach to civil society', in Gary Sampson and W Bradnee Chambers (eds) *Trade, Environment, and the Millennium*, Tokyo: United Nations University Press

Esty, D C and D Geradin (1997) 'Market access, competitiveness, and harmonization: Environmental protection in regional trade agreements', *Harvard Environmental Law Review*, vol 21, no 2, pp265–336

Esty, D C and D Geradin (1998) 'Environmental protection and international competitiveness: A conceptual framework', *Journal of World Trade* 32 (3, pp5–46

Esty, D C and D Geradin (2000) 'Regulatory co-opetition', *Journal of International Economic Law*, vol 3, no 2, pp235–255

Ethyl Corp (1998a) 'Ethyl welcomes government of Canada decision', press release, 20 July, Richmond, VA: Ethyl Corporation

Ethyl Corp (1998b) *Information About MMT*, Richmond, VA: Ethyl Corporation

European Commission (1992) *Proposal for a Council Directive Introducing a Tax on Carbon Dioxide Emissions and Energy*, COM(92) 226 final, Brussels: Commission of the European Communities

European Commission (2000a) *Draft Proposal for a European Parliament and Council Directive on Waste Electrical and Electronic Equipment*, Brussels: Commission of the European Communities

European Commission (2000b) *Communication from the Commission on the Precautionary Principle*, COM(2000) 1, Brussels: Commission of the European Communities

European Communities (1997) 'Amended proposal for a Council Decision concerning the signing and conclusion of an Agreement on international humane trapping standards between the European Community, Canada, and the Russian Federation', *Official Journal of the European Communities*, C 207, 8 July 1997, pp14–30

European Communities (1998) 'Proposal for a Council Decision concerning the signing and conclusion of an International Agreement in the form of an Agreed Minute between the European Community and the United States of America on humane trapping standards', *Official Journal of the European Communities*, C 32, 30 January 1998, pp8–18

European Communities (1999) *EC Approach to Trade and Environment in the New WTO Round – Communication from the European Communities*, WT/GC/W/194, Geneva: World Trade Organization

European Communities (2000a) *Sustainability Impact Assessment Study, Phase Two Main Report*, report by Colin Kirkpatrick and Norman Lee, Manchester: Institute for Development Policy and Management and Environmental Impact Assessment Centre

European Communities (2000b) *Resolving the relationship between WTO rules and multilateral environmental agreements – submission by the European Community*, WT/CTE/W/170, Geneva: World Trade Organization

European Parliament (1998) *Resolution on the MAI*, A4–0073/98, 11 March, Strasbourg: European Parliament

Falkner, R (2000) 'Regulating biotech trade: The Cartagena Protocol on Biosafety', *International Affairs*, vol 76, no 2, pp299–313

FAO (1999) *The FAO International Plan of Action for the Management of Fishing Capacity and Related Initiatives for Sustainable Fisheries – Communication from the Food and Agriculture Organization (FAO)*, WT/CTE/W/126, Geneva: World Trade Organization

Feenstra, R C (1998) 'Integration of trade and disintegration of production in the global economy', *Journal of Economic Perspectives*, vol 12, no 4, pp31–50

FIELD et al (2001) *European Communities – Measures affecting asbestos and asbestos-containing products, Report of the Panel: Submission of written brief by non-parties*, London et al.: Foundation for International Environmental Law and Development, Ban

Asbestos Network, Greenpeace International, International Ban Asbestos Secretariat and WWF

Financial Post (1999) 'Ottawa's flip-flop on PCBs cost $85M, with suit pending', *Financial Post*, 25 November 1999

Financial Times (2000) 'Mexico loses NAFTA case', *Financial Times* 1 September 2000

Finus, M and B Rundshagen (1998b) 'Renegotiation-proof equilibria in a global emission game when players are impatient', *Environmental and Resource Economics*, vol 12, no 3, pp275–306

Finus, Michael and Bianca Rundshagen (1998) 'Toward a positive theory of coalition formation and endogenous instrumental choice in global pollution control', *Public Choice*, vol 96, no 1–2, pp145–186

FitzGerald, E V K, R Cubero-Brealey and A Lehmann (1998) *The Development Implications of the Multilateral Agreement on Investment*, A report commissioned by the UK Department for International Development, Oxford: Finance and Trade Policy Research Centre

FoE (1999a) *WTO Scorecard – WTO and Free Trade versus Environment and Public Health: 4–0*, Washington, DC: Friends of the Earth

FoE (1999b) *Green Scissors '99 Campaign*, Washington, DC: Friends of the Earth

FoE (1999c) *The Emperor has no Clothes: Why it's Time to Change the Way we Trade*, London: Friends of the Earth International

Freedom House (1999) *Annual Survey of Freedom Country Scores 1972–73 to 1998–99*, Washington, DC: Freedom House

French, Hilary F (1994) 'Making environmental treaties work', *Scientific American*, vol 271, no 6, pp62–65

FSC (2000) *Homepage*, Oaxaca: Forest Stewardship Council, online at www.fscoax.org

Gallup, G H Jr, A M Gallup and R E Dunlap (1993) *Health of the Planet: A George H Gallup Memorial Survey*, Princeton, New Jersey: Gallup International Institute

Ganesan, A V (1998) *Strategic Options Available to Developing Countries with Regard to a Multilateral Agreement on Investment*, Discussion Paper No 134, UNCTAD/OSG/DP/134, New York and Geneva: United Nations Conference on Trade and Development

GATT (1983) *United States – Prohibition of Imports of Tuna and Tuna Products from Canada*, Panel report, adopted on 22 February 1982, L/5198, BISD 29, Geneva: World Trade Organization

GATT (1987a) *United States – Taxes on Petroleum and Certain Imported Substances*, BISD 34th Supplement, pp136–166, Geneva: General Agreement on Tariffs and Trade

GATT (1987b) *Canada – Measures Affecting Exports of Unprocessed Herring and Salmon*, Panel report, adopted on 22 March 1988, BISD 35S/98, Geneva: World Trade Organization

GATT (1990) *Thailand – Restrictions on Importation of and Internal Taxes on Cigarettes*, Panel report, adopted on 7 November 1990, BISD 36S/200, Geneva: World Trade Organization

GATT (1993) *United States – Restrictions on Imports of Tuna*, Panel report, not adopted, BISD 39S/155, Geneva: World Trade Organization

GATT (1994a) 'United States – taxes on automobiles', *International Legal Material* 33, pp1397–1460

GATT (1994b) 'United States – restrictions on imports of tuna', *International Legal Material* 33, pp839–902

Gentry, B S (1999) *The Environmental Effects of International Portfolio Flows*, Working Paper, ENV/EPOC/GEEI(98)32/FINAL, Organisation for Economic Co-operation and Development, Paris

Goldman, P and J Scott (1999) *Our Forests at Risk: The World Trade Organization's Threat to Forest Protection*, Seattle and Bellingham: Earthjustice Legal Defense Fund and Northwest Ecosystem Alliance

Government of Canada (1999) *Statement of Defence in the Matter of an Arbitration under Chapter Eleven of the North American Free Trade Agreement between S D Myers Inc and the Government of Canada*, Ottawa: Government of Canada

Greenpeace (1993a) *The Impact of the North American Free Trade Agreement on the Environment*, Testimony of Greenpeace before the Subcommittee on Environment and Natural Resources, Committee on Merchant Marine and Fisheries, United States House of Representatives, Washington, DC: Greenpeace

Greenpeace (1993b) *NAFTA and the North American Agreement on Environmental Cooperation (NAAEC): Side-stepping the Environment*, Washington, DC: Greenpeace

Greenpeace (1997) *WTO Against Sustainable Development*, Amsterdam: Greenpeace International

Greenpeace (1999) *Safe Trade in the 21st Century: A Greenpeace Briefing Kit*, Amsterdam: Greenpeace International

Grossman, G M and A B Krueger (1993) 'Environmental impacts of a North American Free Trade Agreement' in P Garber (ed) *The Mexico–US Free Trade Agreement*, Cambridge, Mass: MIT Press

Hamilton, J T (1995) 'Pollution as news: Media and stock market reactions to the toxics release inventory data', *Journal of Environmental Economics and Management* 28, pp98–113

Harrison, G W, T F Rutherford, and D G Tarr (1996) 'Quantifying the Uruguay Round' in Will Martin and L Alan Winters (eds) *The Uruguay Round and the Developing Countries*, Cambridge: Cambridge University Press

Harrop, S R (2000) 'The international regulation of animal welfare and conservation issues through standards dealing with the trapping of wild animals', *Journal of Environmental Law*, vol 12, no 3, pp333–360

Heal, G (1994) 'Formation of international environmental agreements', in Carlo Carraro (ed) *Trade, Innovation, Environment*, Dordrecht: Kluwer

Henderson, D (1999) *The MAI Affair: A Story and its Lessons*, London: Royal Institute of International Affairs

Hettige, H, M Huq, S Pargal and D Wheeler (1996) 'Determinants of pollution abatement in developing countries: evidence from South and Southeast Asia', *World Development*, vol 24, pp1891–1904

Hillyard, M (1998) *Multilateral Agreement on Investment*, Research Paper 98/31, London: House of Commons Library, Economic Policy and Statistics Section

Hilton, F G and A Levinson (2000) *Measuring Environmental Compliance Costs and Economic Consequences: A Perspective from the US*, mimeo, Washington, DC: Georgetown University

Housman, R and D Zaelke (1995) 'Mechanisms for integration', in R Housman, D Goldberg, B van Dyke and D Zaelke (eds) *The Use of Trade Measures in Select Multilateral Environmental Agreements*, Nairobi: United Nations Environment Programme

Howse, R and D Regan (2000) *The Product/Process Distinction: An Illusory Basis for Disciplining Unilateralism in Trade Policy*, mimeo, Michigan: University of Michigan Law School

Hudec, R E (1996) 'GATT legal restraints on the use of trade measures against foreign environmental practices', in J N Bhagwati and R E Hudec (eds) *Fair Trade and Harmonization*, vol 2, Cambridge, Mass: MIT Press

ICC (1999) *TRIPs and the Biodiversity Convention: What Conflict?*, Paris: International Chamber of Commerce

ICC (2000) *The Business Charter for Sustainable Development: Principles for Environmental Management*, Paris: International Chamber of Commerce

ICSID (1999a) 'Disputes before the centre', *ICSID News*, vol 16, no 2, Washington, DC: International Centre for Settlement of Investment Disputes

ICSID (1999b) *Award – Robert Azinian, Kenneth Davitian and Ellen Baca versus The United Mexican States*, Washington, DC: International Centre for Settlement of Investment Disputes

ICSID (2000) *Award – Waste Management Inc versus The United Mexican States*, Washington, DC: International Centre for Settlement of Investment Disputes

ICTSD (1998a) 'Discussion launched on TRIPs Article 27.3(b) review but relationship with biodiversity convention remains unclear', *BRIDGES between Trade and Sustainable Development Monthly Review*, vol 3, no 6, p7

ICTSD (1998b) 'Shrimp-turtle report raises systemic concerns', *BRIDGES between Trade and Sustainable Development Monthly Review*, vol 2, no 8, p8

ICTSD (1999a) *Report on the WTO's High-level Symposium on Trade and Environment*, Geneva, 15–16 March 1999, Geneva: World Trade Organization

ICTSD (1999b) *Report on the WTO's high-level symposium on trade and development*, Geneva, 17–18 March 1999, Geneva: World Trade Organization

ICTSD (1999c) 'No change in NAFTA investor-state provisions', *BRIDGES between Trade and Sustainable Development Monthly Review*, vol 3, no 3, p9

ICTSD (1999d) 'US release list of 'certified' shrimp exporters', *BRIDGES Weekly Trade News Digest*, vol 3, no 19, 17 May 1999

ICTSD (1999e) 'Dispute settlement review peters out', *BRIDGES between Trade and Sustainable Development Monthly Review*, vol 3, no 6, p9

ICTSD (2000a) 'EU–US beef dispute update', *BRIDGES Weekly Trade News Digest*, 21 March 2000

ICTSD (2000b) 'EU seeks consultations with Chile in trade and environment conflict', *BRIDGES Weekly Trade News Digest*, vol 4, no 29, 25 July 2000

ICTSD (2000c) 'US in murky waters over shrimp-turtle', *BRIDGES Weekly Trade News Digest*, 2 February 2000

ICTSD (2000d) 'The battle between environmental co-operation and trade embargoes flares up with possibility of tuna dolphin III', *BRIDGES between Trade and Sustainable Development Monthly Review*, vol 4, no 6, pp1ff

ICTSD (2000e) 'WTO members reach agreement in principle on SPS measures', *BRIDGES Weekly Trade News Digest*, vol 4, no 11, 21 March 2000

ICTSD (2000f) 'Prospects for new round depend on flexibility', *BRIDGES Weekly Trade News Digest*, vol 4, no 12, 28 March 2000

ICTSD (2000g) 'In brief', *BRIDGES Weekly Trade News Digest*, vol 4, no 9, 7 March 2000

ICTSD (2000h) 'US announcement of TRIPs and TRIMs cases antagonises developing countries', *BRIDGES between Trade and Sustainable Development Monthly Review*, vol 4, no 4, p5

ICTSD (2000i) 'African convention parties to address traditional knowledge and agricultural trade', *BRIDGES between Trade and Sustainable Development Monthly Review*, vol 4, no 3, pp9ff

ICTSD (2000j) 'Dispute settlement briefs', *BRIDGES between Trade and Sustainable Development Monthly Review*, vol 4, no 4, p6

ICTSD (2000k) 'Trade and environment après-Seattle', *BRIDGES between Trade and Sustainable Development Monthly Review*, vol 4, no 2, pp3ff

ICTSD (2000l) 'Shrimp-turtle: the return?', *BRIDGES between Trade and Sustainable Development Monthly Review*, vol 4, no 6, p7

ICTSD (2000m) 'In brief: Gore's advisor proposes global environmental organisation', *BRIDGES Weekly Trade News Digest*, vol 4, no 32, 22 August 2000

ICTSD (2000n) 'The swordfish in peril: The EU challenges Chilean port access restrictions at the WTO', *BRIDGES between Trade and Sustainable Development Monthly Review*, vol 4, no 6, pp11ff

ICTSD (2000o) 'WTO General Council slaps appellate body on amicus briefs', *BRIDGES Weekly Trade News Digest*, vol 4, no 45, 28 November 2000

ICTSD (2001a) 'Canada challenges NAFTA tribunal's jurisdiction', *BRIDGES Weekly Trade News Digest*, vol 5, no 6, 20 February 2001

ICTSD (2001b) 'Dispute settlement update: swordfish', *BRIDGES Weekly Trade News Digest*, vol 5, no 3, 30 January 2001

ICTSD and IUCN (1999) *Fish for Thought: Fisheries, International Trade and Sustainable Development*, Geneva and Cambridge: International Centre for Trade and Sustainable Development and The World Conservation Union

IISD and IUCN (1999) *A Standing Conference on Trade and Environment*, Winnipeg and Gland: International Institute for Sustainable Development and The World Conservation Union

IISD and UNEP (2000) *Environment and Trade: A Handbook*, Winnipeg and Nairobi: International Institute for Sustainable Development and United Nations Environment Programme

IMD (1999) *World Competitiveness Yearbook*, International Institute for Management Development, Lausanne

IMF (1998) *Government Finance Statistics Yearbook*, International Monetary Fund, Washington, DC

Indigenous Peoples' Statement (1999) *Indigenous Peoples' Statement on the Trade-related Aspects of Intellectual Property Rights (TRIPs) of the WTO Agreement*, Geneva

Inglehart, R, M Basanez and A Moreno (1998) *Human Values and Beliefs: A Cross-Cultural Sourcebook – Political, Religious, Sexual, and Economic Norms in 43 Societies: Findings from the 1990–1993 World Values Survey*, Ann Arbor: University of Michigan Press

Institute of Science in Society (1999a) *Open Letter from World Scientists to All Governments*, Milton Keynes: Institute of Science in Society

Institute of Science in Society (1999b) *Why Patents on Life-forms and Living Processes should be Rejected from TRIPs – Scientific Briefing on TRIPs Article 27.3(b)*, Milton Keynes: Institute of Science in Society

Irwin, D A (1996) 'The United States in a new global economy? A century's perspective', *American Economic Review Papers and Proceedings*, vol 86, no 2, pp41–46

Jaffe, A B, S R Peterson and R N Stavins (1995) 'Environmental regulation and the competitiveness of US manufacturing: What does the evidence tell us?', *Journal of Economic Literature*, vol 33, pp132–163

Jha, V, A Markandya and R Vossenaar (1999) *Reconciling Trade and the Environment: Lessons from Case Studies in Developing Countries*, Cheltenham: Edward Elgar

Johnson, P M and A Beaulieu (1996) *The Environment and NAFTA: Understanding and Implementing the New Continental Law*, Washington, DC: Island Press

Kahn, M E (2000) *United States Pollution Intensive Trade Trends from 1972 to 1992*, mimeo, New York: Columbia University

Keller, W and A Levinson (1999) *Environmental Compliance Costs and Foreign Direct Investment Inflows to US States*, Working Paper 7369, Cambridge, Mass: National Bureau of Economic Research

Kenya (1999a) *Contribution to the Preparatory Process – Communication from Kenya*, WT/GC/W/233, Geneva: World Trade Organization

Kenya (1999b) *The TRIPs Agreement – Communication from Kenya on Behalf of the African Group*, WT/GC/W/302, Geneva: World Trade Organization

Kettlewell, U (1992) 'GATT: Will liberalized trade aid global environmental protection?', *Denver Journal of International Law & Policy*, vol 21, no 1, pp55–76

Keuschnigg, M (1999) *Comparative Advantage in International Trade: Theory and Evidence*, Heidelberg: Physica-Verlag

Khor, M (1999) *New Battles Begin Soon in the WTO*, Penang (Malaysia) Third World Network

Kodama, Y (1998) 'The Multilateral Agreement on Investment and its legal implications for newly industrialising economies', *Journal of World Trade*, vol 32, no 4, pp21–40

Körber, A (2000) *The Political Economy of Environmental Protectionism*, Cheltenham: Edward Elgar

Krasner, S D (1983) 'Structural causes and regime consequences: Regimes as intervening variables' in S D Krasner (ed) *International Regimes*, Ithaca: Cornell University Press

Kriström, B and P Riera (1996) 'Is the income elasticity of environmental improvements less than one?', *Environmental and Resource Economics*, vol 7, no 3, pp45–55

Krueger, J (1999) *International Trade and the Basel Convention*, London: Earthscan and Royal Institute of International Affairs

Kuruvila, P E (1997) 'Developing countries and the GATT/WTO dispute settlement mechanism', *Journal of World Trade*, vol 31, no 6, pp171–208

Kuznets, S (1955) 'Economic growth and income inequality', *American Economic Review*, vol 45, no 1, pp1–28

Lal Das, B (1997) *A Critical Analysis of the Proposed Investment Treaty in WTO*, Penang: Third World Network, online available at http://www.twnside.org.sg

Lal Das, B (1998) 'The steamroller rolls on', *Third World Economics*, vol 182, April, pp1–15

Lal, D (1993) 'Trade blocs and multilateral free trade', *Journal of Common Market Studies*, vol 31, no 3, pp349–358

Lalumiere, C and J-P Landau (1998) *Report on the Multilateral Agreement on Investment*, Intermediary Report, September 1998, Paris

Lang, T and C Hines (1993) *The New Protectionism: Protecting the Future Against Free Trade*, London: Earthscan

Laplante, B and P Rilstone (1995) *Environmental inspections and emissions of the pulp and paper industry: the case of Quebec*, Policy Research Paper 1447, Washington, DC: World Bank

Lappé, M and B Bailey (1999) *Against the Grain: The Genetic Transformation of Global Agriculture*, London: Earthscan

Leonard, J H (1988) *Pollution and the Struggle for the World Product*, Cambridge: Cambridge University Press

Levinson, A (1996) 'Environmental regulations and manufacturers' location choices: Evidence from the census of manufactures', *Journal of Public Economics*, vol 62, pp5–29

List, J A and C Y Co (2000) 'The effects of environmental regulations on foreign direct investment', *Journal of Environmental Economics and Management*, vol 40, no 1, pp1–20

Low, P (1992) 'Introduction and overview', in Patrick Low (ed) *Trade and the Environment*, Discussion Paper 159, Washington, DC: World Bank

Lucas, R E B, D Wheeler and H Hettige (1992) *Economic Development, Environmental Regulation, and the International Migration of Toxic Industrial Pollution 1960–88*, Working Paper 1062, Washington, DC: World Bank

Mabey, N and R McNally (1999) *Foreign Direct Investment and the Environment: From Pollution Havens to Sustainable Development*, Surrey: World Wide Fund for Nature United Kingdom

Maddison, A (1991) *Dynamic Forces in Capitalist Development: A Long-run Comparative View*, Oxford: Oxford University Press

Maestad, O (1998) 'On the efficiency of green trade policy', *Environmental and Resource*, vol 11, no 1, pp1–18

Mander, J and E Goldsmith (eds) (1996) *The Case Against the Global Economy: And for a Turn Toward the Local*, San Francisco: Sierra Club Books

Mani, M and D Wheeler (1997) *In Search of Pollution Havens? Dirty Industry in the World Economy 1960–1995*, background document OECD Conference on FDI and the Environment (The Hague, 28–29 January 1999), Paris: OECD

Mani, M, S Pargal and M Huq (1996) *Does environmental regulation matter? Determinants of the location of new manufacturing plants in India in 1994*, Policy Research Paper 1718, Washington, DC: World Bank

Mann, H and K von Moltke (1999) *NAFTA's Chapter 11 and the Environment: Addressing the Impacts of the Investor-state Process on the Environment*, Winnipeg: International Institute for Sustainable Development

Marceau, G (1999) 'A call for coherence in international law: Praises for the prohibition against "clinical isolation" in WTO dispute settlement', *Journal of World Trade*, vol 33, no 5, pp87–152

Markandya, A (1994) 'Is free trade compatible with sustainable development?', *UNCTAD Review*, pp9–22

Markusen, J R, E R Morey and N Olewiler (1995) 'Competition in regional environmental policies when plant locations are endogenous', *Journal of Public Economics*, vol 56, no 1, pp55–77

Martin, R B (2000) 'When CITES works and when it does not' in Jon Hutton and Barnabas Dickson (eds) *Endangered Species, Threatened Convention: The Past, Present and Future of CITES, the Convention on International Trade in Endangered Species Of Wild Fauna and Flora*, London: Earthscan, pp29–37

McConnell, V D and R M Schwab (1990) 'The impact of environmental regulation on industry location decisions: The motor vehicle industry', *Land Economics*, vol 66, no 3, pp67–81

McGinn, C (1998) *Trade Body Threatens Democracy*, Washington, DC: Public Citizen Global Trade Watch

Menyasz, P (2000) 'Negotiations experts divided on developing nations' role in further multilateral negotiations in WTO', *WTO Reporter*, 2 June 2000, Washington, DC: Bureau of National Affairs

Methanex (1999a) *Q&A Background on Methanex's NAFTA Claim and MTBE*, Vancouver: Methanex Corp

Methanex (1999b) *Bullet Point background on Methanex's NAFTA Claim and MTBE*, Vancouver: Methanex Corp

Methanex (1999c) *Letter by President and CEO Pierre Choquette to the Commission for Environmental Cooperation*, Vancouver: Methanex Corp

Methanex (1999d) 'Methanex seeks damages under NAFTA for California MTBE ban', news release, 15 June 1999, Vancouver: Methanex Corp

Metrick, A and M L Weitzman (1996) 'Patterns of behavior in endangered species preservation', *Land Economics*, vol 72, no 1, pp1–16

Morris, D (1990) 'Free trade: The great destroyer', *The Ecologist*, vol 20, no 5, pp190–195

MSC (2000) *Homepage*, London: Marine Stewardship Council, online at www.msc.org

Muradian, R and J Martinez-Alier (2001) 'Trade and the environment from a "Southern" perspective', *Ecological Economics*, vol 36, no 3, pp281–297

Myers, N and J Kent (1998) *Perverse Subsidies: Tax $s Undercutting our Economies and Environments Alike*, Winnipeg: International Institute for Sustainable Development

Nader, R (ed) (1993) *The Case against Free Trade: GATT, NAFTA, and the Globalization of Corporate Power*, San Francisco and Berkeley: Earth Island Press and North Atlantic Books

Neumayer, E (1999a) 'Multilateral agreement on investment: Lessons for the WTO from the failed OECD-negotiations', *Wirtschaftspolitische Blätter*, vol 46, no 6, pp618–628

Neumayer, E (1999b) 'Developing countries in the WTO: Support or resist a new "Millennium" round of trade negotiations?', *Development in Practice*, vol 9, no 5, pp592–595

Neumayer, E (1999c) *Weak versus Strong Sustainability: Exploring the Limits of Two Opposing Paradigms*, Cheltenham: Edward Elgar

Neumayer, E (2000a) 'Trade and the environment: A critical assessment and some constructive suggestions for reconciliation', *Journal of Environment and Development*, vol 9, no 2, pp138–159

Neumayer, E (2000b) 'Trade measures in multilateral environmental agreements and WTO rules: Potential for conflict, scope for reconciliation', *Aussenwirtschaft*, vol 55, no 3, pp403–426

Neumayer, E (2001a) 'Do we trust the data? On the validity and reliability of cross-national environmental surveys', *Social Science Quarterly*, vol 82

Neumayer, E (2001b) 'Greening the WTO agreements: can the Treaty establishing the European Community be of guidance?', *Journal of World Trade*, vol 35, no 1

Neumayer, E (2001c) 'How regime theory and the economic theory of international environmental cooperation can learn from each other', *Global Environmental Politics*, vol 1, no 1

Neumayer, E (2001d) 'Pollution havens: an analysis of policy options for dealing with an elusive phenomenon', *Journal of Environment & Development*, vol 10, no 2, pp147–177

Neumayer, E (2001e) 'Do countries fail to raise environmental standards? An evaluation of policy options addressing "regulatory chill"', *International Journal of Sustainable Development*, vol 4

Neumayer, E (2001f) *A blueprint for making the prospective Mediterranean Free Trade Zone an environmental role model*, mimeo, London: London School of Economics

Newell, P and J Whalley (1999) 'Towards a World Environment Organisation?' *IDS Bulletin*, vol 30, no 3, pp16–24

New Zealand (1999) *Benefits of Eliminating Trade Distorting and Environmentally Damaging Subsidies in the Fisheries Sector – Submission by New Zealand*, WT/CTE/W/121, Geneva: World Trade Organization

Nordström, H and S Vaughan (1999) *Trade and Environment*, Special Studies 4, Geneva: World Trade Organization

North, R D (2000) *Fur and Freedom: In defence of the Fur Trade*, London: Institute of Economic Affairs

Norway (1999) *Trade and Environment – Communication from Norway*, WT/GC/W/176, Geneva: World Trade Organization

Nova, S and M Sforza-Roderick (1997) 'Multilateral Agreement on Investment: "The constitution of a single global economy"', *The Ecologist*, vol 27, no 1, p5

Oates, W E and R M Schwab (1988) 'Economic competition among jurisdictions: Efficiency enhancing or distortion inducing?', *Journal of Public Economics*, vol 35, no 3, pp333–354

OECD (1988) *Development Co-operation 1987*, Paris: Organisation for Economic Co-operation and Development

OECD (1995) *Report on Trade and Environment to the OECD Council at Ministerial Level, Vol III*, Working Paper No 47, Paris: Organisation for Economic Co-operation and Development

OECD (1996) *Pollution Abatement and Control Expenditure in OECD Countries*, Paris: Organisation for Economic Co-operation and Development

OECD (1997) *Experience with the Use of Trade Measures in the Convention on International Trade in Endangered Species of Wild Fauna and Flora (CITES*, OCDE/GD(97)106, Paris: Organisation for Economic Co-operation and Development

OECD (1997) *Trade Measures in the Basel Convention on the Control of Transboundary Movements of Hazardous Wastes and Their Disposal*, COM/ENV/TD(97)41/FINAL, Paris: Organisation for Economic Co-operation and Development

OECD (1997a) *Eco-labelling: Actual Effects of Selected Programmes*, OCDE/GD(97)105, Paris: Organisation for Economic Co-operation and Development

OECD (1997b) *Freight and the Environment: Effects of Trade Liberalisation and Transport Sector Reforms*, OCDE/GD(97)213, Paris: Organisation for Economic Co-operation and Development

OECD (1997c) *Experience with the Use of Trade Measures in the Montreal Protocol on Substances that Deplete the Ozone Layer*, Paris: Organisation for Economic Co-operation and Development

OECD (1998a) *The MAI Negotiating Text (as of 24 April 1998)*, Paris: Organisation for Economic Co-operation and Development

OECD (1998b) 'Ministerial Statement on the Multilateral Agreement on Investment (MAI)', press release, 28 April, Paris: Organisation for Economic Co-operation and Development

OECD (1998c) *Environment and Labour in the MAI: Chairman's Proposals*, March 1998, Paris: Organisation for Economic Co-operation and Development

OECD (1998d) 'Informal consultations on international investment', press release, 3 December 1998, Paris: Organisation for Economic Co-operation and Development

OECD (1998e) *Open Markets Matter: The Benefits of Trade and Investment Liberalisation*, Paris: Organisation for Economic Co-operation and Development

OECD (1998f) *Recent Trends in Foreign Direct Investment*, Paris: Organisation for Economic Co-operation and Development

OECD (1998g) *International Direct Investment Statistics Yearbook 1998*, Paris: Organisation for Economic Co-operation and Development

OECD (1998h) *Statement of Intent on Officially Supported Export Credits and the Environment*, Paris: Organisation for Economic Co-operation and Development

OECD (1998i) *Improving the Environment through Reducing Subsidies*, Paris: Organisation for Economic Co-operation and Development

OECD (1999a) *Development Co-operation 1998*, Paris: Organisation for Economic Co-operation and Development

OECD (1999b) *Main Economic Indicators*, Paris: Organisation for Economic Co-operation and Development

OECD (1999c) *Methodologies for Environmental Assessment of Trade Liberalisation Agreements*, report of the OECD workshop held on 26–27 October 1999, Paris: Organisation for Economic Co-operation and Development

OECD (1999d) *Trade Measures in Multilateral Environmental Agreements: Synthesis Report of Three Case Studies*, COM/ENV/TD(98)127/FINAL, Paris: Organisation for Economic Co-operation and Development

OECD (2000) *The OECD Guidelines for Multinational Enterprises*, Paris: Organisation for Economic Co-operation and Development

Olofsdotter, K (1998) 'Foreign Direct Investment, Country Capabilities and Economic Growth', *Weltwirtschaftliches Archiv*, vol 134, no 3, pp534–547

Olson, M (1965) *The Logic of Collective Action: Public Goods and the Theory of Groups*, Cambridge, Mass: Harvard University Press

OTA (1992) *Trade and Environment: Conflicts and Opportunities*, Washington, DC: Congress of United States Office of Technology Assessment

Oxfam (1997) *The OECD Multilateral Agreement on Investment (MAI)*, Oxfam UK and Ireland Briefing Paper

Oxfam (1999) *Loaded Against the Poor: World Trade Organization*, Oxford: Oxfam

Panel Report (1998) *Report of the Article 1704 Panel Concerning a Dispute between Alberta and Canada regarding the Manganese-based Fuel Additives Act*, Winnipeg: Agreement on Internal Trade

Pargal, S and M Mani (2000) 'Citizen activism, environmental regulation, and the location of industrial plants: evidence from India', *Economic Development and Cultural Change*, vol 48, pp 829–846

Peoples' Global Action (1999) *Peoples' Global Action Against 'Free' Trade and the World Trade Organization*, Ottawa: Peoples' Global Action

Picciotto, S (1998) 'Linkages in International Investment Regulation: The Antinomies of the Draft Multilateral Agreement on Investment', *University of Pennsylvania Journal of International Economic Law*, vol 19, no 3, pp731–768

Porter, G (1999) 'Trade competition and pollution standards: "Race to the bottom" or "stuck at the bottom"?', *Journal of Environment & Development*, vol 8, no 2, pp133–151

Public Citizen (2000) *NAFTA's broken promises*, online at http://www.citizen.org/pctrade/nafta, Washington, DC: Public Citizen

Puls, B (1999) 'The murky waters of international environmental jurisprudence: A critique of recent WTO holdings in the shrimp/turtle controversy', *Minnesota Journal of Global Trade*, vol 9, pp343–379

Quinet, E (1994) 'The social costs of transport: evaluation and links with internalisation policies' in OECD (ed) *Internalising the Social Costs of Transport*, Paris: OECD

Rauscher, M (1991) 'Foreign trade and the environment' in Horst Siebert (ed) *Environmental Scarcity: the International Dimension*, Tübingen: Mohr

Rauscher, M (1994) 'On Ecological Dumping', *Oxford Economic Papers*, vol 46, pp822–840

Reichert, W M (1996) 'Resolving the trade and environment conflict: The WTO and NGO consultative relations', *Minnesota Journal of Global Trade*, vol 5, pp219–246

Reppelin-Hill, V (1999) 'Trade and environment: An empirical analysis of the technology effect in the steel industry', *Journal of Environmental Economics and Management*, vol 38, no 3, pp283–301

Retallack, S (1997) 'The WTO record so far – Corporations: 3, humanity and the environment: 0', *The Ecologist*, vol 27, no 4

Revesz, R L (1998) *Federalism and Environmental Regulation*, mimeo, New York: New York University Law School

Ricardo, D (1817) *Principles of Political Economy and Taxation*, London: John Murray

Richards, E L and M A McCrory (2000) 'The sea turtle dispute: Implications for sovereignty, the environment, and international trade law', *University of Colorado Law Review*, vol 71, no 2, pp295–341

Roberts, J T (1996) 'Predicting participation in environmental treaties: A world-system analysis', *Sociological Inquiry*, vol 66, pp38–57

Rock, M T (1996) 'Pollution intensity of GDP and trade policy: Can the World Bank be wrong?', *World Development*, vol 24, no 3, pp471–479

Røpke, I (1994) 'Trade, development and sustainability: A critical assessment of the "free trade dogma"', *Ecological Economics*, vol 9, no 1, pp13–22

RSPCA (1999) *Conflict or Concord? Animal Welfare and the World Trade Organization*, Horsham: Royal Society for the Prevention of Cruelty to Animals

Ruggiero, R (1997) 'Speech on trade and sustainable development', *BRIDGES between Trade and Sustainable Development Monthly Review*, vol 1, no 6, pp7ff

Ruggiero, R (1999) *Opening Remarks to the High Level Symposium on Trade and the Environment*, 15 March, Geneva: World Trade Organization

Rutgeerts, A (1999) 'Trade and environment: Reconciling the Montreal Protocol and the GATT', *Journal of World Trade*, vol 33, no 4, pp61–86

Sachs, J D and A Warner (1995) 'Economic reform and the process of global integration', *Brookings Papers on Economic Activity*, vol 1, pp1–118

Saladin, C (1999) WTO *'Supremacy Clause' in the POPs Convention*, Working Paper, Washington, DC: Center for International Environmental Law

Sampson, G P (1999) *Trade, Environment, and the WTO: A Framework for Moving Forward*, ODC Policy Paper February 1999, Washington, DC: Overseas Development Council

Sand, P H (ed) (1992) *The Effectiveness of International Environmental Agreements*, Cambridge: Grotius

Saunders, J O (1997) 'The NAFTA and the North American Agreement on Environmental Cooperation' in Lyndon K Caldwell and Robert V Bartlett (eds) *Environmental Policy: Trans-national issues and National Trends*, Westport: Quorum Books

Sauvé, P (1994) 'A first look at investment in the Final Act of the Uruguay Round', *Journal of World Trade*, vol 28, no 5, pp5–16

Schoenbaum, T J (1997) 'International trade and protection of the environment: The continuing search for reconciliation', *American Journal of International Law*, vol 91, no 2, pp268–313

Scholte, J A, R O'Brien and M Williams (1998) *The WTO and Civil Society*, CSGR Working Paper 14/98, Warwick: University of Warwick, Centre for the Study of Globalisation and Regionalisation

Scoffield, H and S Chase (1999) 'Methanex to sue US under free-trade deal', *The Globe and Mail*, 16 June 1999

Sforza, M (1998a) *MAI Provisions and Proposals: An Analysis of the April 1998 Text*, Washington, DC: Public Citizen's Global Trade Watch

Sforza, M (1998b) *The Multilateral Agreement on Investment and the Environment*, Washington, DC: Public Citizen's Global Trade Watch

Shahin, M (1997) 'Trade and environment in the WTO: Achievements and future prospects', *Third World Economics*, no 156, 1–15 March 1997

Sierra Club of Canada (1997) *Fact Sheet: MAI and the Environment*, Ottawa: Sierra Club of Canada

Sizer, N, D Downes and D Kaimowitz (1999) *Tree Trade – Liberalization of International Commerce in Forest Products: Risks and Opportunities*, Washington, DC: World Resources Institute and Center for International Environmental Law

Smith, C (1998) 'Carbon leakage: An empirical assessment using a global econometric model' in J Köhler (ed) *International Competitiveness and Environmental Policies*, Cheltenham: Edward Elgar

Snape, R H (1992) 'The environment, international trade and competitiveness' in Kym Anderson and Richard Blackhurst (eds) *The Greening of World Trade Issues*, Michigan: Michigan University Press

Soloway, J A (1999a) 'Environmental trade barriers under NAFTA: The MMT fuel additives controversy', *Minnesota Journal of Global Trade*, vol 8, pp55–95

Soloway, J A (1999b) 'NAFTA's Chapter 11: The challenge of private party participation', *Journal of International Arbitration*, vol 16, no 2, pp1–14

South Centre (1997) *The TRIPs Agreement: A Guide for the South*, Geneva: South Centre

South Centre (1999) *Issues Regarding the Review of the WTO Dispute Settlement Mechanism*, Geneva: South Centre

Staffin, E B (1996) 'Trade barrier or trade boon? A critical evaluation of environmental labeling and its role in the "greening" of world trade', *Columbia Journal of Environmental Law*, vol 21, pp205–286

Stewart, R B (1993) 'Environmental regulation and international competitiveness', *Yale Law Journal*, vol 102, pp2039–2106

Strand-Rangnes, M (1999) *MAI: WTO Jump Start of MAI Attempted*, contribution to IGC Internet Conference on 10 March, San Francisco: Institute for Global Communications

Stumberg, R (1999) *Supreme Court Review of the Burma-law Decision*, Washington, DC: Georgetown University Law Center, Harison Institute for Public Law

Swenarchuk, M (2000) *The Cartagena Biosafety Protocol: Opportunities and Limitations*, mimeo, Toronto: Canadian Environmental Law Association

Swire, P P (1996) 'The race to laxity and the race to undesirability: Explaining failures in competition among jurisdictions in environmental law', *Yale Journal on Regulation*, Symposium Issue: Constructing a New Federalism, pp67–110

Switzerland (2000) *Clarification of the relationship between the WTO and multilateral environmental agreements – submission by Switzerland*, WT/CTE/W/168, Geneva: World Trade Organization

't Sas-Rolfes, M (2000) 'Assessing CITES: Four case studies' in J Hutton and B Dickson (eds) *Endangered Species, Threatened Convention: The Past, Present and Future of CITES, the Convention on International Trade in Endangered Species Of Wild Fauna and Flora*, London: Earthscan, pp69–87

Tarasofsky, R G (ed) (1999) *Assessing the International Forest Regime*, Gland: The World Conservation Union (IUCN)

Third World Intellectuals (1999) *Third World Intellectuals and NGOs Statement Against Linkage (TWIN-SAL)*, Jaipur: CUTS Centre for International Trade, Economics and Environment

Third World Network (1998) *Call to Reject any Proposal for Moving the MAI or an Investment Agreement to the NGO*, Penang, Malaysia: Third World Network

Thompson, P and L A Strohm (1996) 'Trade and environmental quality: a review of the evidence', *Journal of Environment & Development*, vol 5, no 4, pp363–388

Tobey, J A (1990) 'The effects of domestic environmental policies on patterns of world trade: An empirical test', *Kyklos*, vol 43, no 2, pp191–209

Transparency International (1999) *Corruption Perceptions Index*, Berlin: Transparency International

Tusse, D and P I Vasquez (1997) 'The FTAA, Mercosur, and the environment', *International Environmental Affairs*, vol 9, no 3, pp232–248

Tussie, D (ed) (2000) *The environment and international trade negotiations – developing country studies*, London: Macmillan

UK Department of Trade and Industry (1999) 'Ministers call for international investment rules to promote sustainable development', press release, 8 February, P/99/111, London: Department of Trade and Industry

UK House of Commons Environmental Audit Committee (1999) *The Multilateral Agreement on Investment, First Report*, London: House of Commons, Environmental Audit Committee

UNCTAD (1991, 1995, 1998c) *Trade and Development Report*, New York and Geneva: United Nations Conference on Trade and Development

UNCTAD (1993, 1994, 1998a) *World Investment Report*, New York and Geneva: United Nations Conference on Trade and Development

UNCTAD (1996) *Incentives and Foreign Direct Investment*, Current Studies, Series A, No 30, New York and Geneva: United Nations Conference on Trade and Development

UNCTAD (1998b) *Bilateral Investment Treaties in the Mid-1990s*, New York: United Nations Conference on Trade and Development

UNCTAD (1999b) *Handbook on Trade and Development Statistics 1996*, New York and Geneva: United Nations Conference on Trade and Development

UNDP (1995) *Human Development Report 1995: Gender and Human Development*, New York: United Nations Development Programme

UNDP (1999) *Human Development Report 1999: Globalization with a Human Face*, New York: United Nations Development Programme

UNEP and UNCTAD (2000) *UNEP–UNCTAD Capacity Building Task Force on Trade, Environment and Development*, WT/CTE/W/138, Geneva: World Trade Organization

United States (1999) *Trade and Sustainable Development – Communication from the United States*, WT/GC/W/304, Geneva: World Trade Organization

US Bureau of Census (1996) *Pollution Abatement Costs and Expenditures: 1994*, Washington, DC: US Department of Commerce

US Department of State (2000) *Pakistan – Sea Turtle Conservation and Shrimp Imports*, Press statement, 12 July 2000, Washington, DC: US Department of State Office of the Spokesman

US Representative (1999) *Letter from Brussels*, 6 August, Brussels: US Representative to the European Union

USCIB (1998) *Civil Society and Trade Negotiations: A Business Perspective*, Washington, DC: United States Council for International Business

USTR (1999) 'Accelerated tariff liberalization in forest products sector expected to have small environmental effects', press release, 2 November 1999, Washington, DC: Office of the United States Trade Representative

US Trade Representative (2000) *Guidelines for implementation of Executive Order 13141*, Washington, DC: Council on Environmental Quality and United States Trade Representative

Valliantos, M (1997) 'In focus: Multilateral Agreement on Investment', *Foreign Policy in Focus*, vol 2, no 39, Washington, DC: Institute for Policy Studies, online available at www.foreignpolicy-infocus.org/briefs/vol2/v2n39mai.html

Valliantos, M and A Durbin (1997) *10 Reasons to be Concerned about the Multilateral Agreement on Investment*, Washington, DC: Friends of the Earth

Van Beers, C and J C J M van den Bergh (2000) *Perseverance of Perverse Subsidies and their Impact on Trade and the Environment*, mimeo, Delft and Amsterdam: Delft University of Technology and Free University

Van Dyke, L B and J B Weiner (1997) *An Introduction to the WTO Decision on Document Restriction*, Geneva: International Centre for Trade and Sustainable Development

Van Long, N and H Siebert (1991) 'Institutional competition versus ex-ante harmonization: The case of environmental policy', *Journal of Institutional and Theoretical Economics*, vol 147, pp296–311

Vandevelde, K J (1998) 'Investment liberalization and economic development: The role of bilateral investment treaties', *Columbia Journal of Transnational Law*, vol 36, no 3, pp501–527

VanGrasstek, C (1992) 'The political economy of trade and the environment in the United States Senate' in Patrick Low (ed) *Trade and the Environment*, Discussion Paper 159, Washington, DC: World Bank

Vogel, D (1995) *Trading Up: Consumer and Environmental Regulation in the Global Economy*, Cambridge, Mass: Harvard University Press

Vogel, D (2000) 'Environmental regulation and economic integration', *Journal of International Economic Law*, vol 3, no 2, pp265–279

von Moltke, K (1997) 'When the appellate body errs', *BRIDGES between Trade and Sustainable Development Monthly Review*, vol 1, no 4, p9

Webb, G J W (2000) 'Are all species equal? A comparative assessment' in J Hutton and B Dickson (eds) *Endangered Species, Threatened Convention: The Past, Present and Future of CITES, the Convention on International Trade in Endangered Species of Wild Fauna and Flora*, London: Earthscan

Western Governors' Association (1997) *Multilateral Agreement on Investment: Potential Effects on State and Local Government*, Denver: Western Governors' Association,

Wheeler, D (2000) '"Green consumerism" and labelling: A retailer's perspective' in H Ward and D Brack (eds) *Trade, Investment and the Environment: Proceedings of the Royal Institute of International Affairs Conference, Chatham House, London, October 1998*, London: Earthscan and Royal Institute of International Affairs

Wheeler, D and A Mody (1992) 'International investment location decisions: the case of US firms', *Journal of International Economics*, vol 33, no 1, pp 57–76

Wheeler, D and P Martin (1992) 'Prices, policies, and the international diffusion of clean technology: The case of wood pulp production' in P Low (ed) *International Trade and the Environment*, World Bank Discussion Paper 159, Washington, DC: World Bank

White House (1999) *Environmental Review of Trade Agreements*, Executive Order of 16 November 1999, Washington, DC: The White House

White, R (1998) 'Foreword' in A Jackson and M Sanger (eds) *Dismantling Democracy: The Multilateral Agreement on Investment (MAI) and its Impact*, Ottawa and Toronto: Canadian Centre for Policy Alternatives and James Lorimer & Co

Witherell, W H (1998) *Environment and Labour in the MAI: Speaking Notes from the Press Seminar 26 March 1998*, Paris: OECD, Directorate for Financial, Fiscal and Enterprise Affairs

Wofford, C (2000) 'A greener future at the WTO: The refinement of WTO jurisprudence on environmental exceptions to GATT', *Harvard Environmental Law Review*, vol 24, no 2, pp563–592

Wold, C (1996) 'Multilateral environmental agreements and the GATT: Conflict and resolution?', *Environmental Law*, vol 26, no 3, pp841–921

World Bank (1992) *Development and the Environment*, Washington, DC: World Bank

World Bank (1997, 1998a, 1999) *World Development Indicators*, Washington, DC: World Bank

World Bank (1998b) *Competitiveness Indicators*, Washington, DC: World Bank

World Bank (2000) *Greening industry. New roles for communities, markets, and governments*, Washington, DC: World Bank

World Development Movement (1999) *Take Action on WTO*, London: World Development Movement

World Economic Forum (1999) *Global Competitiveness Report*, Geneva: World Economic Forum

WTO (1994) *Trade Measures for Environmental Purposes taken Pursuant to Multilateral Environmental Agreements: Recent Developments*, Note by the Secretariat, PC/SCTE/W/3, Geneva: World Trade Organization

WTO (1995a) *Negotiating History of the Coverage of the Agreement on Technical Barriers to Trade with Regard to Labelling Requirements, Voluntary Standards, and Processes and Production Methods Unrelated to Product Characteristics*, note by the Secretariat, WT/CTE/W/10, Geneva: World Trade Organization

WTO (1995b) *Environment and Services*, WT/CTE/W/9, Geneva: World Trade Organization

WTO (1996) *Procedures for the Circulation and Derestriction of WTO Documents*, Decision adopted by the General Council on 18 July 1996 – Revision, WT/L/160/Rev.1, Geneva: World Trade Organization

WTO (1996a) *The Effects of Environmental Measures on Market Access, Especially in Relation to Developing Countries, in Particular to the Least Developed Among Them*, note by the Secretariat, WT/CTE/W/26, Geneva: World Trade Organization

WTO (1996b) *United States – Standards for Reformulated and Conventional Gasoline*, Appellate body report and panel report, adopted on 20 May 1996, WT/DS2/9, Geneva: World Trade Organization

WTO (1996c) *Report (1996) of the Committee on Trade and Environment*, WT/CTE/1, Geneva: World Trade Organization

WTO (1997a) *Environmental Benefits of Removing Trade Restrictions and Distortions*, WT/CTE/W/67, Geneva: World Trade Organization

WTO (1997b) *The Relationship between Trade and Foreign Direct Investment*, note by the Secretariat, WT/WGTI/W/7, Geneva: World Trade Organization

WTO (1998a) *United States – Import Prohibition of Certain Shrimp and Shrimp Products*, Panel report, WT/DS58/R, Geneva: World Trade Organization

WTO (1998b) *United States – Import Prohibition of Certain Shrimp and Shrimp Products*, Appellate body report, adopted on 12 October 1998, WT/DS58/AB/R, Geneva: World Trade Organization

WTO (1998c) *EC Measures Concerning Meat and Meat Products (Hormones)*, Appellate body report, adopted on 16 January 1998, WT/DS26/AB/R and WT/DS48/AB/R, Geneva: World Trade Organization

WTO (1998d) *GATT/WTO Dispute Settlement Practice Relating to Article XX, Paragraphs (b), (d) and (g) of GATT*, note by the Secretariat, WT/CTE/W/53/Rev.1, Geneva: World Trade Organization

WTO (1998e) *Japan – Measures Affecting Agricultural Products*, Appellate body report, WT/DS76/AB/R, Geneva: World Trade Organization

WTO (1998f) *Australia – Measures Affecting Importation of Salmon*, Appellate body report, WT/DS18/AB/R, Geneva: World Trade Organization

WTO (1998g) *The Impact of Investment Incentives and Performance Requirements on International Trade*, note by the Secretariat, WT/WGTI/W/56, Geneva: World Trade Organization

WTO (1998h) *European Communities – Measures affecting asbestos and asbestos-containing products – Request for the Establishment of a Panel by Canada*, WT/DS135/3, Geneva: World Trade Organization

WTO (1999a) *Background Document for High Level Symposium on Trade and Environment*, Geneva, 15–16 March 1999, Geneva: World Trade Organization

WTO (1999b) *Background Document for High Level Symposium on Trade and Development*, Geneva, 17–18 March 1999, Geneva: World Trade Organization

WTO (1999c) *Communication from the Secretariat for the Vienna Convention and the Montreal Protocol*, UNEP, WT/CTE/W/115, Geneva: World Trade Organization

WTO (1999d) *WTO and Transparency, Preparations for the 1999 Ministerial Conference, Communication from Canada*, WT/GC/W/350, World Trade Organization, Geneva

WTO (2000a) *United States – Imposition of Countervailing Duties on Certain Hot-rolled Lead and Bismuth Carbon Steel Products Originating in the United Kingdom*, Report of the Appellate Body, WT/DS138/AB/R, Geneva: World Trade Organization

WTO (2000b) *European Communities – Measures affecting asbestos and asbestos-containing products*, Report of the Panel, WT/DS135/R, Geneva: World Trade Organization

WTO (2001) *European communities – Measures affecting asbestos and asbestos-containing products*, Report of the Appellate Body, WT/DS135/AB/R, Geneva: World Trade Organization

WWF (1993) *NAFTA Fact Sheet: The Attacks of the Critics of the NAFTA Environmental Package Have No Foundation*, Washington, DC: World Wildlife Fund

WWF (1996) *Trade Measures and Multilateral Environmental Agreements: Backwards or Forwards in the WTO?* Gland: World Wide Fund For Nature

WWF (1999a) *A Reform Agenda for the WTO Seattle Ministerial Conference*, Gland: World Wide Fund For Nature

WWF (1999b) *Initiating an Environmental Assessment of Trade Liberalisation in the WTO (Vol II)*, Gland: World Wide Fund For Nature

WWF (1999c) *Directing WTO Negotiations Towards Sustainable Agriculture and Rural Development*, Discussion Paper, November 1999, Gland: World Wide Fund For Nature

WWF (2000) *Environmental Assessment Of Trade Agreements: Implementing Executive Order 13141*, briefing materials, Washington, DC: World Wildlife Fund

WWF et al (2000) *A 'critique' of the EC's WTO sustainability impact assessment study and recommendations for phase III*, World Wide Fund For Nature, Oxfam, Save the Children and ActionAid

WWF, Oxfam, Center for International Environmental Law and Community Nutrition Institute (1998) *Dispute Settlement in the WTO: A Crisis for Sustainable Development*, Discussion Paper, Gland, Oxford, Conches and Washington, DC

Xing, Y and C D Kolstad (1998) *Do Lax Environmental Regulations Attract Foreign Investment?*, mimeo, University of California, Department of Economics, Santa Barbara

Zarsky, L (1997) 'Stuck in the mud? Nation-states, globalisation, and environment', in OECD (ed) *Globalisation and Environment: Preliminary Perspectives*, Paris: Organisation for Economic Co-operation and Development

Zarsky, L (1999) *Havens, Halos and Spaghetti: Untangling the Evidence about Foreign Direct Investment and the Environment*, background document, OECD Conference on FDI and the Environment (The Hague, 28–29 January 1999), Paris: Organisation for Economic Co-operation and Development

Index